Reference Manual for Office Workers

LOUIS C. NANASSY
Professor of Business Education
Montclair State College

WILLIAM SELDEN
State Supervisor, Business Education
Pennsylvania Department of Education

JO ANN LEE
Assistant Professor of Business
Pasadena City College

GLENCOE PUBLISHING CO., INC.
Encino, California
Collier Macmillan Publishers
London

Acknowlegment is made to Glencoe Publishing Co., Inc., for permission to adapt sample letters from *Advanced Typewriting for the College Student* by Kenneth Zimmer.

Printed in the United States of America

Glencoe Publishing Co., Inc.
17337 Ventura Boulevard
Encino, California 91316
Collier Macmillan Canada, Ltd.

Library of Congress Catalog Card Number: 74-6627

3 4 5 6 7 8 9 78 79 80

Contents

Preface

This reference manual attempts to answer questions office workers are likely to encounter in their daily work. Where should *manifest* be divided when it occurs at the end of a typewritten line? What information should be included in the letter of transmittal that accompanies a business report? What graphic formats can be used to present statistics, and how are such illustrations prepared on the typewriter? These and countless other subjects are thoroughly explored in this text.

The office worker's job is no longer limited to relatively mechanical duties. Traditional responsibilities have been expanded to include many areas formerly reserved for supervisory or professional personnel; in addition to typing the final report or letter, a secretary or administrative assistant may also be asked to take part in the planning and writing stages. Thus, the chapter on business reports offers detailed information on outline, footnote, and bibliography preparation. The chapter on grammar not only lists and explains the basic rules of good English usage, but also serves as a guide to clear writing style as well.

The business world is changing in response to technological and social changes of recent decades. Up-to-date information concerning the most significant of these developments is incorporated here. The chapter on office procedures, for example, contains a section on word processing, and the chapter on measurement includes the proper use of metric terminology.

Perhaps the single most important feature of the *Manual* is the accessibility of information, explained under "How To Use This Manual," on the next page. All topics are indexed and numbered to enable the reader to locate the desired information easily. Further aid is provided by the use of color to highlight topic headings, paragraph numbers, key words within the text, and illustrations.

Reference Manual for Office Workers, then, is dedicated not only to office workers, but also to students, teachers, business executives, librarians, and others for whom good communication and organizational skills are essential.

Acknowledgments

The authors acknowledge with thanks the encouragement and assistance received from colleagues, students, and businesses too numerous to mention. Special thanks and appreciation go to Dr. Kenneth Zimmer, Professor of Business Education, California State University, Los Angeles, and Jennifer Alkire, Development Editor, Glencoe Publishing Co., for their many contributions to the success of this book.

Louis C. Nanassy
William Selden
Jo Ann Lee

How To Use This Manual

This reference manual has been designed to provide quick and easy access to the information it contains. Each item of information is given a reference number that identifies the topic. These numbers are the keys to locating information.

How To Read the Numbers

Reference numbers are printed in blue in the left margin of each page. The inclusive reference numbers for each two-page spread are prominently displayed in the upper left corner. Each number is made up of two parts. The part to the left of the decimal refers to the chapter number; the part to the right of the decimal refers to the topic number within the chapter. All topics in a chapter are numbered consecutively.

Example: **10.25**

10 = Chapter Number; 25 = Topic Number

How To Use the Index

When specific information is desired, refer to the index at the back of the manual. The index lists all topics in alphabetical order and gives a reference number for each topic and a page number for each illustration. To look up a specific topic:

1. Locate the entry in the index and note the reference number that follows it.

2. Flip through the pages of the manual. Scan the top left corners of the pages and look for the page containing the reference number of the desired topic.

3. Open the book to the page that contains the desired reference number. Look down the left margins for the reference number that identifies the topic desired.

How To Use the Chapter Contents

When you want to locate several items of related information, refer to the table of contents on page iii to find the page number of the chapter you want. Turn to the page indicated in the table of contents. The first page of each chapter contains an alphabetical listing of the topics contained in that chapter. From this list you can identify the topics you wish to look up and find them by using the reference numbers listed after each topic.

One
Grammar

Introduction: Sentence Structure and Parts of Speech

1.1 Grammar is the study of the structure of a language—the forms of words and their arrangement in sentences. Words are classified into eight categories—**noun, pronoun, verb, adverb, adjective, preposition, conjunction,** or **interjection**—according to their functions and relationships in a sentence. An understanding of the process by which words are organized into complete thoughts is essential for clear writing.

The analysis of sentence structure below is followed by a discussion of each part of speech, with a separate section on subject-predicate agreement (1.94–1.113).

SENTENCE STRUCTURE

1.2 Sentence structure refers to the sequence of words in the sentence, the kinds of words contained in the sentence (parts of speech), and the length of the sentence.

1.3 A **sentence** is a unit of speech: a word or group of words arranged to convey a thought. A sentence usually contains a subject and a predicate. Sentences are classified according to the type of statement or the arrangement of words, as follows.

1. A **declarative sentence** makes a statement.

   Mr. Roberson will be going to Chicago this week.

2. An **interrogative sentence** asks a question.

   Is Mr. Roberson going to Chicago this week?

3. An **imperative sentence** gives a command or makes a request.

   Mr. Roberson, you must go to Chicago this week.

4. An **exclamatory sentence** expresses strong emotion.

   Oh, no! I can't go to Chicago!

CLAUSES

1.4 A clause is a group of words containing a subject and predicate. Clauses may be **independent** or **dependent (subordinate)**.

Independent Clauses

1.5 An independent clause can stand alone as a complete sentence.

Paul Mendez [subject] **is** [predicate] a capable supervisor.

The **meeting** [subject] **took place** [predicate] in Robbins Hall.

Dependent (Subordinate) Clauses

1.6 A dependent clause cannot stand alone as a complete sentence even if it contains a subject and predicate. This kind of clause depends on the independent clause for its meaning.

The president, **who lives in Detroit,** called the meeting for 2 p.m. in Flint.

Please let us know immediately **when the order arrives.**

A representative will be selected **as soon as all applicants have been interviewed.**

The dispute, **if it is not satisfactorily settled,** must then be resolved in court.

Whether the factory is to be rebuilt is a question to be decided by the Board of Directors.

CORRELATIVE EXPRESSIONS

1.7 Certain expressions are written in pairs because they convey a related thought. Examples of such expressions are **both . . . and, either . . . or, neither . . . nor, not . . . but,** and **not only . . . but also.** Maintain consistency in the form and tense of the words used with these expressions.

Either Ellen Fong **or** Glenda Baldwin would qualify for the teller's position.

Neither the employee **nor** the supervisor would admit any difficulty.

[In these examples, the words connected by the correlative expressions are singular; therefore, the verb forms used must also be singular.]

Neither the students **nor** the teachers expected such an entertaining speech.

[The words connected by the correlative expressions—*students* and *teachers*—are plural; therefore, the verb form must also be plural.]

She excels **not only** in her academic subjects **but also** in her extracurricular activities.

FRAGMENTS

1.8 A sentence fragment, or incomplete sentence, occurs when words necessary to complete the thought are missing. A fragment also occurs when a punctuation mark is used incorrectly to chop the sentence into phrases.

Fragment: Thank you for your letter. **Regarding your shipment of October 20.**

Sentence: Thank you for your letter **regarding your shipment of October 20.**

1.9 Dependent (subordinate) clauses that begin with such words as **although, as, because, if, since,** and **when** are often punctuated as complete sentences when in fact they are fragments.

Although we are leaving on Flight No. 415. [contains a subject and predicate but is only a subordinate clause]

The economy is facing the prospects of a depression. **Because of the inflationary period.** [The dependent clause should be in the same sentence as the independent clause, separated from it by a comma.]

1.10 **Verbal clauses** (those beginning with a verb form) are often incorrectly punctuated as complete sentences.

The Miami Beach office, **trying to meet the June 15 deadline.** [The independent clause is incomplete.]

Superior Court Judge Tierney dismissed the jurors. **Thanking them for their service.** [The subordinate clause should be in the same sentence and should be separated by a comma.]

1.11 Descriptive or explanatory expressions (**appositives**) are often incorrectly punctuated as complete sentences.

Honored on her anniversary, Linda Yamauchi was credited for establishing many modern office procedures. **Methods that provided greater productivity at less cost.** [The appositive further describes the office procedures and should be set off with a comma.]

MODIFIERS

1.12 A **modifier** is a word or group of words that limits, restricts, or qualifies the meaning of another word. The relationship between and among words in a sentence is developed by their sequence.

Ambiguous Modifiers

1.13 A modifier is ambiguous when the word modified is not obvious to the reader. Place words and groups of words close to their related thoughts, or rearrange the words to form a sentence that is logical in thought. Leave no doubt as to the meaning of the sentence.

Ambiguous: There was an important meeting he could not attend **at 10 a.m.**

Improved: He could not attend an important meeting **at 10 a.m.**

Ambiguous: We received your letter concerning the shipment of goods **on December 10.** [Was the *letter* or the *shipment* dated December 10?]

Improved: We received your letter **of December 10** concerning the shipment of goods.

Confusing Connectives

1.14 Words used as connectives should be chosen carefully so their meanings are clear. Some common connectives are **and, or, as, when,** and **while.**

Confusing: Jones was elected a trustee **and** is employed as a systems analyst.

Improved: Jones, who was elected a trustee, is employed as a systems analyst.

Confusing: **While** our manager resigned, our sales have decreased dramatically. ["While" could mean *because, since, inasmuch as, seeing that,* or *during the time that.*]

Improved: **Because** our manager resigned, our sales have decreased dramatically.

PARALLEL CONSTRUCTION

1.15 Related ideas should be stated in parallel grammatical style, whether in a series, in comparisons, within linking verbs, or with correlative expressions.

Nonparallel: John will go to the meeting, speak to the group, and is leaving at 3 p.m. [verb phrases not consistent]

Parallel: John will **go** to the meeting, **speak** to the group, and **leave** at 3 p.m.

Nonparallel: The dictionary shows us how to spell a word, its pronunciation, meaning, and where it originated. [words in the series not consistent]

Parallel: The dictionary shows us the **spelling, pronunciation, meaning,** and **origin** of a word.

PHRASES

1.16 A phrase is a group of words without a predicate and its subject that cannot stand alone as a complete sentence.

McLaren Towers, the new office building, is **22 stories high.** [adjectival phrase]

The lecturers presented their topics in a **clear and concise manner.** [adverbial phrase]

A new representative **qualifying for the job** has been selected. [restrictive or essential phrase]

The stock, **which sold at $200 per share,** has just split 3 for 1. [nonrestrictive or nonessential phrase]

On the job for only three weeks, the new file clerk was asked to resign. [prepositional phrase]

SUBORDINATION

1.17 See clauses, 1.4–1.6 and 1.9–1.10.

SENTENCE LENGTH

1.18 To avoid monotony of style, sentence length should be varied. Short sentences add spontaneity, while longer sentences help to achieve continuity. Too many short, simple sentences result in choppy thoughts and loss of continuity. The four principal types of sentence construction are identified by the complexity and organization involved.

Simple Sentence

1.19 A simple sentence contains one independent clause.

Mr. Johnson is our new supervisor.

Compound Sentence

1.20 A compound sentence contains more than one independent clause joined by a comma and conjunction or a semicolon. Omitting the comma and conjunction or the semicolon creates grammatically incorrect run-on sentences.

Mary received an appointment in the Personnel Department, but her sister did not.

or

Mary received an appointment in the Personnel Department; her sister did not.

Complex Sentence

1.21 A complex sentence contains one independent clause and one or more dependent clauses.

> Don Redman will be the next supervisor, although he has been here only a year.

Compound-Complex Sentence

1.22 A compound-complex sentence contains two or more independent clauses and one or more dependent clauses.

> Janice Redman will be the next supervisor, although she had been here only a year; Don Jackson was here for three years, but he never had the opportunity for the job.

Run-on Compound Sentence

1.23 A run-on sentence consists of two or more independent clauses (compound sentences) that are incorrectly separated by a comma. A run-on sentence is two complete sentences that should be separated by a **comma and conjunction** or by a **semicolon.**

Run-on: A successful office worker is one who arrives at work on time, he or she gives a full day's work for a day's pay.

Sentence: A successful office worker is one who arrives at work on time**;** he or she gives a full day's work for a day's pay.

or

A successful office worker is one who arrives at work on time**, and** he or she gives a full day's work for a day's pay.

Consistency

1.24 Regardless of sentence length and complexity, maintain one point of view per sentence and stay on the subject. Switching from one point of view or from one subject to another creates confusion.

Incorrect: When **you** purchase our product, **we** guarantee it for one year.

Correct: When **you** purchase our product, **you** have our one-year guarantee.

Nouns

1.25 A noun is the name of a person, place, or thing. Nouns may be common or proper.

1. A **common noun** is the name used to identify a class of things (such as dog, house, tree, pen, scissors), persons (boy, girl, teacher, minister, artist), or places (city, country, park, beach). A common noun that identifies a specific group—company, council, faculty, crowd, audience, committee— is called a **collective noun.**

2. A **proper noun** is the name used to identify a particular person, place, or thing (Alan Jones, Oregon, Grand Canyon, the Empire State Building).

NOUN AS SUBJECT

1.26 A noun as the subject of a sentence is the word about which the sentence is written. A **singular subject** refers to *one* person, object, or place. Singular subjects take singular predicates.

John is a student.

The **train** leaves at 12 noon.

Collective Nouns

1.27 The following collective nouns are considered singular subjects and take singular predicates.

audience	council	herd
board	crowd	jury
class	department	management
club	faculty	society
committee	family	staff
community	firm	team
company	flock	union
corporation	group	

The committee **has voted** unanimously in favor of the fund-raising project.

The jury **has returned** a guilty verdict.

That crowd **has remained** very orderly.

Our football team **deserves** a great deal of admiration.

1.28 The following collective nouns are considered *plural* subjects and take *plural* verbs.

goods	proceeds	savings	shears
pants	remains	scissors	thanks
pliers	riches		

These scissors **are** safe enough for small children.

His thanks **were conveyed** to the audience.

1.29 The following collective nouns may be used as either singular or plural subjects.

counsel	minority	series	species
deer	moose	sheep	swine
majority	number		

His counsel **are studying** the implications of the proposal.

My counsel **is drafting** a copy of the agreement.

The series of programs **is** very popular.

Which ticket series **are** still available at the Music Center?

Compound Subject

1.30 A compound subject refers to two or more objects, persons, or places and takes a plural predicate.

English and Math **are** my favorite subjects.

Tom and Mona **were** in charge of registration.

NOUN AS DIRECT OBJECT

1.31 A **direct object** receives the action of a verb or a verb form directly. The direct object answers the question of who or what receives the action of the verb.

The bookkeeper mailed the **statements.**

Professor Muha delivered his **speech.**

NOUN AS INDIRECT OBJECT

1.32 An indirect object receives the action of a verb indirectly. The indirect object is often preceded by a preposition (such as **to, of, by,** or **at**).

She gave the guest list to **Mr. McDowell.**

He aimed the attack at **Gibbs.**

NOUN AS COMPLEMENT

1.33 A complement is a word or phrase (predicate noun) that completes the meaning of the verb and explains or describes the subject. The subject is connected to the predicate noun by a linking verb, such as **am, appear, are, become, is, look, seem, was,** and **were.**

Brenton Wilks became the **East Coast representative.**

Don't those copies seem like the **originals?**

NOUN AS OBJECT OF A PREPOSITION

1.34 When a noun follows a phrase beginning with a preposition, the noun becomes the **object** of the preposition. Some common prepositions are:

about	before	from	of	under
after	by	in	through	upon
at	for	into	to	with

Send a copy **of the book** today.

Mr. DeVries will stop **at the Anchorage Inn.**

Pronouns

1.35 A pronoun takes the place of a noun and refers to the person, place, or thing named, asked for, or understood in the context. Pronouns are classified as **personal, relative, indefinite, demonstrative, interrogative, reflexive,** and **reciprocal.**

PERSONAL PRONOUNS

1.36 Personal pronouns are divided into three cases: *nominative, objective,* and *possessive.*

	Nominative Case		Objective Case		Possessive Case	
PERSON	***SINGULAR***	***PLURAL***	***SINGULAR***	***PLURAL***	***SINGULAR***	***PLURAL***
First	I	we	me	us	my, mine	our, ours
Second	you	you	you	you	your, yours	your, yours
Third	he, she, it	they	him, her, it	them	his, hers, its	their, theirs

TABLE 1-1. PERSONAL PRONOUNS

Nominative Case: I, you, he, she, it, we, they

1.37 Use the nominative case:

1. When the pronoun replaces the noun as the subject of the sentence.

   Dona and I study together, but **she** earns better grades on tests. [*She* refers to Dona.]

   He and Nancy will develop audiovisual materials for the lecture tour.

2. When the pronoun is the complement of a form of the verb *to be.*

   It was **I.**

   If I were **he,** I would have resigned.

3. When the verb form **to be** does not have a subject but is followed by a pronoun.

   The foreman was thought to be **he.**

   Is it going to be **she?**

Objective Case: me, you, him, her, it, us, them

1.38 Use the objective case:

1. When the pronoun is a direct object of a verb.

   The police officer called **us.**

   Captain Deneauve tried punishing **me.**

2. When the pronoun is an indirect object of a verb.

   The stock market gave **me** a scare.

   Mary read **them** their rights.

3. When the pronoun is the object of a preposition.

   Don and Joan are going with **him** now.

   Leave the job to **them.**

4. When the pronoun is the subject of an infinitive.

Would you expect **us** to collect the debt?

It is up to **them** as buyers to provide insurance coverage.

5. When the pronoun is the second of two objects and the pronouns are connected by **and.**

Dr. Engel presented Sue and **me** with a plaque.

His parents are coming to visit Vic and **me.**

6. When the pronoun is the subject of the verb **to be.**

We expected **him** to be a better salesman.

It was like **her** to be waiting.

Possessive Case: my, mine, your, yours, his, hers, her, its, our, ours, their, theirs

1.39 Use the possessive case:

1. When the pronoun precedes the noun it modifies, use **my, your, his, her, its, our,** or **their.**

It is **their** annual awards banquet.

The annual statement reflects **its** best year of sales to date.

2. When the pronoun immediately precedes a verb form ending in *ing* (gerund), use **my, your, his, her, its, our,** or **their.**

We appreciate **your** shipping the goods so promptly.

They planned on **our** completing construction by the 10th.

3. When the pronoun does not immediately precede the noun, use **mine, yours, his, hers, its, ours,** or **theirs.**

Dr. Herrera is a loyal customer of **ours.**

The selection is **hers** to make.

RELATIVE PRONOUNS

1.40 *Relative pronouns* are used to relate to the antecedent of the relative pronoun.

Nominative Case	*Objective Case*	*Possessive Case*
that	that	that
who	whom	whose
whoever	whomever	
which	which	which, whose
what	what	

TABLE 1-2. RELATIVE PRONOUNS

1.41 Relative pronouns are divided into the nominative, objective, and possessive cases, and each pronoun has its own function in sentences.

That refers to people, places, and things and is used in the nominative, objective, and possessive cases. *That* is used to introduce restrictive or essential clauses.

What refers to places and things and is used in the nominative and objective cases. *What* is often written in place of *that which* or *those which*.

Which refers to things and is used in the nominative, objective, and possessive cases. *Which* is always used to introduce nonrestrictive or nonessential clauses.

Who and **whoever** refer to people and are used in the nominative case.

Whom and **whomever** refer to people and are used in the objective case.

Whose refers to people and is used in the possessive form.

Nominative Case: that, who, whoever, which, what

1.42 Use the nominative form of relative pronoun:

1. When the pronoun is the subject of the sentence. (Substitute a personal pronoun—**I, he, she,** or **it**—to test the correctness of the relative pronoun.)

The situation **that** came up was exceptional.

Could **that** have been it?

What happened to the flow charts is not known.

The method **which** we adapted for our use was the most up-to-date.

The culprit, **whoever** committed the burglary, was extremely clever.

The girl **who** has maintained perfect attendance records is Mayling.

2. When the pronoun **what** is used for **that which** or **those which.**

What seemed so simple was actually quite puzzling.

The homes, parks, and stables were **what** suffered most from the winds.

Objective Case: that, whom, whomever, which, what

1.43 Use the objective form:

1. When the pronoun is the object of a verb. (Substitute such personal pronouns as **you, me, him, her,** or **them** to test the choice of the relative pronoun.)

The salesman disregarded **that.**

Hans Winneberger, **whom** we considered to be a clever scientist, declined the position.

Invite **whomever** you want.

2. When the pronoun is used as the object of the preposition.

This is the account in **which** you were overcharged.

The woman in **whom** you confided was my sister.

Possessive Case: whose

1.44 Use the possessive form to indicate ownership.

Among Hinckley, Benedetti, and Rice, **whose** territory is doing the best?

It was obvious **whose** error it was.

INDEFINITE PRONOUNS

1.45 Indefinite pronouns do not refer specifically to any one person or thing. The words that relate to these indefinite pronouns must agree in number and tense. Most indefinite pronouns are singular, some are plural, and a few are either singular or plural.

The following **singular** indefinite pronouns must be written with singular verbs.

another	each one	everything	one
anybody	either	much	some one
any one	every	neither	somebody
anyone	every one	no one	someone
anything	everybody	nobody	something
each	everyone	nothing	

Singular Form

1.46 Use the **singular form** of the indefinite pronoun:

1. When the pronoun is the subject of a sentence and indicates a single person or thing. (Use a singular predicate with this form.)

Each has an undivided interest in the estate.

Something is to be presented to the speaker.

Nothing is to be accomplished or gained by his bitter attitude.

2. When two indefinite pronouns joined by the word "and" are used as the subject of a sentence.

Anything and **everything** is likely to happen at the auction Saturday.

3. When the pronoun is used as an **adjective** to modify a noun.

Every man is to report for roll call at 7 a.m.

It occurred that **no one** person was really liable for the damage.

Feminine or Masculine Gender

1.47 To avoid confusion when indefinite pronouns are used to refer to either the feminine or masculine gender, or both, follow these rules.

1. When the pronoun is used to refer exclusively to the masculine gender, use the possessive personal pronoun **his:**

Has **everyone** put **his** wife's name on the list?

Anyone who is willing may place **his** name on the list for the men's doubles match.

2. When the pronoun is used to refer exclusively to the feminine gender, use the possessive personal pronoun **her:**

Everyone on the girls' swim team selected **her** own endurance goal.

3. When the pronoun is used to refer to both feminine and masculine genders, **he or she** and **his or her** may be used. It is best to reword the sentence so that no pronoun is needed. (Often a simple substitution of a plural subject will solve the problem.)

Each applicant must pass **his or her** aptitude test to qualify.
Each applicant must pass the aptitude test to qualify.

When **someone** agrees to the contract terms, **he or she** accepts full responsibility for **his or her** part of the bargain.
When borrowers agree to the contract terms, they accept full responsibility for **their** part of the bargain.

If a sentence cannot be reworded without making it awkward, **he** or **his** may be used to refer to both genders:

The child wanted **his** favorite toy. [sentence cannot be made plural, and *his or her* sounds awkward in this context]

Plural Form

1.48 The following indefinite pronouns are **plural** and must be written with plural verbs.

both **few** **many** **others** **several**

1.49 Use the **plural form** of an indefinite pronoun when the pronoun is the subject of a sentence and indicates more than one person, place, or thing. (Use a plural verb with this form.)

Many of the crew were ill during the cruise.

Several have already enrolled for the course.

Singular or Plural Form

1.50 The following indefinite pronouns are either singular or plural, depending on their use in the sentence as singular or plural subjects.

all **more** **other** **such**
any **none** **some**

1.51 Use the correct verb form with these indefinite pronouns.

We **all** are taking advantage of the current low tour prices.
All we need is evidence to substantiate our client's case.

None of the word processors have been installed as requested.
None of the four mechanics has been absent in the last six months.

There is a shortage of parks and recreation areas in the country; **more** are needed.
Much **more** is needed in the way of training in filing and records management.

Such are the circumstances of the boycott.
Such is the law of the land.

INTERROGATIVE PRONOUNS: who, whose, whom, what, which

1.52 Interrogative pronouns are used in sentences that ask a question. Each of these pronouns has a different function.

1. **What:** nominative and objective cases

   What is the agenda for the April 5 meeting?

   From **what** country does the United States import the most oil?

2. **Who:** nominative case

   Is she the girl **who** is most likely to succeed?

3. **Whom:** objective case

   For **whom** is this work to be done?

4. **Which:** nominative and objective cases

   Which will you be willing to supervise?

   In **which** department is the accident rate the highest?

   Which medium offers the largest storage capacity?

5. **Whose:** possessive case

   Whose desk is this?

DEMONSTRATIVE PRONOUNS: this, that, these, those

1.53 Demonstrative pronouns limit the number or kind of items being discussed. This class of pronouns is used in the nominative case as subjects. **This** and **these** are used to point out items nearest us in distance or time; **that** and **those** are used to point out items further away from us either in distance or time.

This is an interesting film.

That film we saw last week was fascinating.

These are our daily computer runs.

Those were recommended by Jon McGregor as being the best models.

1.54 Note that the demonstrative pronouns **this** and **that** are singular pronouns requiring singular verb forms; the pronouns **these** and **those** are plural, requiring plural verb forms.

REFLEXIVE PRONOUNS: myself, yourself, itself, himself, herself

1.55 Reflexive pronouns are formed by adding "-self" to the possessive personal pronouns. These words are used for emphasis following the subject of the sentence; they are also used as objects.

The building **itself** was nearly demolished.

She saw **herself** on video tape.

RECIPROCAL PRONOUNS: each other, one another

1.56 Reciprocal pronouns relate specifically to another person discussed. **Each other** relates to two persons; **one another** relates to more than two persons.

Greg and Jan appear to work well with **each other.**

Linda, Anita, and Lori are in competition with **one another** for Campus Representative.

PRONOUN USAGE PROBLEMS

Possessives and Contractions

1.57 The possessive case of pronouns is often confused with contractions. Use the **possessive pronouns** to indicate ownership or other relationship between a pronoun and its antecedent. Use the **contractions** sounding like the possessive pronouns to indicate a subject-predicate relationship.

Possessive Pronouns	*Sound-Alike Contractions*
its	it's (it is, it has)
their	they're (they are)
theirs	there's (there is, there has)
whose	who's (who is)
your	you're (you are)

Our company offers **its** employees a comprehensive fringe benefit package. [possessive pronoun referring to *company*]

It's the policy of the agency to charge a 15 percent placement fee. [contraction of *It is*]

Their microfilm operations include several rotary and flatbed cameras and different models of readers for reels and fiche. [possessive pronoun]

They're performing the three-act play in fourteen cities across the state. [contraction of *They are*]

Theirs has been the highest-paying dividend since 1972. [possessive pronoun]

There's a solution to the problem if we can only meet to discuss it. [contraction of *There is*]

Whose application for district representative was filed first? [possessive pronoun]

Who's going to be responsible for auditing the safe-deposit contents? [contraction of *Who is*]

Your family should have the added protection offered by this new insurance policy. [possessive pronoun]

You're never better protected against loss from fire or theft than now. [contraction of *You are*]

Comparison, Identification, and Compounds

1.58 To avoid errors in using either nominative or objective pronouns, follow these rules.

1. When a pronoun is used with the comparison words **than** or **as,** use either the nominative or objective pronoun depending on how the sentence is constructed.

Roger is more effective as a supervisor than **I** [am]. [nominative as complement of verb *to be*]

The cashier would prefer to work with Mr. Saracho rather than [work with] **her.** [objective as object of a preposition]

2. When a pronoun identifies (is in apposition with) a noun, read the sentence without the noun to determine the construction.

We union officials must meet soon. [We . . . must meet soon; nominative as subject]

One of **us** executives will be promoted. [One of us . . . will be promoted; objective as object of preposition]

3. When a pronoun and a noun form a compound, read the sentence without the noun to determine the construction.

Danny wanted Jeff and **me** to work overtime tonight. [Danny wanted . . . me to work overtime tonight; objective as object of verb]

Lyn spoke to both Lillian and **me.** [Lyn spoke to . . . me; objective as object of preposition]

Verbs

1.59 A **verb** is a word used to express an action, state of being, or condition of the subject in a sentence. Like other parts of speech, verbs are classified according to their functions.

ACTIVE AND PASSIVE VERBS

1.60 The **active voice** places emphasis on the subject acting upon the verb. The active voice shows **action.** The **passive voice** places emphasis on the object or receiver of the action or **deemphasizes** the action.

Active: Lambert Architects, Inc., **drew up** a design for the new school.

Passive: A design for the new school **was drawn up** by Lambert Architects, Inc.

Use the active voice to convey a more direct and concise message. Use the passive voice to convey bad news or a "no" response as tactfully as possible.

Active: You **did not endorse** your check properly.
Passive: Your check **was not** properly **endorsed.**

Active: We **cannot make** refunds on sale merchandise.
Passive: Because the sweater you purchased was on sale, a refund **cannot be made.**

GERUNDS

1.61 A **gerund,** a verb form that ends in **-ing,** is used like a noun—as the subject of a sentence or as an object.

Interviewing possible award winners is a difficult task for the committee. [gerund used as noun and subject of sentence]

Did you get any results in **discussing** the problem with them? [gerund used as a noun and object of preposition]

AUXILIARY (helping) VERBS

1.62 An auxiliary verb is joined to another verb to help convey the action, state of being, or condition of the subject. Some helping verbs are **be, can, could, do, have, may, might, must, ought, shall, should, will,** and **would.** Each of these words can stand alone as a main verb; they can also be combined with one another as auxiliary and main verb. The auxiliary verb always *precedes* the main verb in the sentence.

I **must fly** to San Francisco this Friday.

If they had the time, they **could spend** a week with us.

Helping verbs are often grouped with each other as follows.

can be	might be	shall have been
can have	might have	should be
could be	might have been	should have
could have	must be	should have been
could have been	must have	will be
had been	must have been	will have
has been	ought to be	will have been
have been	ought to have	would be
may be	ought to have been	would have
may have	shall be	would have been
may have been	shall have	

It **could have been** a total disaster.

She **has been** a loyal employee for fifteen years.

They **may have** to abandon the project because of insufficient public support.

I **would have been** a sales engineer for three years now, had I not become a banker.

Would it **have been** feasible ten years ago?

1.63 Some helping verbs used to convey a specific thought are often confused with other similar verbs.

Can indicates ability or capacity to do something in the present or future tenses.

Could indicates ability or capacity to do something in the past or future tense.

> **Can** the mechanic fix the carburetor immediately?
>
> That assignment **could** be accomplished in about three days.
>
> The witnesses **could** have been mistaken about what they saw.

May indicates request for permission in the present tense; used for the first person.

Might indicates request for permission in the future or past tense; used for the second and third persons.

> **May** I introduce you to Councilman Snyder from the 14th District?
>
> Public relations **might** be responsible for the successful ad campaign.
>
> There **might** be a reasonable explanation for his peculiar action.

Must indicates an act that is commanded, requested, or determined to be done. Used in the first person as well as second and third persons.

Ought to indicates an act that is commanded, requested, or determined to be done. Used in the second and third persons in the present, past, or future tenses.

> I **must** leave to catch the 4:45 plane.
>
> You **ought to** check your company's safety regulations regularly.

Shall indicates future tense and is used in the first person [*I shall*].

Will indicates future tense and is used in the first person [*I will*] in a definitive statement. Also, it is usually used in the second and third persons [*he, she, it, they, you,* or *we will*].

> I **shall** subscribe to *Fortune* next year. [statement in future tense, first person]
>
> I **will** complete my income tax statement by April 15. [definitive statement, first person]

Should indicates a duty or obligation. It is used in the first person in the future tense for a definitive statement and in the second and third persons for the past and future tenses.

Would indicates some condition or state of being and is used in the second and third persons in the past and future tenses.

> My committee **should** plan the itinerary for the forthcoming tour.

The foreman said he **would** be pleased to conduct a tour of the plastics manufacturing plant.

Knowing you as I do, I knew you **would** consider the position of treasurer.

INFINITIVES

1.64 An infinitive is a verb in the present tense (first person singular) preceded by **to**. An infinitive may be used as a noun, adjective, or adverb.

It is our pleasure **to introduce** our newest associate, Cynthia S. Miller. [adverb modifying *pleasure*]

To deny him an impartial hearing would deny him a constitutional right. [noun, as subject of the sentence]

Those films seem **to be** inadequate for the intended audience. [noun as object]

There are six more manuscripts **to review.** [adjective modifying *manuscripts*]

Please ask all parties **to read** the attached exhibits, **to initial** the changes, and **to return** all copies to me. [nouns]

See 1.74–1.75 for a discussion of split infinitives.

INTRANSITIVE VERBS

1.65 An intransitive verb is a verb that **does not need a direct object** to complete the meaning of the sentence. (A **direct object** tells who or what receives the action of the verb.)

Verbs that are always intransitive include the various forms of **to be** and the following words: **appear, become, feel, grow, look, remain, seem, smell, sound, stay,** and **taste.**

They **were** anxious to go on the African safari.

Jackson **was** not **feeling** well.

IRREGULAR VERBS

1.66 An irregular verb does not conform to the ending patterns for past tenses described under Regular Verbs (1.73). Refer to the chart on page 22 when you are uncertain about the spelling of a verb in one of the past or perfect tenses (see 1.81–1.87). Irregular verbs are used as follows:

To stay healthy, **drink** at least eight glasses of water each day.
They **drank** a toast to the newly elected board officers.
Manny **should** not **have drunk** as much as he did.

Please **lay** those papers here on the desk.
The builders **laid** the foundation yesterday.
Our company **had laid** off several engineers last year because of insufficient contracts.

Note that auxiliary verbs are used with the past participle of irregular verbs but not with the past tense.

Present	Past	Past Participle	Present	Past	Past Participle
am, are, is*	was, were	been	hang	hung	hung
become	became	become	hide	hid	hidden
begin	began	begun	know	knew	known
bid (to tell)	bade	bidden	lay	laid	laid
bid (to offer)	bid	bid	leave	left	left
bite	bit	bitten	lend	lent	lent
blow	blew	blown	lie	lay	lain
break	broke	broken	pay	paid	paid
bring	brought	brought	ride	rode	ridden
burst	burst	burst	ring	rang	rung
buy	bought	bought	rise	rose	risen
catch	caught	caught	run	ran	run
choose	chose	chosen	see	saw	seen
come	came	come	set	set	set
do	did	done	shake	shook	shaken
drag	dragged	dragged	shine†	shone	shone
draw	drew	drawn	shrink	shrank	shrunk
drink	drank	drunk	sing	sang	sung
drive	drove	driven	sit	sat	sat
eat	ate	eaten	speak	spoke	spoken
fall	fell	fallen	spring	sprang	sprung
fight	fought	fought	steal	stole	stolen
flee	fled	fled	strike	struck	struck
fly	flew	flown	swear	swore	sworn
forget	forgot	forgotten	swim	swam	swum
freeze	froze	frozen	take	took	taken
get	got	got	tear	tore	torn
give	gave	given	throw	threw	thrown
go	went	gone	wear	wore	worn
grow	grew	grown	write	wrote	written
hang (to put to death)	hanged	hanged			

TABLE 1-3. PRINCIPAL PARTS OF COMMON IRREGULAR VERBS

*Forms of "to be."

†When shine means "to polish," the parts are shine, shined, shined.

Adapted from *Business English and Communication,* 4th ed., Marie M. Stewart et al. (New York: McGraw-Hill, 1972). Reprinted by permission.

LINKING VERBS

1.67 Linking verbs are used to connect a subject with a predicate adjective or noun. The present and past tense forms of **to be** are commonly used as linking verbs: **am, are, is, was,** and **were.** **Appear, become, feel, grow, look, seem, smell, sound,** and **taste** are other linking verbs. These linking verbs do not convey any action between the subject and verb; the connecting words should be adjectives rather than adverbs.

Scott **looks** pale; **is** he **feeling** well?

The music over the loud speaker **sounds** too raucous for the office.

PARTICIPLES

1.68 A participle is a verb that is combined with another verb to indicate differences in time. The participle is written in the present, past, and perfect forms.

- **Present participle:** ends in **ing.**

  The word processing center **is finishing** its work on the report.

- **Past participle:** ends in **d** or **ed** for regular verbs; irregular verbs end in their particular verb form. (The past participle is used to form the present perfect, past perfect, and future perfect tenses. See 1.66, 1.84–1.87.)

  They **had leased** three office suites for a twenty-year period.

- **Perfect participle: having** plus the past participle.

  Having leased the building to Hotchkiss & Co., we can boast a 100 percent occupancy factor.

Participle as Adjective

1.69 A participle standing alone functions as an adjective and modifies a noun or pronoun.

The **growing** number of inhabitants on the island is alarming.

Weakened by his recent illness, Mr. Farrell is not working long hours.

Participle as Verb

1.70 A participle can assume the characteristics of a verb and can take an object or be modified by an adverb.

Giving his support, Admiral LaCroix lauded the candidates for their platform. [verb is *giving;* object is *support*]

Walking slowly to the podium, Dr. Agatha Guntermann impressed the audience with her dignity. [verb is *walking;* adverb is *slowly*]

PREDICATE

1.71 A predicate consists of a verb by itself, a verb and its complement, or two or more predicates in one sentence.

- **Simple predicate:** the verb itself.

  The repairman **fixed** the appliances.

- **Verb and complement:** the verb and its object, predicate noun, or predicate adjective.

  Mae Ling-Tsam **has rewritten** the office manual. [verb and its object]

  Delmas Bugelli **is our department chairperson.** [verb and its predicate noun]

  The secretarial program here **is comprehensive.** [verb and its predicate adjective]

- **Compound predicate:** two or more predicates in the sentence.

  Their legal counsel **will determine the probable cause of action** and **will seek punitive damages.**

PRINCIPAL VERBS

1.72 The principal verb in a sentence is a single word that is the main verb. When used with an auxiliary verb, the principal verb follows the helping verb.

Stacey **writes** shorthand well. [principal verb]

Stacey **is learning** to type this semester. [auxiliary verb is *is*; principal verb is *learning*]

REGULAR VERBS

1.73 A regular verb is a verb whose past tense and past participle are formed by adding **d** or **ed** to the present tense. In other words, the root of the verb is spelled the same in all tenses.

We usually **walk** to the engineering library every day. [present tense]

Jack Robbins **walked** two miles on his new sales route. [past tense]

Glenda and Dottie **have walked** as far as a mile to find a telephone. [past tense]

SPLIT INFINITIVES

1.74 A split infinitive is an infinitive with a modifier between **to** and the verb. The modifier is an adverb that generally follows the object of the verb.

Infinitive: Dr. Bugelli wants **to review** our proposals carefully.
Split Infinitive: Dr. Bugelli wants **to** carefully **review** our proposals.

1.75 Whenever possible, word sentences to avoid split infinitives. Place the modifier (adverb) close to the word being modified so the meaning of the sentence is clear. Follow these guidelines:

1. Place the modifier after the object of the infinitive.

Our choice at this time is **to make** an offer **immediately.**

2. Place the modifier either before or after the infinitive.

Their idea was **apparently to propose** a stock split.

It is difficult **to remember exactly** the words of the Gettysburg Address.

3. When the infinitive must be split to form a clearer sentence, be sure the modifier is placed so it clearly refers to the word it modifies. Splitting an infinitive often results in a misplaced modifier.

Awkward: **To deny** them a fair hearing **arbitrarily** by the Senate does not seem equitable in the circumstances.

Clear: **To arbitrarily deny** them a fair hearing by the Senate does not seem equitable in the circumstances.

SUBJUNCTIVE MOOD

1.76 The subjunctive mood is used (1) to describe an impossible or uncertain condition or situation; (2) to express a wish or doubt; and (3) to indicate a request, command, or resolution. The subjunctive mood is introduced by such words as **if, that, though, unless,** or **whether.**

1.77 The verbs **be** and **were** are used for the subjunctive mood rather than **is** and **was** (is and was indicate definite conditions or assumed facts).

1. To indicate an impossible or uncertain condition or situation, use the verbs **be** and **were.**

> If I **were** only taller, I could easily reach that book on the top shelf.
>
> If this **be** the case, I shall be the first to apologize.

If a condition or situation is possible or could be true, use the verbs **was** and **are.**

> If Ron **was** promoted last week, he has not told us anything about it.

2. To express a wish or a doubt, use the verb **were** (rather than was).

> I wish I **were** coming to visit you next month.

3. To indicate a request, command, or resolution when preceded by the word **that,** do not use the verbs **shall** or **should** to complete the predicate:

> The company insists that all **customers obtain** credit approval before orders are shipped. [Not: . . . that all customers *should* obtain . . .]
>
> Their instruction was that **I be required** to remain in Texas for another two weeks. [Not: . . . that I *should* be required . . .]

TRANSITIVE VERBS

1.78 A *transitive verb* is a verb that needs a direct object to complete the meaning of a sentence. A direct object tells who or what receives the action of the verb.

> Messrs. Freeling and Myers **wrote** the first three chapters of the operations manual.
>
> The vice president, Carla J. Rapp, **acknowledged** the efforts of the entire staff.

VERB TENSES

1.79 Verbs are written in different tenses to indicate various time relationships with their subjects. The three principal verb tenses are present, past, and future.

Present Tense

1.80 Use the present tense when an action is currently taking place, when a condition is stated, and when a state of being is expressed.

The board **is** meeting in the conference room now.

Accounting for Taxes **begins** at 9:30 a.m.

Our legal department **has** the subpoena.

Past Tense

1.81 Use the past tense to indicate an action that has already taken place or a condition that no longer exists. The past tense of regular verbs is formed by adding **d** or **ed;** the past tense of irregular verbs is formed as indicated in Table 1-3.

The *Sunset Gazette* **advertised** 153 jobs this week.

The cost-of-living index **rose** again last month.

Future Tense

1.82 Use the future tense to indicate an action that will take place or a condition that will exist in the future. The word **shall** or **will** precedes the present tense form of the verb. In most cases, use *shall* for the first person and *will* for the second and third persons.

I **shall work** on the manuscript next weekend.

The DeAzevedo estate **will be liquidated** soon.

1.83 In an emphatic statement, use **will** for the first person and **shall** for the second and third persons:

I **will** not **go,** even if they insist.

On the contrary, you most certainly **shall go.**

Perfect Tenses

1.84 There are three additional tenses formed with the past participle: present perfect, past perfect, and future perfect.

1.85 Use the **present perfect** tense to indicate action that began in the past and has been completed in the present. The word **has** or **have** precedes the past participle.

The auditors **have completed** the reports that were begun last month.

Gene Pinchuk **has assumed** the note as the cosigner.

1.86 Use the **past perfect** tense to indicate action that began and was completed in the past. The word **had** precedes the past participle.

Both witnesses **had testified** on behalf of the defendant

1.87 Use the **future perfect** tense to indicate action that will be completed by some future date. The phrase **shall have** or **will have** precedes the past participle.

> The incoming president, Angus Mothershead, **will have presented** his new board by the end of the meeting.
>
> I **shall have rescheduled** our counseling patients by the end of the week.

Progressive Tenses

1.88 The progressive tenses (present, past, future, and perfect) are used to indicate some immediate action or existing condition or action that is in progress or taking place over a period of time.

1.89 Use the **present progressive** tense to indicate an uncompleted action or condition.

> Our programmers and analysts **are being defended** by their supervisors.

1.90 Use the **past progressive** tense to indicate an action or condition that has already taken place.

> She **was preparing** the escrow instructions when the buyer arrived.

1.91 Use the **future progressive** tense to indicate an action or a condition that will be taking place.

> McMahan and Allister **will be thinking** seriously about a new office site.

1.92 Use the **perfect progressive** tenses as follows.

> *Present:* The workmen **have been completing** the finishing touches to the hospital wing.
>
> *Past:* Our representatives **had been dealing** with Jalisco Importers in Mexico.
>
> *Future:* By Friday, we **will have been deciding** on a new design for three weeks.

Emphatic Tenses

1.93 The emphatic tenses are used to emphasize the action, condition, or state of being. The words **do, does** and **did** are used to form the present and past tenses.

> *Present:* She **does read** all letters carefully before sorting them.
>
> We **do give** special attention to all court-appointed guardians.
>
> *Past:* They **did mention** the deadline to us, but we apparently forgot.
>
> I **did** not **say** I would volunteer for that task.

Subject-Predicate Agreement

1.94 The subject and predicate of the sentence must agree with each other in number (singular or plural) and tense. The subject can be a noun, a pronoun, a clause, or a phrase.

A pronoun within the sentence must agree with its antecedent in number and gender. A modifier must agree with the noun or pronoun it describes.

Generally speaking, any verb ending in *s* is singular.

BOOKS AND MAGAZINES

1.95 Names of books or magazines, and the chapter or article titles from these works, are considered singular subjects and should be written with singular predicates and pronouns.

Consumer Reports **is** published to provide valuable information to all segments of the consuming public.

Economics **has been** recently published in **its** seventh edition.

COLLECTIVE NOUNS

1.96 As noted under 1.27, collective nouns that are singular in form and represent one unit or group take a singular predicate; collective nouns that are plural in form and represent one or more units within the group take a plural predicate.

COMPANIES AND INSTITUTIONS

1.97 Names of companies and institutions (such as hospitals and schools) usually are written as singular subjects, which take singular predicates and the pronouns **it, its, which,** and **that.**

Lawrence & Tyson, Inc., one of the larger medical groups in this area, **is noted** for **its** research in endocrinology.

1.98 However, if a company or institution name is to be used as a plural subject, use a plural predicate and the pronouns **they, their,** and **who.**

Kral, Leslie and Davis, Certified Public Accountants, **have prepared their** financial statements as of December 31.

When in doubt about subject-predicate agreement, rewrite the sentence so the company name is not the subject.

The medical group of Lawrence & Tyson, Inc., one of the largest in this area, **is noted** for **its** research in endocrinology. [subject is *group*]

COMPOUND SUBJECTS

1.99 A compound subject, consisting of two singular nouns (names of people, places, or things) joined by the conjunction *and,* should be written with a plural predicate. Be sure that plural modifiers and pronouns, as well as predicates, are used with compound subjects.

Peter and Roger **were** sitting quietly at the opera when **they** noticed a small mouse in **their** box.

1.100 When a subject consists of two singular nouns joined by the conjunction *and,* but the subject refers to *one* person or thing, use a singular predicate:

The vice president and cashier **has approved** the new management policy. [compound subject refers to one person with a combined title]

The vice president and the cashier **have approved** the new management policy. [compound subject refers to two people]

1.101 When a compound subject is joined by either *or* or *nor,* the predicate should agree with the subject nearer it.

Neither Helen nor the operators **have seen** the film on telephone techniques.

Neither the operators nor Helen **has seen** the film on telephone techniques.

FOREIGN NOUNS

1.102 Many foreign words that have become part of the English language retain the foreign singular or plural endings. To identify a foreign word as singular or plural, refer to Table 1-4.

Singular	*Plural*
addendum	addenda
alumna (feminine)	alumnae
alumnus (masculine)	alumni (masculine or both)
analysis	analyses
appendix	appendixes or appendices
basis	bases
crisis	crises
criterion	criteria
datum	data
formula	formulae or formulas
index	indexes or indices
medium	media
memorandum	memoranda or memorandums
parenthesis	parentheses

TABLE 1-4. FOREIGN SINGULAR / PLURAL ENDINGS

1.103 Use a singular predicate with a singular foreign noun.

Mary Ellen Reyes, an **alumna** of Central College, **works** as an airline pilot traveling throughout the state.

The **basis** for the choice of plant site **was** its proximity to the railroad.

One **criterion** for filing a joint tax return **is** the advantage of a better tax rate.

1.104 Use a plural predicate with a plural foreign noun.

Their **analyses demonstrate** that the project is neither financially nor practically feasible.

The research **data reveal** a startling 40 percent retention rate.

HERE OR THERE

1.105 The words **here** and **there** at the beginning of sentences are *not* the subjects of those sentences. When a sentence begins with either of these words, the subject usually follows the predicate. If the subject is singular, use a singular predicate; if the subject is plural, use a plural predicate.

Here **are** 24 **copies** of the policy manual for your staff.

Here **is** our latest price **quotation.**

There **are** four **typewriters** in that office.

There **is** one **book** missing from the shelf.

INDEFINITE PRONOUNS

1.106 Some indefinite pronouns are used as singular subjects, some are used as plural subjects, and some may be either singular or plural subjects. The predicates used with these indefinite pronouns must agree in number and tense, as described under 1.45–1.51.

INTERVENING WORDS

1.107 Some sentences are constructed so that the normal subject-verb order is separated by one or more intervening words, but the predicate should agree with its subject in any case. Locate the subject, disregarding the noun or pronoun that may be the object of the verb or preposition.

The **reason** for his difficulties **was** his lack of enthusiasm.

Susan, as well as her friends, **was going** to lunch.

NUMBER

1.108 The word **number** can be used as either a singular or plural subject, depending on its meaning in the sentence, its antecedent, and any modifiers. Intervening words between the subject and predicate do not affect the verb tense.

A number is used as a plural subject.

A number of senior citizens **are planning** a three-week cruise to the West Indies.

The number is used as a singular subject:

The number of accidents on the highways **has decreased** since the lower speed limit was enforced.

PHRASES AND CLAUSES

1.109 A **phrase** is a group of words with no subject or predicate. When a phrase is used as the subject of a sentence, the predicate should be singular.

Establishing friendly relations with the community is the company's chief concern. [gerund phrase]

Whichever offers the most reasonable rate is the one we shall purchase.

1.110 A **subordinate clause** is a group of words that includes a subject and verb but cannot stand by itself as a sentence because the verb is not a complete predicate. Subordinate clauses that begin with *what* may take either a singular or plural predicate to make them full sentences, depending on the words that complete the meaning.

What this world needs *is* compassion.

What this company strives for *are* higher ideals and goals.

RELATIVE PRONOUNS

1.111 The relative pronouns **who** and **whoever** belong to the nominative case; they are used as subjects in place of *he, she, it, they,* or *we*. These relative pronouns may be either singular or plural subjects, depending on their use in the sentence.

Who **is** responsible for the textbook exhibit? [*who* replaces *he, she,* or *it*]

Whoever **meets** the requirements **will** be elected. [*who* replaces *he, she,* or *it*]

Who **are** the new officers for the club? [*who* replaces *they* or *we*]

SUBJECT AND VERB INVERTED

1.112 When the usual subject-predicate-complement form is not followed in constructing the sentence and the verb precedes the subject, the verb must still agree with the number and tense of the inverted subject.

Enclosed *is* a **copy** of our contract.

Attached *are* three **sets** of blueprints and specifications for your approval.

TIME, AMOUNTS, QUANTITIES

1.113 Expressions of time, amounts, and quantities can be either singular or plural subjects, depending on whether they refer to a single unit or several individual units:

Four days *is* ample time to prepare the amendment.

The **$5,595** *is* to be repaid over a two-year period.

The last **six months** of each year *have given* us many clues as to potential problem areas.

Adverbs

1.114 An **adverb** is a word, phrase, or clause that modifies, describes, limits, or qualifies an adjective, a verb, or another adverb. Adverbs are words that indicate some type of action and usually answer such questions as How? When? Where? Why? and To what extent?

How: It was done **well.**

When: It was done **yesterday.**

Where:	It was done **outside.**
Why:	It was done **because it rained.**
To what extent:	It was done **everywhere.**

ADVERB FUNCTIONS

Modifying an Adjective

1.115 An adverb can be used to modify an adjective (adjectives modify the meaning of nouns or pronouns).

Fotiou and Sons will offer a **rather** reasonable rate.

Inflation dealt a **very** sharp blow to our purchasing power.

Modifying a Verb

1.116 An adverb can be used to modify a verb (verbs express actions, states of being, and conditions).

Annie punched the cards **quickly,** but she did so **inaccurately.** [How? Quickly but inaccurately.]

The consignor delayed shipment **until April 10.** [How long? Until April 10.]

Modifying Another Adverb

1.117 An adverb can modify another adverb either before or after the verb; but it should reflect the action of that verb.

Those contractors fulfilled their obligations quite carefully. [*quite* modifies *carefully*]

Phyllis Brzozowski almost always allowed them a week's leeway. [*almost* modifies *always*]

Adverbs with Two Forms

1.118 Some adverbs are written in two forms, and each has a somewhat different meaning and function. In many instances, one word may sound more correct than the other; however, in most cases, only one form is correct. (Note that the first word of each pair may also function as an adjective. When in doubt, consult the dictionary.)

clear, clearly	hard, hardly	quick, quickly
close, closely	heavy, heavily	quiet, quietly
deep, deeply	high, highly	sharp, sharply
direct, directly	late, lately	short, shortly
fair, fairly	light, lightly	slow, slowly
free, freely	loud, loudly	wide, widely

Our descriptive brochure will be sent **free** to anyone requesting it.

Recognition should be given **freely** to all who deserve it.

Merchandise on Invoice 14793-C will be shipped **direct** to Baton Rouge.

Both assembly line workers were **directly** responsible for the faulty parts.

The order was shipped **clear** to Alaska.

He spoke **clearly** into the microphone.

ADVERBIAL CLAUSES AND PHRASES

1.119 An **adverbial clause** or **phrase** is a dependent clause used with the independent or main clause that indicates the time, place, manner, or extent. (A **clause** is a group of words containing a subject and predicate; some can stand alone as independent thoughts. A **phrase** is a group of words, lacking either a subject or a predicate, that cannot stand alone as a complete sentence.)

> **When you receive the invoice,** please call our accounts receivable clerk. [adverbial clause at the beginning of the sentence that tells *when*]

> His assignment was **near his home** on the west side of town. [adverbial phrase in the middle of the sentence that tells *where*]

> Our factories will be temporarily closed **because of the flood damage.** [adverbial phrase at the end of a sentence tells *why*]

FORMS OF ADVERBS

Connective Adverbs

1.120 A **connective adverb** is a word that joins a dependent (subordinate) clause to the main or independent clause. Connective adverbs are used in introductory clauses and phrases and in transitional expressions. (See 2.37 and 2.38 for placement of commas with connective adverbs.)

accordingly	consequently	so
after	furthermore	then
also	however	therefore
although	if	thus
as	nevertheless	when
because	otherwise	while
before	since	yet
besides	still	

> **After** the examination, we must go for an interview with Sara Hawkins in the Personnel Department. [When?]

> The police escort was a success **because** motorists were forced to drive slower. [Why?]

Adverbs Followed by Prepositions

1.121 When a preposition follows an adverb, the *-ly* form of the adverb is usually preferred (see 1.118). In some instances, however, the other form is used.

agreeable to	differently from	previous to
agreeable with	exclusively of	regardless of
consistent with	independently of	separately from
consistently with	irrespective of	subsequently to

> Students should attempt to learn and study **independently of** their teacher's direct guidance.

> **Irrespective of** that fact, Burns Construction Company was still awarded the contract.

Intervening Adverb with Split Infinitive

1.122 An adverb placed between "to" and the verb that follows usually produces an awkward sentence:

Awkward: It is not possible to **impartially** judge this contest.
Better: It is not possible to judge this contest **impartially.**

Sometimes, however, a split infinitive is not only acceptable but necessary (see section 1.75).

Note that "to be" followed by an adverbial clause is *not* an infinitive. Thus, an adverb may precede the clause.

Awkward: The new mayor is thought **essentially** to be moderate in her political views.
Better: The new mayor is thought to be **essentially** moderate in her political views.

Negative Adverbs

1.123 Certain adverbs are used to convey a negative meaning. These negative adverbs should be used carefully to avoid forming a double negative, which consists of two negative expressions in the same sentence. Remember that *not* expresses a negation; *never* is an absolute term that means "at no time" or "in no way."

but	not
hardly	only
never	scarcely

The Johannsen Co. **never** considered opening a store within a block of its competitor.

He **hardly** could type the 45 words per minute required for passing the test.

1.124 The double negative may sometimes be used to express a thought more emphatically.

This is **not** an **unpleasant** task.

We **couldn't** care **less.**

When improperly used, the double negative cancels out the desired meaning instead of emphasizing it:

He **couldn't hardly** type the 45 words per minute required for passing the test.

Adjectives

1.125 An *adjective* is a word, clause, or phrase that modifies—describes, limits, or qualifies—a noun or pronoun. Adjectives answer such questions as What kind? How many? and Which one?

What kind: Our survey covered a **limited** market.

How many: Please order **twelve** reams of bond paper.

Which one: The **April 14** codicil is the most recent one.

ADJECTIVE FUNCTIONS

Modifying Subject of Sentence

1.126 Adjectives are used to modify both nouns and pronouns as subjects. (An adverb should not be used for this purpose, as it indicates the action of a verb.)

1.127 The verb forms of **feel, look, smell, sound,** and **taste** are followed by adjectives. (Substitute the verbs are, is, was, or were for the other verbs to determine the correct use of an adjective to modify the subject.)

Mr. Rinaldi appears **healthy.** [Mr. Rinaldi *is* healthy.]

Mount Wilson looked **distant.** [Mount Wilson *was* distant.]

Modifying a Noun

1.128 Within a sentence, an adjective is used to modify a noun.

Millions of readers were amused by the **clever** cartoons. [What kind of cartoons? Clever.]

Adjective Clauses

1.129 An *adjective clause* is a dependent clause modifying a noun or pronoun in the independent clause. The relative pronouns **that, which, who, whom,** and **whose** are used to introduce the adjective clause. (A *clause* is a group of words containing a subject and predicate. Some clauses can stand alone as an independent thought while others cannot.)

The topic **that was being debated** did not draw much audience participation.

Hartmann Co., Ltd., **which distributed auto parts statewide,** recently became insolvent.

Adjective Phrases

1.130 An *adjective phrase* is an infinitive phrase, a participial phrase, or a prepositional phrase that functions as an adjective to modify a noun or pronoun. (A *phrase* is a group of words without a subject or predicate that cannot stand alone as a complete sentence.)

Our salesmen have a lot more territory **to cover.** [infinitive phrase]

Alfred and Ida, **having driven across the state,** were glad to get home. [participial phrase]

The microfiche **on the counter** was returned today. [prepositional phrase]

Compound Adjectives

1.131 A compound adjective includes two or more words that function like adjectives and are written as one unit to convey a single thought. A compound adjective may be used in place of an adjective clause or phrase.

1.132 Some forms of compound adjectives require a hyphen, some require a comma, and some require no punctuation.

1.133 **Adjective and adjective.** When two or more adjectives are combined to modify a noun, a hyphen is not used.

black leather case	**manila kraft** envelope
blue denim shirt	**pretty young** woman

1.134 When two independent adjectives modify the same noun, separate the adjectives with the conjunction **and.**

German and French ancestry
long and tedious task

1.135 When two independent adjectives modify the same noun and there is no conjunction between the adjectives, use a comma to indicate the omission of the word **and.** (Insert the word **and** between the two independent adjectives to test the correct use of the comma.)

old, decrepit building
tall, slender youngster

1.136 **Adjective and past participle.** The following compound adjectives consist of an adjective and a verb ending in -ed (or an irregular form—see 1.66). These words are always hyphenated when they precede a noun.

air-conditioned	high-priced	old-fashioned
double-spaced	low-priced	small-sized
good-natured	lowest-priced	smaller-sized
heavy-handed	medium-sized	soft-spoken
high-flown	middle-aged	triple-spaced

1.137 **Adjective and noun.** An adjective and a noun are combined as a compound adjective to modify a noun. If the compound adjective immediately precedes the noun, hyphenate the compound adjective. If the compound adjective appears elsewhere in the sentence, it is not hyphenated.

fine-quality merchandise [merchandise of fine quality]

high-income property [property yielding a high income]

1.138 Certain adjective-and-noun combinations are spelled as one word without the hyphen. Consult the dictionary when you are in doubt.

bylaws	cutrate
checkbook	taxpayer
clearinghouse	underrated

1.139 **Adjective and present participle.** A participle is a word that ends in *-ed* or *-ing* or is the past tense form of an irregular verb. When used by itself, a participle functions as an adjective modifying a noun or pronoun. Hyphenate adjective-present participle modifiers before a noun.

high-ranking official **strange-sounding** noise

1.140 **Adverb and adjective.** An adverb and adjective compound adjective is not hyphenated since the adverb is used to modify the adjective.

more complicated plot	**very intelligent** person
most exciting experiences	**very jealous** child

1.141 **Adverb and participle.** An adverb and a participle used as a compound adjective are hyphenated when they precede the noun. When the participle is written as part of the predicate, a hyphen is not used.

best-known reporter
[reporter who is best known]

faster-moving train
[train that is moving faster]

1.142 Certain adverb-participle compounds are hyphenated even when they follow a noun.

clear-cut responsibilities
[responsibilities are clear-cut]

far-reaching effects
[effects are far-reaching]

1.143 **Adverb and participle.** An *-ly* ending adverb and a past participle are not hyphenated.

highly respected administrator	**privately operated** shop
newly decorated home	**poorly written** letter
oddly shaped room	**richly deserved** award

1.144 An adverb and an *-ing* ending participle are hyphenated.

highly-motivating lecture
exceptionally-pleasing meal

1.145 **With suspended hyphen.** A series of hyphenated adjectives may be written with a suspended hyphen after each adjective. The noun is stated only after the last adjective. Leave one space after each suspended hyphen.

a **ten-** or **twenty-year** bond
short- or **long-term** loan
$40-, $50-, or **$60-a-day** suites
three- to **four-week** training

1.146 **Compound noun.** A compound noun consists of two nouns combined to modify another noun. A hyphen is not used with these compound nouns.

charge account customer
community college degree
income tax laws
life insurance coverage
real estate license
word processing center

1.147 **Compound phrase.** A phrase used as a compound adjective is hyphenated when it precedes the noun.

on-the-job training
on-the-scene reporter
$1,000-a-month salary
out-of-pocket expenses
out-of-town address
question-and-answer period

1.148 When foreign words and phrases are used as adjectives, they should not be hyphenated.

ad hoc committee
au gratin potatoes
bon voyage party
bona fide complaint
de facto segregation
ex officio member

1.149 **Number and noun.** A number and noun combined as a compound adjective are hyphenated when the adjective precedes the noun. If the compound adjective appears elsewhere in the sentence, it is not hyphenated. The noun following the number is written in its singular form. Numbers below ten and numbers that can be written in one word are spelled out.

two-month leave
four-week vacation
twenty-pound bond
thirty-year lease
55-mile limit
136-page transcript

1.150 When a number (numeral or spelled out) is used with such nouns as **percent, million,** or **billion,** do not hyphenate the compound adjective.

a **nine percent** increase
$14 million project
120 percentage points

1.151 Ordinal numbers combined with nouns as compound adjectives also are hyphenated. The words should be spelled in full if they can be written in one word.

first-rate campaign
first-run film
second-hand information

1.152 **Proper adjective.** When proper names are used to modify other nouns, they are not hyphenated.

Western Union Mailgram	**Superior Court** docket
Municipal Court case	**Wilshire Boulevard** address

1.153 When two or more proper names are combined as one modifying unit, a hyphen is used to connect the words. If the sentence is rewritten, the proper names are not hyphenated, except when the compound adjective is intended as a single unit.

The **Los Angeles-to-Honolulu** flight takes about 4½ hours. [The flight from Los Angeles to Honolulu takes about 4½ hours.]

FORMS OF ADJECTIVES

1.154 Adjectives are not easily identified by their form, since they may also be used as adverbs and as verb forms.

Descriptive Adjectives

1.155 A *descriptive adjective* is a word that describes the quality of a noun or pronoun. This type of adjective answers the question *What kind?*

James Smith decided to retire early because he was a **sick** man.

Please rearrange those **conference** chairs.

Demonstrative Adjectives

1.156 **This, that, these,** and **those** are *demonstrative adjectives* that limit the noun or pronoun.

This (singular form) and **these** (plural form) are used to point out people or objects nearest us in distance or time.

The data on **this** microfiche need to be updated.

These cities had the largest increase in air pollution since 1965.

That (singular) and **those** (plural) are used to point out people or objects further removed in distance or time.

I believe **that** date was November 30.

Those administrative secretaries are the most efficient people.

Limiting Adjectives

1.157 A *limiting adjective* is a word that limits the quantity of a noun or pronoun and specifies *which* one.

1.158 The articles **a** and **an** are indefinite adjectives used to refer to one person, place, or thing. Use *a* before a noun beginning with a consonant.

> **A** mistake has been discovered in our recent statement.

Use *an* before a noun beginning with a vowel.

> Lyn Clark and Don Busche were to submit **an** opinion in two weeks.

When the letter *h* at the beginning of a noun is pronounced, use the article *a*. If the letter *h* is not pronounced, use the article *an*.

> **A** hangar on Field 13 is available for the light plane.
>
> We will take a break for **an** hour.

When the letter *u* at the beginning of a word is pronounced *yoo,* use the article **a.** When the letter *u* is pronounced in other than the long *u* sound, use the article **an.**

> He has developed **an** unusual formula.
>
> **A** union strike would cripple all transportation services.

1.159 The article **the** is a definite adjective used to designate a specific person, place, or thing or a group or class.

> Savings accounts are insured by **the** Federal Deposit Insurance Corporation (FDIC).
>
> **The** truth is quite obvious.

Proper Adjectives

1.160 A *proper adjective* is an adjective derived from a proper noun and is capitalized.

> The **Russian** cosmonauts and the **American** astronauts have made great strides in space.

Similar Adjectives and Adverbs

1.161 Many of the words classified as adjectives and adverbs are similar or identical, although their function in sentences and their meanings are different. The similarities and differences may be classified under absolute adjectives and adverbs, comparisons of words, and words ending in -ly.

ABSOLUTE ADJECTIVES AND ADVERBS

1.162 An *absolute* adjective or adverb is a limiting or descriptive word that represents the highest degree or quality and cannot be compared with anything else. No comparison is possible with these words.

absolutely (adv)	conclusive (adj)
always (adv)	correct (adj)
complete (adj)	correctly (adv)
completely (adv)	dead (adj and adv)

eternal (adj and adv)	perfectly (adv)
exact (adv)	perpendicular (adj)
final (adj)	real (adv)
forever (adv)	round (adj and adv)
full (adj)	square (adj and adv)
ideal (adv)	supreme (adj and adv)
immaculate (adj)	unanimous (adj)
impossible (adv)	unique (adj)
never (adv)	universal (adv)
perfect (adj)	wrong (adv)

The **eternal** light shines over John F. Kennedy's grave.

These printed solutions in the back of the book are **wrong.**

1.163 When necessary to indicate the degree to which a person or object reaches the absolute quality, use the words **hardly, less, more, nearly, more nearly,** or **most nearly** before the absolute adjective or adverb.

Sherwood's solution was **more nearly perfect** than Rollie's.

Mr. LaCroix's secretary performs her laboratory analyses in a **most nearly perfect** way.

-LY ENDING WORDS

1.164 Words that end in **-ly** are usually adverbs; some are adjectives; others can function as both adjectives and adverbs.

Adverbs	*Adjectives*	*Both*
badly	costly	daily
carefully	fatherly	early
clearly	friendly	likely
completely	motherly	monthly
immediately	neighborly	only

It was the **only** way to keep our overhead expenses down. [adj]

It was **only** yesterday that we noticed the patient's change in blood pressure. [adv]

Jim Clark arrived **early** for the meeting with his editor. [adv]

The Los Angeles *Times* is a **daily** publication. [adj]

COMPARISONS

1.165 Adjectives and adverbs indicate degrees of comparisons between and among persons, places, and things. The three degrees of comparison are the **simple, comparative,** and **superlative.**

A *simple adjective or adverb* is used by itself or with another adjective or adverb to make a simple statement. No comparison is being made in the statement.

A *comparative adjective or adverb* compares a higher or lower degree between two persons, places, or things.

A *superlative adjective or adverb* compares the highest or lowest degree among three or more persons, places, or things.

Simple: The new street was made **wide** for the flow of traffic.

Comparative: The new street was made **wider** than the other streets.

Superlative: The new street was made the **widest** of all the streets in the area.

Simple: Ken is a **tall** boy.

Comparative: David is **taller** than Tracy.

Superlative: Ken is the **tallest** boy of the three.

One-Syllable Words

1.166 The **comparative form** is written by adding *-er* to the simple form of one-syllable words. (Note the slight change in spelling of some words when *-er* is added.)

1.167 The **superlative form** is written by adding *-est* to the simple form of one-syllable words. (Note the slight change in spelling when *-est* is added.)

Simple	Comparative	Superlative
big (adj/adv)	bigger	biggest
cheap (adj/adv)	cheaper	cheapest
close (adj/adv)	closer	closest
deep (adj/adv)	deeper	deepest
fast (adj/adv)	faster	fastest
fine (adj/adv)	finer	finest
hard (adj/adv)	harder	hardest
large (adj/adv)	larger	largest
loud (adj/adv)	louder	loudest
nice (adj/adv)	nicer	nicest

1.168 A few one-syllable words are written with the words **more** or **less** in the comparative form and **most** or **least** in the superlative form.

Simple	Comparative	Superlative
prompt	more/less prompt	most/least prompt
tired	more/less tired	most/least tired

Simple: The Dobbings are **prompt** people.

Comparative: The Dobbings are **more prompt** than most people realize.

Superlative: The Dobbings are the **most prompt** people in the world!

Two-Syllable Words

1.169 The **comparative form** is written by adding either *-er* to the simple form or *more* or *less* before the simple form.

1.170 The **superlative form** is written by adding either *-est* to the simple form or *most* or *least* before the simple form.

Simple	*Comparative*	*Superlative*
active (adj)	more/less active	most/least active
careful (adj)	more/less careful	most/least careful
clever (adj)	more/less clever	most/least clever
costly (adj)	more/less costly	most/least costly
happy (adj)	happier	happiest
jolly (adj/adv)	jollier	jolliest
lonely (adv)	lonelier	loneliest
lovely (adj/adv)	lovelier	loveliest
mild (adj)	milder	mildest
often (adv)	more/less often	most/least often

Simple: Production recommended a **costly** proposal to management.

Comparative: Production recommended to management a **more costly** proposal than was expected.

Superlative: Production recommended the **most costly** proposal in the company's history.

Simple: I found the test **easy.**

Comparative: I found this test **easier** than the one I took in psychology.

Superlative: I found this test the **easiest** of the tests in psychology, biology, and English.

Polysyllabic Words

1.171 The **comparative form** is written by adding *more* or *less* before the simple form.

1.172 The **superlative form** is written by adding *most* or *least* before the simple form.

Simple	*Comparative*	*Superlative*
acceptable	more/less acceptable	most/least acceptable
beautiful	more/less beautiful	most/least beautiful
capable	more/less capable	most/least capable
enthusiastic	more/less enthusiastic	most/least enthusiastic

Simple: The company's work standards were **acceptable** to her.

Comparative: The company's work standards were **more acceptable** to her than to her coworkers.

Superlative: The company's work standards were the **most acceptable** of the five comparable organizations in the city.

Irregular Adjectives and Adverbs

1.173 Irregular words are those where the word itself is changed in the comparative and superlative degrees. There are few words in this category, but they are commonly used.

Simple	***Comparative***	***Superlative***
bad (adj/adv)	worse	worst
far (adj/adv)	farther/further	farthest/furthest
good (adj/adv)	better	best
ill (adj/adv)	worse	worst
late (adj/adv)	later, latter	latest, last
little (adj/adv)	littler, less, lesser	littlest, least
many (adj)	more	most
much (adj/adv)	more	most
well (adj/adv)	better	best

Simple: The company's credit position is **bad.**

Comparative: The company's credit position is getting **worse.**

Superlative: The company's credit position is at the **worst** point in its history.

Simple: Her associates were **many.**

Comparative: Her firm had **more** associates than the other medical groups.

Superlative: Her firm had the **most** associates of the groups in the association.

COMPARISONS WITHIN THE SAME GROUP

1.174 When a comparison is made between particular persons, places, or things in the same group, use the **comparative form** of the adjective or adverb and the word **other** or **else** to clarify the comparison.

Their pharmacy is better stocked than any **other** in town.

Our cheerleaders yelled louder than anyone **else** at the game.

1.175 When a comparison is made between *one* person, place, or thing and *several others* within the same class, use the **superlative form** and the phrase **of all** after the adjective or adverb.

Of all diseases known to medical science, cancer is the most puzzling. [an inverted sentence with the dependent clause written first]

TROUBLESOME ADJECTIVES AND ADVERBS

1.176 Some words that can function as either an adjective or an adverb are often confused; the definitions below may help you avoid some of these problems.

Fewer/Less

1.177 *Fewer* is an adjective used to refer to **number** with plural nouns.

There were **fewer** than five students at the tryouts.

Less is an adjective used to refer to **degree** or **amount** with singular nouns.

Less interest on our savings is paid at the college foundation than at a savings and loan association.

Good/Well

1.178 *Good* is an adjective used to modify a noun.

Many feel that Mrs. Willis is a **good** teacher.

Well is either an adjective or an adverb. As an adjective, it modifies a noun or another adjective. *Well* can refer to health.

Dr. Norman Vincent Peale is a **well**-known lecturer on positive thinking.

He is in fine health; his doctor says Mac is **well** enough to return to work.

As an adverb, *well* describes the action of the verb.

For a drama student, she sings **well.**

Most/Almost

1.179 *Most* is the superlative form of the adjectives **much** and **many.**

She is the **most** dedicated person I know.

Almost is an adverb.

Almost all the basketball players are at least six feet tall.

Real/Really

1.180 *Real* is an adjective used to modify a noun.

It wasn't a hairpiece; it was **real** hair.

Really is an adverb describing the action of a verb. Substitute the word *very* to test the correctness of *really* in a sentence.

He has been a **really** enthusiastic worker.

Some/Somewhat

1.181 *Some* is an indefinite adjective used to modify a noun.

There is **some** rumor of financial difficulties.

Somewhat is an adverb that answers the question, What? Substitute the words "a little bit" to test the correctness of *somewhat*.

She was only **somewhat** positive in her description of the runaway car.

Sure/Surely

1.182 *Sure* is an adjective used to modify a noun. Substitute the word *certain* to test the correctness of *sure*.

He will be a **sure** winner in the next election.

Surely is an adverb used to describe the action of a verb. Substitute the word *certainly* to test the correctness of *surely*.

It was **surely** an unusual coincidence.

Prepositions

1.183 A *preposition* is a word that shows the relationship between a noun or pronoun and another word in the sentence. The noun or pronoun becomes the object of the preposition.

The following are commonly used prepositions:

about	at	but	of	under
above	before	by	off	until
after	below	except	on	up
against	beside	into	over	upon
among	between	like	to	with

WORDS THAT REQUIRE PREPOSITIONS

1.184 Certain prepositions are commonly used with certain words to convey a more precise meaning.

account **for** someone or something
account **to** someone

agree **on** something
agree **to** something
agree **with** a person or an idea

angry **at** something
angry **with** someone

argue **about** something
argue **with** someone

compare **to** something similar
compare **with** by analyzing for differences

couple **of** persons, places, or things

differ **from** something else
differ **with** someone
different **from** something else

discrepancy **in** one thing
discrepancy **between** two things
discrepancy **among** three or more things

identical **to** somebody
identical **with** something

part **from** someone
part **with** something

retroactive **to** a date

speak **to** someone (to tell)
speak **with** someone (to discuss)

similar **to** something

We finally **agreed on** a plan of action for the staff meeting. [We worked out a plan . . .]

All parties **agreed to** the stipulation that air travel be minimized to cut expenses. [All parties accepted . . .]

Eleanor requested a **couple of** brochures on Hawaii. [not a couple brochures]

PREPOSITIONAL PHRASES

1.185 A prepositional phrase consists of a preposition followed by a noun or pronoun (the object of the preposition). It may be used either as an adjective or as an adverb.

As Adjective

1.186 When used as an adjective, the prepositional phrase is placed after the noun it modifies. (Note that the preposition and its object may be separated by one or more adjectives.)

The automatic typewriter is a tool **with great timesaving potential.**

As Adverb

1.187 When used as an adverb, the prepositional phrase may follow either the verb or its object.

He hit the ball **into the grandstand.**

A prepositional phrase used as an adverb may also be placed at the beginning of the sentence as an introductory, dependent element.

During that month, sales increased by 10 percent.

PREPOSITION USAGE PROBLEMS

1.188 Difficulties may arise with prepositions in four contexts: when used improperly at the end of a sentence, used improperly in a series, inserted in a sentence when they should be omitted, and confused with similar prepositions.

At End of Sentence

1.189 It is generally preferable to avoid prepositions at the end of a sentence unless any other placement would produce an awkward sentence.

That is the kind of nonsense up **with** which I will not put.
—*Winston Churchill*

In some cases, placement depends on whether a formal or an informal tone is desired.

Informal: Whom did he give the report **to**?

Formal: **To** whom did he give his report?

Short questions may end with a preposition.

What is this needed **for**?

How many people can we count **on**?

In a Series

1.190 When a sentence includes a series of prepositional phrases or parallel clauses using words that require certain prepositions, be sure that each item in the series begins or ends with the appropriate preposition.

The settlers traveled **over** a mountain range, **across** a plain, and **through** dangerous Indian territory to reach their destination.

He had a deep **devotion to,** and a sincere **interest in,** the work of the late composer.

When Unnecessary

1.191 Some colloquial speech patterns insert unnecessary prepositions after the verb; these are incorrect and should be omitted.

Does Jaime know where it is [**at**]?

Where are they going [**to**]?

We sent [**in**] for a free trial subscription.

Pairs of Similar Prepositions

1.192 Certain prepositions cause problems because their meanings may be confused with those of similar words or phrases.

1.193 **Beside/Besides.** *Beside* is a preposition meaning "next to."

She sat **beside** Jill at the luncheon.

Besides as a preposition means "except."

No one is going **besides** me.

Besides as an adverb means "in addition to."

Besides the fact that we are overloaded, we are already behind schedule in our work.

1.194 **Between/Among.** *Among* is a preposition used to refer to three or more persons, places, or things.

Among the three of us, I feel that I am the most fortunate.

Between is a preposition used to refer to two persons, places, or things.

The choice was **between** Dick and me.

1.195 **Except.** Use the objective form of the personal pronoun after the preposition *except.*

Everyone had an opportunity to speak **except** Tom Rooney and **me.** [*not* . . . except Tom Rooney and I.]

1.196 **Help/help from.** Do not use the expression "help from" except when the word *help* is used to mean "assistance" or "aid."

She couldn't **help** offering all her ideas.

The Credit Bureau requested **help** [assistance] **from** our credit clerks.

1.197 **In to/into.** *In* means something or someone located within or inside. *Into* implies some motion from the outside to the inside.

At the theatre, we ran **in** to see the manager. [*To* is part of the infinitive *to see.*]

The cattle were herded **into** the corral from the prairie.

1.198 **Of/have.** *Of* is a preposition used to indicate a relationship. *Have* is a verb. These two words are misused because of poor pronunciation in speaking. The following verb forms are used with *have:*

could have	must have	should have
may have	ought to have	would have
might have		

She should **have** realized her skills earlier. [*not* She should of . . .]

1.199 **On to/onto.** *On to* implies physical movement or the physical action of placing a person or object. *Onto* refers to the direction of movement.

He went **on to** the presidency.

She maneuvered her car **onto** the shoulder of the highway.

Conjunctions

1.200 A *conjunction* is a word used to connect two words, phrases, or clauses. The three types are coordinating, correlative, and subordinating conjunctions.

COORDINATING CONJUNCTIONS

1.201 A coordinating conjunction connects grammatical elements that are alike, such as two or more words, two or more phrases, or two or more clauses. The most common are:

and but for or nor yet

Other coordinating conjunctions, also known as conjunctive adverbs, are used to join independent clauses only. They include:

accordingly	however	notwithstanding
also	likewise	now
besides	moreover	so
consequently	neither	therefore
furthermore	nevertheless	thus
hence		

Coordinating conjunctions are used as follows:

Miss Reasons **and** Miss Lesley reserved a room in Las Vegas for the weekend. [conjunction *and* connecting two words]

Joe and Sam will fly to Reno **and** to San Francisco. [conjunction *and* connecting two phrases]

Our sales have decreased, **but** we do not know the reasons. [conjunction *but* connecting two independent clauses]

Dick Carter ordered the new equipment **but** requested that it not be installed immediately. [conjunction *but* connecting two verb phrases]

In Compound Sentences

1.202 A compound sentence consists of two or more independent clauses connected by a coordinating conjunction or conjunctive adverb. (A comma is generally used before the conjunction to separate the two clauses.)

Jake Mercado is handling the convention reservations, **and** Millicent Reese is planning the workshops.

Those books will be returned to the publishers; **therefore,** they should be packed carefully.

In a Series

1.203 A series is a group of words, phrases, or clauses. The items in the series are usually separated by commas, and the conjunction precedes the last item in the series.

We placed our order for paper clips, rubber bands, **and** fasteners.

1.204 The items in the series, however, may be separated by coordinating conjunctions rather than commas if the items are short.

Is Billy **or** Ana **or** DeeDee going to the store?

CORRELATIVE CONJUNCTIONS

1.205 A *correlative conjunction* is a pair of words that connects two elements of equal grammatical value—words, phrases, or clauses. These conjunctions include:

both . . . and	not . . . but
either . . . or	not only . . . but also
neither . . . nor	whether . . . or

They are used as follows.

Either Professor Tannenbaum **or** his assistant will perform the experiment.

Neither Ben **nor** I remembered that request.

She is **not only** an effective supervisor **but also** an expert in communication skills.

Both Florence **and** Milan were delightful cities to visit.

1.206 Care must be taken to use the correct verb form with these correlative conjunctions. Use a singular verb form with the singular noun and conjunction; use the plural verb form with the plural noun and conjunction.

SUBORDINATE CONJUNCTIONS

1.207 A *subordinate conjunction* is a noun, adverb, or adjective used to connect clauses of unequal grammatical value, such as dependent clauses and independent clauses. (The conjunction introduces the dependent clause.) The most common are:

after	if	that	whereas
although	in case that	then	wherever
as	in order that	though	whether
as if	inasmuch as	unless	which
as though	otherwise	until	while
because	provided	when	who
before	since	whenever	whom
for	so that	where	why

As we must move by the tenth, our rent should be prorated for that month.

Whether or not she receives a raise, she plans to quit her job soon.

CONJUNCTION USAGE PROBLEMS

1.208 The following pairs of conjunctions cause some difficulty in proper usage.

And/But

1.209 *And* means an addition. *But* indicates a contrasting view.

June **and** Lilly are both going.

She is going, **but** I am staying.

As . . . as/So . . . as

1.210 *As . . . as* is used to make a positive statement. *So . . . as* is used to make a negative statement.

He is **as** witty **as** he is clever.

Our fiscal policies are not **so** clear-cut **as** they ought to be.

Like/As, As if, As though

1.211 *Like* is a preposition and should not be used as a conjunction. Use the words *as, as if,* or *as though* to mean "similar to" when a conjunction is needed.

Doesn't he look **as though** he were on top of the world?

Mamie's acting **as if** she didn't care.

Whether/If

1.212 *Whether* is used to express a question or to convey a doubt. *If* is used to state a condition.

We have wondered **whether** he would be the suitable man for the job.

If the company receives another government contract, everyone will be assured of a job for the next five years.

Interjections

1.213 An *interjection* is a word that expresses strong emotion. The word may stand by itself, or it may be used within a sentence. An exclamation mark is usually written at the end of the sentence or word.

The following are common interjections.

Ha!	Great!	Ouch!	Wow!
Hooray!	Oh!	Wonderful!	Boy!

Oh! What a beautiful parade!

Ouch! That bee stung me!

Two

Punctuation

Introduction

2.1 Punctuation marks are written signals that clarify the meaning of sentences and separate structural units of writing. To use punctuation marks correctly, keep these points in mind:

1. The chief purpose of punctuation is to help the reader understand the message.

2. Toward this end, punctuation marks can be as effective as a speaker's pauses and voice inflections.

3. Punctuation marks help to clarify the basic structure of the sentence; they cannot change a poorly written sentence into a well-written one.

4. Incorrect use of punctuation marks can drastically alter the meaning or emphasis of a sentence.

2.2 Punctuation marks are discussed in alphabetical order.

Apostrophe '

2.3 Use an apostrophe:

1. To form a **possessive** to show ownership.

To determine whether a word is possessive, change the expression to read "the bicycle *of* Joe." If the word *of* can be inserted, the apostrophe is correctly used. To form the possessive of a noun that ends in *s,* add only the apostrophe. To form the possessive of a noun that doesn't end in *s,* add the apostrophe and *s* (*'s*).

`They only had a minute's notice before the tornado struck.`

`These will be the managers' decisions.`

2. To indicate **contractions.**

`it's` [for *it is*]
`I've` [for *I have*]
`don't` [for *do not*]
`she'll` [for *she will* or *she shall*]
`they're` [for *they are* or *they were*]

3. In place of an **omitted letter or letters.**

`class of '70` [for *1970*]

`8 o'clock` [for *of the* clock]

4. With a noun preceding a gerund. (A gerund is a verb form that ends in *ing.*)

`Paul's leaving upset the family.`

5. As a symbol for **foot, feet, minutes.**

`The carpet is 9' long.` [9 feet]

`He ran the mile in 5'.` [5 minutes]

6. As a **single quotation mark.**

```
Arlis shouted, "I  read the article 'Traveling
Abroad' in twenty minutes."
```

7. To indicate a **quotation within a quotation.**

```
"Did you read that chapter entitled 'Improving
Your Success Quotient'?" asked Betty.
```

8. To indicate **plurals of letters** and letters followed by periods.

```
Cross those t's and dot those i's.

M.A.'s and M.D.'s
```

Do not use the apostrophe, however, to indicate plurals of words, numbers, or uppercase letters.

```
Omit the therefores and furthermores.

Learn your ABCs and the three Rs.

Sometime between the 1920s and the 1950s, the
automobile became an American institution.
```

Asterisk *

2.4 Use an asterisk:

1. To indicate a **footnote** (where only one appears in the entire document) and its related reference or explanation.

```
Zimmer and Jones* suggest that one margin setting
be used for all report styles.

______________________________

  *Kenneth Zimmer and Vauncille Jones, Basic
Typewriting for the College Student (Beverly Hills,
Calif.:  Glencoe Press, 1972), p. 32.
```

2. To indicate an **omission** of an entire paragraph.

* * *

Brace }

2.5 Use a brace to connect **related information.** A brace can be typed by using the right or left parenthesis key, or it may be drawn in pen.

```
Alouisius Stevens,  )
Plaintiff,          )
vs.                 )      or      }
MacGraw Farnham,    )
et al.,             )
Defendants,         )
```

Brackets [ ]

2.6 Use brackets:

1. To **make a correction** or to **insert a comment** within quoted material. The brackets separate the information from the rest of the quoted material.

```
"These [Civil War] statistics are crucial to the
date."
```

2. To indicate a **parenthetical expression** within parentheses.

```
(See Exhibit D [Deed of Trust and Assignment of
Rents] attached.)
```

2.7 If brackets are not on the typewriter, they are made as follows: To type the left bracket, type the diagonal, backspace, and type an underscore. Roll the paper back one line and type an underscore. To type the right bracket, type the underscore and the diagonal. Roll the paper back one line, backspace, and type an underscore. The brackets may also be written in pen.

Colon :

2.8 Use a colon:

1. **After the salutation** in a business letter with mixed punctuation.

```
Gentlemen:      Dear Madeline:
```

2. In typing **reference initials,** to separate the writer's initials from the typist's.

```
TG:wat
```

3. Between **hours and minutes,** parts of **ratios,** parts of **biblical citations,** or **dates and page numbers** in periodical citations.

```
9:30 a.m.      Luke 3:1
20:1           Journal of Psychology 4 (1973):  24–26
```

4. To introduce a list of items following a complete sentence. The items listed may be words, phrases, clauses, or sentences. Key words used to introduce many listings are **the following, namely,** and **for example.**

```
Common business communications are:

announcements       memoranda
letters             reports
```

The following pronouns take a singular verb: anybody, anyone, each, either, everybody, everyone, neither, nobody, no one, somebody, and someone.

Do not use a colon in the following instances:

When the anticipatory expression appears near the beginning of a long sentence, use a period at the end of the sentence before the listing.

We must adhere to the following rules for our training program to be successful.

1. Eat three regular meals a day.

2. Get sufficient sleep and awake refreshed.

When there is an intervening sentence between the anticipatory expression and the listing, use a period at the end of both sentences.

The following items are to be included. Note the quantity needed.

one ream white paper
twelve sheets red construction paper
three pair scissors

5. To **emphasize a statement** following a complete sentence.

Remember what John F. Kennedy said: "Ask not what your country can do for you. . . ."

6. To **introduce quoted material** or information placed in quotes following an explanatory or introductory sentence. (A quotation of one, two, or three lines is incorporated in the paragraph; however, a quotation of four or more lines is set off as a separate paragraph, indented from both margins and typed in single spacing.)

An English textbook may give the following rule concerning dangling modifiers:

> Gerunds, infinitives, and participial phrases should be placed in sentences so that their relationship to the words modified is instantly clear.

Comma ,

2.9 Commas help the reader slow down and pause before reading further. Commas are used to separate thoughts within a sentence and to help the reader properly interpret the meaning of the sentence.

APPOSITIVE

2.10 An appositive is a noun or pronoun phrase that identifies or explains the noun or pronoun that immediately precedes it. Use commas to set off an appositive.

```
Wilma Carrol, the business teacher, has become a
new member of our organization.

Obeying his first instinct, to leave the podium,
would have caused him embarrassment later.
```

Closely Related Appositive

2.11 **Do not use commas** to separate a noun from a closely related appositive. The noun and its appositive are considered one unit that is essential to the meaning of the sentence.

```
Richard himself knew his future job potential was
limited in that field.

The year 1976 was the country's bicentennial.
```

OR *as Explanatory Word or Phrase*

2.12 Use commas to set off an identifying or explanatory word or phrase beginning with *or*.

```
Set off an appositive, or an apposition, with
commas.

Stenography, or writing in shorthand, will be
taught this year.
```

Professional Degrees

2.13 Use commas to set off a professional degree from the person's name. The degree may either be abbreviated or written out.

```
"Jasper R. Munro, Doctor of Philosophy," was
inscribed on his certificate.

Judy Bradley, CPS, works as a consultant to
business.
```

Personal Titles

2.14 Use commas to set off personal titles written after a person's name to designate rank. Such abbreviations as **Esq., Jr.,** and **Sr.** are followed by a period.

```
Francis Galloway, Jr., has been named
representative for the shipping firm.
```

When Roman or Arabic numerals are used as personal titles to indicate rank, the commas may be omitted.

```
Francis Galloway III
Henry VIII
Alexander Van Wickle 2d
```

DATES

2.15 Use commas to set off the year from the month and day when written in a sentence.

```
The deadline for submitting the bid is May 10, 1977.
```

2.16 When only the month and year are written, the comma between them may be omitted.

```
That discovery took place in May 1974.
```

GEOGRAPHIC LOCATIONS

2.17 Use commas to set off the names of a city and state; city and county; city, county, and state; or state and country.

```
The Notary Public acknowledged the signatures in
Los Angeles, County of Los Angeles, State of
California, at 2:30 p.m.
```

```
Our itinerary included Paris, France; Rome, Italy;
and Munich, Germany.
```
[Semicolons instead of commas may be used to separate series with internal commas.]

NAMES AND ADDRESSES

2.18 Use commas to separate the name, street address, city, and state of an individual or a business.

```
Please send the magazines to Ms. Marcia Rose
Trevino, 1604 Lawndale Boulevard, Parma, ID 83660.
```

2.19 Use commas to set off a descriptive or explanatory statement that includes the name of a business within a city, state, or country.

```
The Reverend Sean Mallory, of the Boys' Academy in
Boston, is addressing the congregation this evening.
```

```
His mother and father, from the Portland, Oregon,
office, are assigned here for the next three months.
```

BUSINESS ABBREVIATIONS

2.20 Use a comma to separate a business abbreviation from the company name, unless a comma is not written in the name. When the abbreviation appears within a sentence, use commas to set it off.

```
Broadway Publishers, Ltd.
Tuttle-Vas & Sons, Inc.
```

```
Massachusetts Petroleum Co., Inc., is offering a
new bonus plan.
```

BUSINESS CORRESPONDENCE: SALUTATION AND CLOSING

2.21 Use a comma after the salutation of an informal business letter or a personal letter. (A colon follows the salutation in business letters when mixed punctuation is used.)

```
Dear Jesse,
```

Use a comma after the complimentary closing when mixed punctuation is used.

```
Sincerely yours,
Very truly yours,
```

CLARIFICATION OF THOUGHTS

2.22 Use a comma to separate words or figures as necessary to avoid a misreading or misunderstanding.

What the problem is, is not known.

Rather than the expected 25, thirty people came to the party.

What the costs are, is for you to determine.

COMPOUND SENTENCES

2.23 Use a comma to separate the clauses of a compound sentence. (A compound sentence contains two or more independent clauses connected by **and, but, or,** or **nor.**)

We have ordered this style in several colors, but we have only received the shipment of green sweaters.

The comma may, however, be omitted between two short independent clauses.

He is the best and he knows it.

2.24 **Do not use a comma** to separate two independent clauses not joined by a coordinating conjunction. Use a **semicolon** or a **dash** or begin a new sentence.

Refer this matter to Personnel; Bill Doud will contact them.

or

Refer this matter to Personnel. Bill Doud will contact them.

CONTRASTING EXPRESSIONS

2.25 Use commas to set off contrasting expressions that begin with such words as **but, not, yet, rather than,** and **instead of.**

Escrow is due to close Tuesday, but only if all conditions have been met.

Eddie, rather than Jimmy, delivered those drawings.

Leave from Daly and Broadway Streets, not from Daly and Normal.

DESCRIPTIVE WORDS AND EXPLANATIONS

2.26 Use commas to set off the following expressions when they further describe or explain the words immediately preceding: **as well as, accompanied by, attached to, in addition to,** and **besides.**

The mother and father, as well as their children, are on vacation.

Submit a written proposal, in addition to all supporting documents, to the Superintendent's Office by Tuesday.

DIRECT ADDRESS

2.27 Use commas to set off a direct address. A direct address is a specific referral to the person's name, title, or other designation.

```
You are correct, Mrs. Ruesge, in saying that your
statement had been paid on June 10.

Madam President, the motion has been made and
seconded.
```

FIGURES

2.28 Use commas to separate numbers and dollar amounts. Use a comma to indicate thousands, hundreds of thousands, and millions.

```
$1,584.95     4,901
347,000       $25,750,680
```

Large numbers normally written without separation may be separated by commas to aid in reading and filing numbers more easily.

```
Invoice No. 458,310
Patent No. 325,600
```

INTERRUPTING EXPRESSIONS

2.29 Use commas to set off expressions that interrupt the flow of the sentence. These expressions may be afterthoughts or words inserted for special emphasis.

```
He was, I suppose, entitled to the promotion.

Interior Decor, I'll have to admit, did a
beautiful job in the executive offices.
```

2.30 Use a single comma when the interrupting expression appears at the end of the sentence.

```
Their anniversary date is February 14, if I recall
correctly.
```

INTRODUCTORY EXPRESSIONS

2.31 An introductory expression is a word, clause, or phrase used to introduce a subordinate clause.

Introductory Clauses

2.32 An introductory clause begins with one of the following subordinating conjunctions:

after	even though	since	until
although	if	so that	when
as	in case	supposing	whenever
as soon as	in order that	then	wherever
as though	inasmuch as	though	whether
because	otherwise	till	while
before	provided	unless	

2.33 Use a comma after an introductory clause at the beginning of the sentence.

```
Since our insurance covers the loss, we'll have
fewer expenses to contend with.
```

Introductory Phrases

2.34 An introductory phrase begins with a preposition, an infinitive, or a participle.

Prepositional. Use a comma after an introductory prepositional phrase.

```
In the meantime, please send us your check for
$485.65.
```

If the introductory prepositional phrase is short (five or fewer words), or if the sentence flows smoothly after the phrase, the comma may be omitted.

```
During our discussion several important decisions
were made.

In March a special benefit performance will be
given.
```

Use a comma after an introductory prepositional phrase that contains a verb form, regardless of how short the phrase is.

```
In reading the newspaper, I noticed an ad for a
Steinway piano.

At the moment you arrived, another customer had
just walked into the store.
```

2.35 **Infinitive.** Use a comma after an introductory infinitive phrase.

```
To obtain ticket information, call 579-7356.
```

2.36 **Participial.** Use a comma after an introductory participial phrase. A participle is a verb form that ends in *-ing, -ed,* or other past tense endings of irregular verbs. A participle may also consist of the verb *having* plus the past participle of a verb.

```
Thinking out loud, she gave the secret away
without realizing it.

Impressed by the responsibilities of the job, he
was able to adjust quite rapidly.
```

Introductory Words

2.37 The following are introductory words.

accordingly	fortunately	namely	perhaps
actually	further	naturally	so
also	hence	nevertheless	still
besides	however	next	then
consequently	indeed	now	therefore
finally	meanwhile	obviously	thus
first	moreover	otherwise	yet

Introductory words are often used as transitional expressions connecting two independent thoughts. Use a comma after them.

The executive suite has been reserved by someone else; consequently, our meeting will be held in the conference chambers.

2.38 Do not use a comma to set off one-syllable transitional expressions used as introductory words.

Arrange these cards in the files; then prepare an index for them.

It can't be done that way. But I'm sure we can find another.

Internal Introductory Expressions

2.39 Use commas to set off prepositional, infinitive, or participial phrases in the sentence (for usage at the start of a sentence, see 2.31–2.36). If the phrases are short, however, the comma is ordinarily omitted.

He told me that, at the recommendation of Miss Lorenzo, we would look at the interior furnishings and designs. [prepositional phrase]

Our teachers told us that, to type business correspondence easily, a secretary must be familiar with various types of letters and reports. [infinitive phrase]

Maria, having worked for the firm for five years, was hesitant to leave. [participial phrase]

The minutes disclosed that during the discussion several important decisions were made. [short prepositional phrase—no comma needed]

INVERTED NAMES

2.40 When an individual's name is inverted, use a comma to separate the surname from the rest of the name.

Coleridge, Samuel Taylor
Johnson, Raymond R.

When a title or degree designation follows the inverted name, use a comma to separate it from the name.

Clark, James L., Jr.
Clark, Sally N., Mrs.
Doud, William R., Ph.D.

NONRESTRICTIVE (nonessential) CLAUSES

2.41 Nonessential or nonrestrictive clauses offer additional information or an explanation but can be omitted from the sentence without changing the meaning of the statement. Use commas to set off nonessential clauses.

Lee Whiting, who is the chairperson, conducted the meeting in a very efficient manner.

The grand opening must be held on March 21, because that is the most convenient day.

NONRESTRICTIVE (nonessential) PHRASES

2.42 Use commas to set off nonessential prepositional, infinitive, and participial phrases that appear within the sentence.

```
When, in your opinion, will the medical center
open?

Our advertising staff, to maintain its fine
reputation, has produced some new
publicity campaigns.
```

OMISSION OF WORDS

2.43 Use a comma to indicate omission of a word or words from a sentence. Omitted words are usually verbs whose meanings are understood.

```
The $25 is due now; $15, in two weeks.

Clerical applicants must take the spelling test;
secretarial applicants, the spelling and vocabulary
tests.
```

PARENTHETICAL EXPRESSIONS

2.44 A parenthetical expression is a word, phrase, or clause that may be omitted from the sentence without changing its meaning. Such expressions are used for emphasis or for transitional purposes.

accordingly
actually
after all
again
also
as a matter of fact
as a result
as you know
besides
certainly
consequently
finally
first
for example
furthermore
hence
however
in addition
in fact
in my opinion
in other words
inclusive
indeed
meanwhile
moreover
namely
naturally
needless to say
nevertheless
next
no doubt
obviously
of course
on the contrary
otherwise
perhaps
personally
respectively
still
that is
then
therefore
thus
too
well
without a doubt
yes

2.45 Use a single comma:

1. To set off a parenthetical expression at the beginning or end of a sentence.

```
Nevertheless, the level of English usage is an
important part of one's total personality.

Phyllis and Don were voted president and vice
president, respectively.
```

2. To set off a parenthetical expression at the beginning of the second independent clause in a compound sentence. Either a semicolon or a period precedes the parenthetical expression in such a sentence.

    Davis Adler has just been promoted; therefore,
    please request a change of status and change in
    office accommodations.

2.46 Use two commas:

1. To set off a parenthetical expression within a sentence. A comma must precede and follow such an expression.

    It is our understanding, furthermore, that Abbott
    Industries must pay the penalty.

    It is apparent, therefore, that he should not have
    acknowledged the letter received from the Beene
    Company.

Commas may be omitted with some parenthetical expressions depending on the emphasis given, the intended meaning of the statement, and whether the expression is essential or nonessential to the sentence.

    Mr. Questa is indeed fortunate.

    We are therefore cancelling our financial
    assistance.

2.47 2. To set off the word *too* (meaning also) used in the sentence other than at the end.

    You, too, can earn a higher rate of interest at
    our association.

Do not set off the word *too* (meaning *also*) when it appears at the end of a phrase or sentence.

    Please extend our invitation to your secretary too.

RESTRICTIVE (essential) CLAUSES

2.48 A restrictive or essential clause is one that is necessary to the meaning of the sentence. Do not use commas to set off essential clauses.

    Those councilmen who favor increasing law
    enforcement personnel are in the minority.

    Anything that is unanimously decided will be
    publicized in the morning papers.

    Telephone service will be discontinued unless your
    60-day overdue bill is paid.

RESTRICTIVE (essential) PHRASES

2.49 Do not use commas to set off essential prepositional, infinitive, or participial phrases within the sentence:

```
The memorandum addressed to Holly Peterson
contained the justification that we were expecting.
```
[participial phrase]

```
Their decision to lay off the workers was reached
after a great deal of discussion.
```
[infinitive phrase]

```
The proposal at the end of the report seems
impractical.
```
[prepositional phrase]

SEPARATING A STATEMENT AND QUESTION

2.50 Use a comma between a statement and a question in the same sentence.

```
I think the annual corporate report is
comprehensive, don't you?
```

SEPARATING PIECES OF INFORMATION

2.51 Use commas to separate pieces of information written within the sentence.

```
Send the subscription to Mrs. Mary C. Seals, 1420
North Ash Avenue, Abilene, Texas 79604.
```

SERIES

2.52 A *series* is a group of related words, phrases, or clauses separated by commas. Use commas to set off items within the series. A comma is generally placed before the conjunction and the last item; it may be omitted if the practice is followed consistently.

Use a comma:

1. To set off words, clauses, or phrases in the series.

```
A dictionary shows the spelling, pronunciation,
meaning, and origins of a word.
```

```
John boarded the plane at 10:30, landed in Reno at
11:45, and arrived at the hotel at 1:15.
```
[series of clauses]

```
They saw Mae at the bookstore, Dona at the market,
and Alicia at the library.
```
[series of phrases]

2. After the last item of the series when there is no conjunction.

```
Red, white, blue, are the colors in our flag.
```

3. Before and after *etc.* as the last item in the series. (*Etc.* means "and so forth," so the conjunction *and* is not written before it.)

Paper, pencils, pens, paper clips, etc., are important supplies to be kept in a desk.

When *etc.* appears at the end of a sentence, a comma is written before the abbreviation only.

Our Spring Clearance will feature office supplies, equipment, furniture, etc.

2.53 **Do not use a comma in a series:**

1. When coordinating conjunctions are written between the items.

We have openings for machinists and draftsmen and chemists.

2. When the ampersand symbol (&) in a company name stands for the word *and*.

Our counsel is Feeney, Bolger & Reickert.

3. After the last item unless the structure of the sentence requires a comma.

January 1, December 25, and July 4, all national holidays, should be noted on our calendars.

COMMA USAGE PROBLEMS

2.54 **Do not use a comma:**

1. Between a subject and its verb.

Our minister is Reverend Jefferson.

2. Between a verb and its complement.

They were heroes in the last war.

3. Between a compound adjective and the noun it modifies.

Those truckers had to drive that long, lonely stretch of highway at night.

4. Before or after a prepositional phrase.

The technician in the laboratory had taken the specimens and had analyzed them by morning.

5. After the coordinating conjunctions *and, but, or,* or *nor* except when the structure of the sentence requires it.

They are a bit disappointed, but they will get over it soon.

See also 2.11, 2.20, 2.23, 2.38, 2.48, 2.49, and 2.53.

Dash --

2.55 The major function of a dash is to emphasize a point. The dash is typed as two hyphens with no space before, between, or after them. (It appears as one long dash in printed matter.) Use a dash:

1. In place of commas to set off a parenthetical expression more clearly.

```
The mechanical aspects of modern writing--
punctuation and capitalization--were absent from,
or inconsistently used in, ancient writing.
```

2. In place of a semicolon for emphasis before the second independent clause.

```
I campaigned the hardest--but she won the
presidency!
```

3. In place of a comma for emphasis in a compound sentence before the conjunction.

```
He was very upset by that confrontation--
and I don't blame him at all.
```

4. In place of parentheses for emphasis or clarity.

```
Refer to the April 10 letter from Corsican
Limited--the one written by the manager--
for the details.
```

5. In place of commas to set off a parenthetical expression when commas appear within the parenthetical expression.

```
Representatives from all western states--
California, Oregon, Washington, and Arizona--are
required to attend the annual sales conference.
```

6. After an introductory statement that needs explanation.

```
Writing began as pictographs--symbols which
resembled definite objects such as a man or a fish.
```

7. Before or after a single word used for emphasis.

```
Read--that is the key to knowledge.

His goals focus on one thing--promotion!
```

8. To repeat, emphasize, or summarize a statement.

```
Test drive our newest model today--Sunday--for the
smoothest ride you'll ever experience.

Meet us on the second floor--not the mezzanine--in
a half hour.
```

9. Before a significant final statement or one that summarizes several ideas.

```
Gladys arrives at work on time, gives a full day's
work for a day's pay, and treats fellow employees
with respect--she is a successful office worker.
```

Diagonal /

2.56 Use the diagonal (or slash):

1. When fractions are typed.

`The sum of 6 1/3 and 2 2/3 is 9.`

Note: All fractions should by typed using the diagonal, even when there are ¼ and ½ keys on the typewriter, unless ¼ and ½ are used alone.

2. To type or write the expression *and/or*.

`Joan and/or John will go to the store.`

3. When certain business terms are indicated.

`2/10, n/30`

4. With certain abbreviations.

A/V	according to value	C/O	carried over
B/F	brought forward	c/o	in care of
B/L	bill of lading	D/O	delivery order
C/A	capital account	L/C	letter of credit
C/D	certificate of deposit	S/D	sight draft

5. In typing reference initials in business correspondence to separate the writer's initials from those of the typist.

`CJS/pm      Morrise/I`

Ellipsis Points . . .

2.57 Ellipsis points are used to indicate the omission of one or more words in quoted material. For instructions on the correct use of ellipses, see 8.80–8.82.

Exclamation Point !

2.58 An exclamation point is used to indicate a strong emotion such as excitement, surprise, anger, or fear.

`Wonderful!  These are the results I was hoping to achieve.`

`He shouted at the top of his voice, "Help!"`

`Several times he said, "I am going to the movies"!` [Note that the exclamation point is typed after the quotation mark because the complete sentence is an exclamation.]

Use the exclamation point to punctuate a one-word expression or a short exclamatory statement.

`Stop! There is a terrible accident ahead.`

Hyphen -

2.59 Use a hyphen:

1. To divide a word at the end of a line.

```
One should not guess in divid-
ing words, and the dictio-
nary should be consulted frequently.
```

2. To write out numbers consisting of two or more words read as a single unit.

```
thirty-five
one hundred fifty-four
ten thousand three hundred seventy-nine
```

3. Between a compound adjective that functions as a single unit to modify a noun (see 1.136–1.153).

```
first-class mail
well-known physician
up-to-date invoice
```

4. In place of the words *to* or *through* (these appear as medium-long dashes in printed matter).

```
1975-76
pp. 56-72
4:30-6:15 p.m.
```

5. With certain prefixes.

```
ex-president
quasi-judicial
self-made
Senator-elect Tunney
```

6. To separate a prefix from a proper noun.

```
mid-Atlantic
post-World War I era
```

7. With improvised words, combining a letter and a word or two different words.

```
L-shaped desks
X-ray picture
kilowatt-hour
```

8. When a fraction is written in words and used as an adjective.

```
He was elected by a two-thirds vote.
```

9. With compound adjectives modifying the same noun (suspended hyphens).

```
The store packages one- and two-pound boxes of
candy.
```

10. In writing out amounts on checks and legal documents.

One Thousand Two Hundred Seventy-Five and 36/100 Dollars

11. When amounts are used as a compound adjective.

75-cent fare
55-mile-an-hour limit
16-cylinder engine

Parentheses ( )

2.60 Use parentheses:

1. To indicate a period of time.

Philologists generally divide the story of the English Language into three periods; namely, Old English (499-1100), Middle English (1100-1500), and Modern English (1500-present day).

2. To express an amount of money when more than one dollar is indicated.

The bill from the attorney was for five hundred dollars ($500).

3. To set off parenthetical expressions when commas would be confusing.

Our new management trainee was transferred from the Springfield (Illinois) office.

4. To set off special references, instructions, or other explanatory statements.

The Bill of Rights (the first ten amendments to the Constitution of the United States) describes the fundamental liberties of the people.

5. To include expressions that help clarify the meaning of a sentence.

A list of some acronyms include radar (radio detecting and ranging), sonar (sound navigation ranging), and laser (light amplification by stimulated emission of radiation).

6. To enumerate items in a sentence.

General requirements include (1) the ability to see relationships, (2) mature judgment, (3) the ability to analyze problems before solving them, and (4) efficient work habits and methods.

7. To indicate the fifth division in an outline.

```
I.
    A.
        1.
            a.
                (1)
```

Period .

2.61 Use a period:

1. After each declarative and imperative sentence.

```
The mechanics of English aid the reader in
understanding the meaning of the sentence and the
intention of the writer.

Please stop playing the piano.
```

2. After abbreviations such as titles, degrees, calendar months, and geographic names. Only one space follows the period at the end of the abbreviation; however, do not space after a period *within* the abbreviation as in degrees or geographic names.

Mr. Arthur Jameson	N.Y.
Lt. Gen.	Dec. 12
Ph.D.	Thurs.
U.S.A. (*or* USA)	U.S.S.R. (*or* USSR)

The two-letter state abbreviations (without periods) should be used for envelope addresses (see 5.14, 7.74).

When a sentence ends with an abbreviation followed by a period, do not use another period.

```
Your order will be sent F.O.B.
```

3. After initials, except for radio and television broadcasting call letters.

```
Arthur R. Jameson     KFOX
```

4. After a sentence containing a request that is phrased in the form of a question. (If a *yes* or *no* response choice is not intended, use a period; otherwise, use a question mark.)

```
Will you please send us your check for $105 today.
```

5. As a decimal point in amounts or percentages.

```
$37.95          44.9%
```

Do not use a decimal point after even dollar amounts. Dollar amounts within tabulations should be written with decimal points and zeros, however.

```
Please submit a requisition for $50 to the
controller's office today.

$57.00      $135.95     $17.90
 49.85        17.00       4.08
  3.92        26.30      15.00
```

Note that the decimals are aligned.

6. In outlines and lists, after all complete sentences.

```
I. Purposes of Typewriting
   A. Language Arts Skill
   B. Vocational Competence

I. Purposes of Typewriting
   A. You will acquire a language arts skill.
   B. Vocational competency will enable you to
      obtain a job.

The following must still be done:
1. Paint the reception area.
2. Carpet the reception area.
3. Order drapery for conference rooms.
```

2.62 *Do not* use a period when numbers or letters are enclosed in parentheses.

```
Carol has taken the following courses: (1)
typewriting, (2) shorthand, and (3) business law.
```

Question Mark ?

2.63 Use a question mark:

1. At the end of a sentence that asks a question.

```
What time is it?
```

2. To express doubt. The question mark is written in parentheses.

```
The captain of the team is 7 (?) feet tall.

His uncle was born in 1921 (?).
```

3. To raise several questions within one sentence. Leave only one space after the internal question marks; the items within the series of questions are not capitalized unless proper names are included.

```
Is he a writer? editor? printer? publisher?
```

Quotation Marks " "

2.64 Use quotation marks:

1. To enclose a direct quotation.

"I shall be home in an hour," John said.

Dr. Philip B. Gove, editor of <u>Webster's New International Dictionary</u>, says: "The proper function of the dictionary maker is to record the language as it is used by the majority of its users, not create it or legislate concerning it."

[Note that the period is placed inside the final quotation mark.]

2. To emphasize a word or phrase.

The word <u>television</u> was invented during the twentieth century by combining the Greek <u>tele</u>, meaning "far," with <u>vision</u>, the Latin root "to see."

What are the correct uses of "to," "too," and "two"?

[Note that the question mark is placed *outside* the last quotation mark because the entire sentence is the question.]

3. To indicate titles of magazine articles, chapters of books, and speeches.

The title of his article in the <u>Business Education Forum</u> is "Business Classroom and Laboratory Equipment."

"American Business" is the title of the first chapter in the book he coauthored.

The title of his speech was listed as "You--The Consumer in the Marketplace."

4. To set off a quotation consisting of a sentence or paragraph. In manuscripts and reports, a quotation of four or more lines is typed in single spacing as a separate paragraph; quotation marks are not necessary, since the quoted material is set apart from the text (see 8.79).

Synonyms may be used in a message to add variety, to adapt the level of vocabulary to the reader, and to be more definitive. While synonyms have the same basic meanings as their counterparts, it should be emphasized that different shades of meaning are involved.

5. With other punctuation marks.

John stated, "Now is the time to make a decision."

"I don't like to go to the dentist," Pete said.

[Note that periods and commas are placed inside the quotation mark.]

I sent you the article, "The Future of Young Americans"; therefore, you shouldn't have trouble with your presentation.

```
The following food items were in the box marked
"Perishable":  bread, butter, and eggs.
```

[Note that semicolons and colons are placed outside the quotation mark because they relate to the entire sentence.]

```
He shouted, "Stop!"

She asked, "What time can I go home?"
```

[Note that the exclamation point and question mark are placed inside the quotation mark because they relate to the statement within the quotes.]

```
He said, "What a piercing shout!"

Did she ask the question, "What time can I go home"?
```

[Note that the exclamation point and question mark are placed outside the quotation mark because they relate to the entire statement, not just the expression within quotes.]

Semicolon ;

2.65 The semicolon holds the reader at a particular point in the sentence before reading on. Use the semicolon:

1. To indicate that a conjunction has been omitted between the independent clauses of a compound sentence.

```
His first payment was due in March; the second
payment was due in April.
```

2. In a compound sentence connected by a coordinating conjunction to provide a longer pause or more emphasis between the clauses.

```
Someone must have realized the error; but
apparently he or she did not think it important
enough to question it.
```

3. When the second clause of a compound sentence begins with an introductory or transitional expression.

```
Spelling is not always logical or consistent;
nevertheless, an educated person is expected to
know how to spell.
```

4. In a series that consists of long items or complete sentences.

```
Dick is preparing the draft of the report; Joanne
is typing the tables, charts, and graphs; and Erik
is proofreading the completed pages.
```

5. To separate clauses that have internal commas.

```
Many common English surnames were derived from
personal characteristics, such as Little, Small,
and Young; from locations, such as Hill, Brooks,
and Wood; and from occupations, such as Baker,
Miller, Shepherd, and Weaver.
```

Underscore

2.66 An underscore is a solid line used to underline words. In typed material, underscore information that would appear in italics in a printed book, as follows:

1. To indicate the titles of books, magazines, and newspapers.

    Gone With the Wind is a book that John thoroughly enjoyed.

2. To identify distinctive names of ships, trains, and planes.

    He sailed from New York on the Queen Mary.

3. To place emphasis on a task or command.

    Please hand-carry this material to the printer.

4. To emphasize a word or expression being defined.

    Knowing the meaning of prefixes helps to define the words. The prefix re means again, con means with, pre means before, and pro means for.

5. To identify unfamiliar or foreign terms. Note that foreign words that have become part of the language are *not* underscored. Refer to a dictionary to determine whether an underscore is needed.

    The hors d'oeuvres were delicious.

6. To refer to a word, letter, or figure.

    The h in Lindbergh is silent.

Three

Capitalization

Introduction

3.1 Proper capitalization helps clarify the meaning of what has been written. In general, capitalize proper nouns—those that specifically identify persons, places, or things. Other parts of speech are not usually capitalized unless they appear at the beginning of a sentence.

Academic Subjects

3.2 Academic subjects are not capitalized unless reference is made to a specific course title. Names of languages, however, are always capitalized.

> During his senior year in high school, John took algebra, chemistry, **E**nglish, **G**erman, and typewriting.
>
> While in college, Mary found **A**lgebra I, **E**nglish III, chemistry, **G**erman I, and **T**ypewriting I to be the most interesting.

Addresses

3.3 Important words in an address are capitalized. (See also 7.18–7.24.)

> Mr. Walter Bilitz
> Burson-Marsteller
> One East Wacker Drive
> Chicago, IL 60601

> Mr. James W. McFall
> President, Educational
> Management Systems
> Automata Corporation
> 2952 George Washington Way
> Richland, WA 99352

Armed Forces

3.4 With a few exceptions, such as those listed below, military terms are capitalized when they refer specifically to a branch of the armed forces.

U.S. Air Force		the brigade
U.S. Army		the corps
U.S. Coast Guard	*but*	the regiment
U.S. Navy		naval shipyard
the Army		naval officer
the Navy		
the Infantry		

Astronomical Bodies

3.5 Names of specific planets (except *earth*), stars (except *sun* and *moon*), and constellations are capitalized. However, if *earth, moon,* and *sun* are in a list of astronomical bodies, capitalize these words to maintain consistency.

the Big Dipper Jupiter the Milky Way Saturn

The four planets nearest the sun are Mercury, Venus, Earth, and Mars.

Businesses

3.6 Important words in business names are capitalized. Such words as *and, of,* and *the,* when written within a name, are not capitalized. *The* is capitalized when it is the first word of a company's name.

American Chemical and Research Corp.
The United Refrigeration Corporation
Dictation Disc Company
John's Barber Shop
Leonard's Restaurant by the Sea
The Kathryn Kienst Salons

Calendar Periods

3.7 Calendar periods include days of the week, months of the year, seasons of the year, historical events, holidays, and periods of time.

DAYS/MONTHS

3.8 Days of the week and months of the year are always capitalized.

Wednesday, February 24
the second Monday in July
the tenth of November

but

in nineteen sixty-nine
the mid-seventies
third-quarter earnings

HISTORICAL EVENTS/TIME PERIODS

3.9 Important words in historical events and periods of time are capitalized.

Battle of Trenton
Civil War years
War between the States
the Ice Age
the Roaring Twenties
the Middle Ages

HOLIDAYS

3.10 Names of holidays are capitalized, including the word *day* written with the event.

Veterans Day Labor Day

SEASONS

3.11 Seasons of the year are not capitalized unless they refer to a specific time period or event.

Fall Quarter, 1976	spring cleaning chores
Spring Clearance Sale at Sears	their winter wardrobe

Common Nouns

3.12 Common nouns—those that refer to people, places, or things in general—should not be capitalized. Note, however, that the following words may be used as common or proper nouns.

act	college	department
avenue	committee	division
board	company	president
board of directors	corporation	state
city	county	supervisor

3.13 When these and similar words are written **as part of a name,** they are capitalized. However, when they are used alone to stand for the entire name or for the general category to which the name belongs, do not capitalize. (See also 3.37, Proper Nouns.)

the Arlington Trust **C**ompany

Their **c**ompany was conducting an involved title search.

U.S. **D**epartment of Agriculture

That **d**epartment publishes several booklets on proper health care and diet for everyone.

He goes to Amherst **C**ollege.

Her hopes for admission to an eastern **c**ollege were soon diminished.

the **B**oard of **D**irectors of U.S. Steel Corporation

Members of the **b**oard of **d**irectors accepted the cost-of-living increase proposed.

Compass Terms

3.14 The points of the compass are not capitalized unless they refer specifically to a particular region or are used as part of a proper name. (See also 3.19–3.21, Geographic Names.)

north side of the street		North Dakota
southwest corner		East Third Street
drive west	*but*	the South (U.S.)
just south of Laguna		the Middle West

3.15 The adjectives **northern, eastern, southern,** and **western** are not capitalized unless they are written as part of a proper name.

northern coastal area	*but*	Northern Ireland
southern Illinois		Southern Section Conference
midwestern drought		Middle Eastern
eastern standard time (EST)		Western world

Derivatives of Proper Names

3.16 Words derived from proper names are capitalized.

New Yorker — Scotch plaid
Elizabethan — Turkish tobacco

3.17 Certain derivatives have acquired a common meaning so that capitalization is not needed. Consult the dictionary for correct capitalization.

french cuff — plaster of paris
manila envelope — roman candle

Family Titles

3.18 Family titles are capitalized when they are followed by a personal name and when the title itself is used as a name.

Uncle Joe was kind to everyone.
His **u**ncle had interesting hobbies.

Grandfather Timpkin was a stamp collector.
It seems **G**randpa was still able to drive his car.

Geographic Names

3.19 Geographic names—of continents, nations, states or commonwealths, cities, towns, mountains, bodies of water—are capitalized. (See also 3.14–3.15, Compass Terms.)

North America	Brownsville	El Monte
Mexico	Atlantic Ocean	Pikes Peak
Idaho	Mount Ranier	New York Harbor

3.20 Regions, localities, and nicknames of cities and states are also capitalized.

the Keystone State — Third Ward
Salem Township — the South Pole

3.21 Sections of countries or other geographic subdivisions should be capitalized; compass points indicating general directions should not be capitalized.

the Midwest
the Middle East
northern New Jersey

John travels south to go home.
The sun sets in the west.

Government Officials and Titles

3.22 The following titles of high-ranking government officials at the international, national, and state levels are capitalized when written before, or in place of, a specific individual's name. They are not capitalized, however, when used to refer to an entire class of officials.

Ambassador
Attorney General
cabinet officials (e.g.,
  Secretary of State
  Secretary of the Interior
  Secretary of the Treasury)
Chief Justice
Chief of Staff
Governor
heads of agencies/bureaus
Lieutenant Governor
Premier
President
Prime Minister
Prince
Princess
Queen
Secretary-General of
the United Nations
Vice-President

President Abraham Lincoln signed the Emancipation Proclamation in 1862.

The **P**resident signed the Emancipation Proclamation.

The Constitution requires that all candidates for **p**resident be at least thirty-five years old.

Governmental Bodies

3.23 The following words are capitalized because they refer to specific governmental **units.**

the Congress
the United States Congress
the Legislature (preceded by state name)
the House (of Representatives)
the Senate (of the United States or a state)

3.24 The names of government **agencies, authorities, boards, commissions,** and **departments** are capitalized.

Pennsylvania's Higher Education
  Assistance Agency
Liquor Control Board
Federal Trade Commission
Department of Justice
California Youth Authority
National Aeronautics and
  Space Administration

Hyphenated Words

3.25 Capitalize only those parts of hyphenated words that are normally capitalized. (See also 3.35 and 3.36, Prefixes.)

Mexican-American
Trustee-elect Sarver
Merriam-Webster dictionaries
mid-August workshops

Institutions

3.26 The names of such institutions as churches, libraries, schools, hospitals, synagogues, colleges, and universities are capitalized.

First Presbyterian Church
Central Hills Public Library
Morris High School
Duffs Junior College
University of Pennsylvania
Beth El Temple
Daniel Freeman Hospital

3.27 School, college, or division names within a university or college are also capitalized.

School of Agriculture
College of Letters and Sciences
Department of English
Business and Social Sciences Division

Legal Terminology

3.28 Important words in legal citations are capitalized.

Galati v. *New Amsterdam Casualty Company,* Mo. App. 381 S.W. 2d 5

Metropolitan Life Insurance Company v. *Wood*

Taft-Hartley Act

3.29 In legal documents, certain **introductory words** are typed in solid capitals.

SECOND: I hereby give, devise, and bequeath. . . .

IN WITNESS WHEREOF, the parties. . . .

WHEREAS, the cooperation of both organizations. . . .

THEREFORE, BE IT RESOLVED, that the establishment and maintenance. . . .

between the PLAINTIFF and DEFENDANT. . . .

Letter Elements

3.30 The first letter of the salutation, attention line, subject line, complimentary closing, and company name are capitalized; sometimes an entire element may be capitalized.

Dear John:
My dear Mr. Hendricks
Attention: Ms. Irene Messina
SUBJECT: Policy No. IR39050

Sincerely yours
Very truly yours
MANAGEMENT
CONSULTANTS, INC.

Names and Nicknames

3.31 Words used as nicknames designating particular people, places, or things, are capitalized.

the First Lady
the Windy City
Old Ironsides

Nationalities and Races

3.32 All nationalities and races are capitalized, but the terms "black" and "white" are not.

Caucasian	German	Mexican	Puerto Rican
Chinese	Italian	Negro	Swedish

Noun Preceding a Letter or Number

3.33 The descriptive word before a number or letter should be capitalized to clarify and place proper emphasis on the term as a single unit. When the noun and the number or letter are separated in the sentence, the descriptive word is not capitalized.

Appendix A	Room 40
Enclosure 3	Conference Room G
Table 15	Public School 39
Form Y	Catalog No. 421

The number of the room where we will meet is 40.
The course number is given as 421 in the catalog.

Organizations

3.34 Organizations include associations, clubs, foundations, political parties, societies, etc. Important words in these names are capitalized.

Future Business Leaders of America
National Education Association
Democratic Party
Republican Party

Prefixes

3.35 Hyphenated prefixes are capitalized only when the sentence begins with the hyphenated word. Even if the prefix precedes a proper noun, only the first letter of the proper noun is capitalized.

ex-President
mid-July wedding
pre-Johnson years
post-war era

Post-war Germany was characterized by economic instability.

Germany's economy suffered during the post-war period.

3.36 Foreign surname prefixes do not follow a specific rule for capitalization. Certain surnames with prefixes begin with a capital letter; others are written with a space between the name and the prefix. In general, follow the individual's preference in spelling his or her name.

de Catur (*or* Decatur)
De La Cruz
de la Torre
Del Prado
DeMille
Di Iorio
MacRae
McCray
M'Creery
McEvily
O'Brien
Van Laanen
Van Osdel
von Kalinowski
Von Posch

Proper Nouns

3.37 The first letter of each significant word in proper names of people, places, and things is capitalized (see also 3.12 and 3.13, Common Nouns).

Blackman Building
Fort Ord
Golden Gate Bridge
Kapiolani Park
Kennedy Center for the Performing Arts
Lincoln Memorial
the Magee Hotel
Norfolk and Western Railroad
Queen Mary
Victory Day Celebration
the White House

Publications

3.38 Important words in titles of books, magazines, newspapers, articles, and historical documents are capitalized. Except for articles and some documents, such titles are also underscored (in print they are in italics) or, less commonly, typed in solid capital letters. Article titles are placed within quotation marks.

New Standard Reference for Secretaries and Administrative Assistants

"Care and Feeding of Persian Cats"

Wall Street Journal or WALL STREET JOURNAL

Declaration of Independence

Encyclopaedia Britannica or ENCYCLOPAEDIA BRITANNICA

Quotations

3.39 If a statement within quotation marks is a complete sentence or a one-word exclamation, the first word should be capitalized. However, a sentence fragment in quotations should not begin with a capital letter.

In opening his speech, Mr. Roberts said, "**T**oday is the tomorrow all of us worried about yesterday."

Referring to the "**s**evere problems facing our modern cities," the speaker expanded in some detail.

After the home team won the game, everyone shouted, "**H**ooray!"

Religious Terms

3.40 Specific religious terms, including names of saints and deities, titles of sacred works, and names of holy days, are capitalized; such general terms as "biblical" and "godlike," however, are not.

Apostles' Creed	Genesis	the Lord
the Bible	God	Mohammed
Buddha	the Holy Ghost	St. Mark
Catholicism	Judaism	Savior
Easter Sunday	the Koran	Ten Commandments

Sentences

3.41 The first word of all sentences begins with a capital letter.

Having a dictionary within easy reach may bring the secretary closer to the revered "dictionary habit."

WITHIN PARENTHESES

3.42 The first word of a complete sentence written within parentheses is capitalized only if the sentence is not part of *another* sentence. Words in sentence fragments in parentheses are capitalized only if they would normally be capitalized.

Because of the late hour, they decided to skip dinner. (Their plane had been delayed before taking off.)

Because of the late hour (their plane had been delayed before taking off), they decided to skip supper.

Our next door neighbors (the Bonnes) will be traveling to South Africa this summer.

IN OUTLINES

3.43 The first word of each item in a **main or secondary heading** is capitalized whether or not the item is a complete sentence. (See also 8.17–8.21, Outline Styles.)

I. Company Fringe Benefits

A. Paid vacations
B. Accumulated sick leave
C. Medical insurance

LISTS WITHIN SENTENCES

3.44 The first word of an enumerated item written within a sentence is not capitalized, even if the item is a complete sentence, unless the first word would normally be capitalized.

The following items must still be taken care of: (1) the Ohio office must make hotel reservations; (2) Artie Maxwell must organize the committee on convention programming; and (3) our New Jersey office must submit a tentative budget.

Titles

3.45 Titles preceding a name are capitalized. Titles that follow a name are capitalized only with positions that indicate special distinction. (See also 7.80, Forms of Address.)

General Saxon	the Mayor of Boston
Vice President Harris	the Reverend David Sork
Justice Tennison	the senior Senator from New Mexico

James Smith, assistant director of purchasing, will be the speaker.

Sales Manager Arthur Brown recently resigned his position.

Trade Names

3.46 Names of common business products or services are capitalized.

Bayer Aspirin	Pyrex
Benrus watches	Vicks VapoRub
Coca Cola	

3.47 Certain trade names that have become accepted as everday words do not require capitalization. (Check the dictionary to determine whether or not a trade name should be capitalized.)

mimeograph	kleenex
nylon	xerox

Four

Spelling & Word Division

Word Endings and Letter Combinations

4.1 In using the general guidelines provided below, remember that there are always exceptions to most spelling "rules." Remember also that many words in the English language are not spelled the way they are pronounced. One rule you *can* depend on is: When in doubt, refer to a dictionary.

-able and *-ible*

4.2 The only guideline offered for the use of these two word endings is to become familiar with the more common words and the correct spelling of the suffix.

-able endings	*-ible endings*
acceptable	admissible
likable	eligible
noticeable	flexible
probable	intelligible
valuable	irresponsible
washable	susceptible

-cede, -ceed, -sede

4.3 Eight words end in *-cede*.

accede	cede	intercede	recede
antecede	concede	precede	secede

Only three words end in *-ceed*.

exceed proceed succeed

Only one word ends in *-sede:*

supersede

4.4 Derivatives of these words are often spelled differently from the root word.

accede	accession
exceed	excess
proceed	procedure, procession
recede	recission
secede	secession
succeed	succession, successive

-ei and *-ie*

4.5 Write the *i* before e except after c and when the sound is pronounced like *a*. (Note the exceptions carefully!)

e *before* i (*after* c)	i *before* e
ceiling	achieve
conceit	belief, believe
conceive	field
receipt	piece
receive	relieve
	reprieve

ei *sounded like* a	*exceptions*
eight	height
heir	leisure
neighbor	neither
vein	seize
weigh	weird

-ize, -ise, -yze

4.6 There are no rules regarding these suffixes. Familiarize yourself with the more common words and the correct spelling of their endings.

-ize	*-ise*	*-yze*
apologize	advertise	analyze
authorize	compromise	paralyze
characterize	enterprise	
criticize	exercise	
liberalize	merchandise	
realize	supervise	
summarize	surprise	

-ll

4.7 Words ending in *-ll* retain the double letters before a suffix. If the suffix is *-ly,* drop one of the consonants. If the suffix is *-like,* hyphenate the words.

full	fuller	fully
install	installed, installment	
skill	skilled, skillful	
shell	shell-like	

COMBINING WORDS

4.8 When a prefix or suffix is added to a word or when words are combined that create a double letter, retain both letters.

boo**kk**eeper	i**rr**espective	roo**mm**ate
di**ss**atisfaction	i**rr**esponsible	sk**ii**ng
di**ss**imilar	mea**nn**ess	unde**rr**ated
di**ss**olve	mi**ss**pelled	wit**hh**olding

CONSONANT BEFORE *y*

4.9 Change the final *y* to *i* when preceded by a consonant before adding a suffix (except for one beginning with *i*).

beauty	beaut**i**ful	beautif**y**ing
biography	biograph**i**cal	
carry	carr**i**es, carr**i**er	carr**y**ing
clumsy	clums**i**ness	

4.10 One-syllable words retain the *-y* before *-ly* and *-ness* suffixes, with some exceptions.

dry	dryly	dryness
sly	slyly	slyness

Exceptions:

day	daily	gay	gaiety
fly	flier	lay	laid

FINAL CONSONANT DOUBLED

4.11 There are several guidelines to follow when the final consonant is doubled. Double the final consonant:

1. After a word that ends in a consonant preceded by a vowel, when the suffix begins with a vowel or *y*.

bag	ba**gg**age	
drop	dro**pp**ed	dro**pp**ing
fit	fi**tt**ed	fi**tt**ing

2. After a word that ends in a consonant preceded by a vowel with the accent on the last syllable when the suffix begins with a vowel.

begin	begi**nn**ing	handicap	handica**pp**ed
confer	confe**rr**ing	recur	recu**rr**ence

Do not double the final consonant:

1. After a word that ends in a consonant preceded by a vowel, when the accent is not on the last syllable.

benefit	benefi**t**ed	benefi**t**ing
cancel	cance**l**ed	cance**l**ing
catalog	catalo**g**ed	catalo**g**ing

2. When a suffix beginning with a *consonant* is added to a word that ends in a consonant preceded by a single vowel.

author**s**hip
develop**m**ent
frac**t**ion
sec**t**ion
ship**m**ent

3. When a suffix is added to a word that ends in a consonant preceded by more than one vowel.

brief	br**ie**fly	br**ie**fing
cheer	ch**ee**rful	ch**ee**ring
cloud	cl**ou**dy	

4. When a word ends in more than one consonant before the suffix.

attach	atta**ch**ment
condemn	conde**mn**ed
length	leng**th**en

SILENT *e*

4.12 Here, as above, several guidelines apply.

Drop the silent "e" when a word ends in silent *e* followed by a suffix that begins with a vowel.

advise	advis**a**ble
desire	desir**o**us
hope	hop**i**ng

Do not drop the silent "e":

1. When a word ending in silent *e* is followed by a suffix beginning with a consonant.

enforce	enforc**e**ment
hope	hop**e**ful
manage	manag**e**ment

Exceptions:

acknowledge	acknowledgment
argue	argument
idle	idly
judge	judgment
nine	ninth
subtle	subtly

2. When a word could be mispronounced or confused if the silent *e* were dropped.

die	di**e**d	dying
dye	dy**e**d	dyeing
eye	ey**e**ing	
hoe	ho**e**ing	

3. When a word ends in -*ce* or -*ge* and is followed by a suffix beginning with a vowel.

courage	coura**ge**ous
manage	mana**ge**able
notice	noti**ce**able

VOWEL BEFORE *y*

4.13 **Do not change "y" to "i"** before adding a prefix when a final *y* is preceded by a vowel.

convey	conveyed	conveyance
employ	employer	employing
relay	relayed	relays

Exceptions:

day	da**i**ly
lay	la**i**d
pay	pa**i**d
say	sa**i**d

Forming Plurals

4.14 The general rule for forming plurals of words is to add an *s* to the singular form of words that do not end in *s* (or an "s" sound). The plural of words ending in *s* is formed by adding *es*. Exceptions are discussed below.

-*f* AND -*fe* ENDINGS

4.15 Few nouns end in -*f* or -*fe*. The -*f* or -*fe* is sometimes changed to *ves* to form the plural. In other cases, however, the plural is formed by adding *s* to the singular form.

brief	briefs	knife	kni**ves**
chief	chiefs	leaf	lea**ves**
dwarf	dwarfs	life	li**ves**
half	hal**ves**	proof	proofs

-*s*, -*x*, -*ch*, -*sh*, AND -*z* ENDINGS

4.16 The plural of words ending in -*s*, -*x*, -*ch*, -*sh*, and -*z* is formed by adding -*es* to the singular form.

bus	buses	rush	rushes
business	businesses	stretch	stretches
church	churches	waltz	waltzes
mix	mixes	wish	wishes
quartz	quartzes		

ABBREVIATIONS

4.17 The plural of most abbreviations is formed by adding *s*.

mo.	mos.
no.	nos.
yr.	yrs.

Capital Letters

4.18 The plural of abbreviations written in capital letters is formed by adding *s* with no apostrophe unless a misreading would otherwise occur.

ABCs	GIs
CPAs	three Rs
CPS's	XYZs

Units of Measurement

4.19 Most abbreviations for weights and measures are written in the same way for the singular and plural forms.

ft.	ft.	mi.	mi.
hr.	hr.	oz.	oz.
in.	in.	qt.	qt. or qts.
lb.	lb. or lbs.	yd.	yd. or yds.

Other Abbreviations

4.20 Other abbreviations are pluralized by doubling the consonants in the singular form.

p. 482
pp. 482–485 (page 482 to or through page 485)
pp. 114 f. (page 114 and the following page)
pp. 114 ff. (page 114 and the following pages)
v. or vv. (verses)

COMPOUND WORDS

4.21 A compound word consists of two or more words combined as a single unit. Some compound words are hyphenated; others are not. Follow the general rules for forming plurals of words and these specific guidelines as well.

1. The most significant word takes the plural form.

adjutant general	adjutant**s** general
court martial	court**s** martial or court martial**s**
deputy chief of protocol	deputy chief**s** of protocol
father-in-law	father**s**-in-law
judge advocate general	judge advocate general**s**
lieutenant colonel	lieutenant colonel**s**
notary public	notar**ies** public or notary public**s**
passer-by	passer**s**-by

2. If both words are of equal significance, both should be written in the plural form.

coat of arms	coat**s** of arm**s**
secretary-treasurer	secretar**ies**-treasurer**s**

3. If there is no one significant word and neither word is a noun, the last word takes the plural form.

go-between	go-betweens
higher-up	higher-ups

CONSONANT BEFORE *o*

4.22 The plural of most words ending in *o* preceded by a consonant is formed by adding *s*. However, some plurals are formed by adding *es;* others may be formed with either ending (first spelling is preferable).

domino	domino**es**	domino**s**
hero	hero**es**	
piano	piano**s**	
steno	steno**s**	
tango	tango**s**	
tomato	tomato**es**	
veto	veto**es**	

CONSONANT BEFORE *y*

4.23 The plural of a word ending in *-y* preceded by a *consonant* is formed by changing the *y* to *ies*. (See also 4.32 and 4.33, Proper Names.)

authority	authorit**ies**
company	compan**ies**
county	count**ies**

FOREIGN ORIGIN WORDS

4.24 The plural forms of foreign origin words deviate from the guidelines for English words. Learning the following singular and plural word endings of these words will make spelling easier.

Singular Ending	*Plural Ending*
a	**ae** or **as**
is	**es**
ix	**ices**
on	**a**
um	**ums** or **a**
us	**i**
addend**um**	addend**a**
alumn**a**	alumn**ae**
alumn**us**	alumn**i**
append**ix**	append**ices** or appendix**es**
bas**is**	bas**es**
cris**is**	cris**es**
criteri**on**	criteri**a**
curricul**um**	curricul**ums** or curricul**a**
dat**um**	dat**a**
executr**ix**	executr**ices**
formul**a**	formul**ae** or formula**s**
matr**ix**	matr**ices** or matrix**es**
medi**um**	medi**ums** or medi**a**
memorand**um**	memorand**ums** or memorand**a**
parenthes**is**	parenthes**es**
stimul**us**	stimul**i**
thes**is**	thes**es**

GEOGRAPHIC NAMES

4.25 The plural of geographic names is formed by adding *s* to the name, regardless of the last letter in the name.

Waterloo (in Iowa, Ontario, Belgium)	the Waterloo**s**
North Carolina and South Carolina	the Carolina**s**

The following geographic words are already plural.

Niagara Falls, New York
Twin Falls, Idaho
United States
West Indies

IRREGULAR PLURALS

4.26 Certain singular words are spelled differently in their plural form.

child	child**ren**	man	m**e**n
foot	f**ee**t	mouse	m**ice**
goose	g**ee**se	tooth	t**ee**th
louse	**lice**	woman	wom**e**n

4.27 When these words are used as suffixes in other words, the irregular plural form is used.

dormouse	dorm**ice**
eyetooth	eyet**ee**th
forefoot	foref**ee**t

NUMBERS

4.28 The plural of numbers written in figures is formed by adding *s*, without an apostrophe.

in the 1980s in the high 20s the middle 200s

4.29 The plural of **numbers spelled out** is formed by adding *s* or *es*, depending on the word ending.

fifty-two	fifty-two**s**
forty	fort**ies**
six	six**es**
sixth	sixth**s**

4.30 When a **fraction** is spelled out, place the plural at the end of the fraction.

three-fourth**s** of an ounce
thirty one-hundredth**s**

PERSONAL TITLES

4.31 The following are the plural forms of personal titles.

Dr. or Doctor	Doctor**s**
Miss	Miss**es**
Mr.	M**essrs.**
Mrs.	M**mes.**
Professor	Professor**s**
Rev. or Reverend	Reverend**s**

When two or more surnames are written with the same personal title, the plural form precedes the surname. The singular form may also be written before each surname—as with *Ms.*, which has no plural.

Messrs. Dvorak and Constant served as hosts for the annual Rotary Club dinner. [or]

Mr. Dvorak and **Mr.** Constant served as hosts for the annual Rotary Club dinner.

Mmes. Busche and Pinchok were elected to serve on the city council for three years. [or]

Mrs. Busche and **Mrs.** Pinchok were elected to serve on the city council for three years.

Misses Wills and Fong received their law degrees last June. [or]

Miss Wills and **Miss** Fong received their law degrees last June.

Ms. Hadden and **Ms.** Carroll have been promoted to executive positions by the Uniontown Bank Board of Directors.

PROPER NAMES

4.32 The plural of surnames is formed by adding either *s* or *es* to the name, depending on the last letter in the name. The spelling of the name is not changed in any way except for the addition of the *s* or *es*.

Judy and Allen Bradley	the Bradley**s**
Marcie and Rich Trevino	the Trevino**s**
the Cox family	the Cox**es**
the Wolf family	the Wolf**s**
the Chiu family	the Chiu**s**
the Dobbings family	the Dobbings**es**
the Guterrez family	the Guterrez**es**

4.33 The plural of first names is formed by adding either *s* or *es* to the name without changing the spelling of the name.

Mary**s**	Mitch**es**	Tracy**s**
Joe**s**	Charles**es**	Margo**es**
Chuck**s**	Kenneth**s**	Jessie**s**
Alex**es**		

SILENT *s*

4.34 Words that end in silent *s* in their singular form retain the same spelling for the plural form.

corp**s**
chassi**s**
faux pa**s**

VOWEL BEFORE *o*

4.35 The plural of words ending in *o* preceded by a vowel is formed by adding *s*.

duo	duo**s**
radio	radio**s**

VOWEL BEFORE *y*

4.36 The plural of a word ending in *y* preceded by a vowel is generally formed by adding *s*. For some words, however, the *y* is changed to *ies*.

attorney	attorney**s** (or attorn**ies**)
bay	bay**s**
display	display**s**
money	money**s** (or mon**ies**)

OTHER WORDS

4.37 The plural of words is formed by adding either *s* or *es* depending on their last letters.

do**s** and don't**s**	in**s** and out**s**
the ay**es** have it	but**s**
pro**s** and con**s**	

4.38 Several words are written in the same way for both the singular and plural forms.

counsel	moose	sheep
deer	number	species
majority	series	swine
minority		

4.39 The following words are always in the plural form.

cattle	pants	remains	scissors
data	pliers	riches	shears
goods	proceeds	savings	thanks
grounds			

Possessives

4.40 The possessive form of a word indicates that something is owned or is part of an item or a place. Possession is indicated by adding an **apostrophe and s** (**'s**) or by adding **only an apostrophe** to the word.

ABBREVIATIONS

4.41 To show possession of abbreviated words, add an *apostrophe plus s*.

CAB'**s** investigation CPS'**s** examination

BUSINESS NAMES

4.42 The possessive of names of businesses, organizations, institutions, and societies is formed by adding an *apostrophe plus s* to names that do not end in *s* or an *s* sound and by adding an *apostrophe* after names that end in *s*. Notice that the possesssive form is added to the last word in the names. (See also 4.53, 4.57.)

California State University, Los Angeles'**s** debating team
Benziger Bruce & Glencoe'**s** publications
Arlen and Ross'**s** tax seminar
General Hospital'**s** Intensive Care Unit

COMPOUND NOUNS

4.43 The possessive of a singular compound noun is formed by adding *apostrophe plus s* to the last word of the compound.

adjutants general'**s** orders
court martial'**s** decision
president-elect'**s** speech

4.44 The possessive of a plural compound word is formed by adding an *apostrophe* to the last word of the compound.

administrative secretaries' classifications
editors in chiefs' remarks
grants-in-aids' requirements

COMPOUND POSSESSIVES

4.45 To indicate the possessive of two or more nouns, add the appropriate possessive form to each word.

the Pinchuk'**s** and the Oakes' boats
the Davises' home and the Nanko'**s** home

4.46 To indicate joint possession, add the appropriate possessive form to the last word only.

Bullock & Yagami'**s** consulting firm
Loui, O'Connor & Stevens' mortuary

PLURAL NOUNS

4.47 The possessive of **regular** plural nouns is formed by adding an *apostrophe*.

directors' decisions
doctors' offices
secretaries' typewriters
students' records

4.48 The possessive of **irregular** plural nouns is formed by adding an *apostrophe and s*.

children'**s** daytime programs
women'**s** rights

POSSESSIVES UNDERSTOOD

4.49 When the item possessed is understood, the word in its possessive form may stand by itself.

David'**s** [grades] are higher than Jaime'**s.**

John'**s** skills in shorthand and typing are more polished than Chris'**s** [skills].

PRONOUNS

Indefinite

4.50 Pronouns ending in "one" are written as one word except for the pronoun "no one" and when the preposition *of* follows the word ("any one of distinction"). The possessive is indicated by adding an *apostrophe and s*.

another'**s** responsibilities
anybody'**s** interest
everyone'**s** ideals
no one'**s** blame

Personal

4.51 The possessive of personal pronouns is formed irregularly.

Personal Pronoun	*Possessive*
I	my, mine
you	you, yours
he	his
she	her, hers
it	its
we	our, ours

Relative

4.52 The possessive of relative pronouns is formed irregularly.

Relative Pronoun	*Possessive*
they	their, theirs
who	whose

PROPER NOUNS

4.53 The possessive of a **singular** proper noun is written with an *apostrophe and s.*

the Clark**'s** desert home
Jan Prentiss**'s** promotion
Fox**'s** Studios
Oklahoma City**'s** population

4.54 The possessive of a **plural** proper noun is written with an *apostrophe.*

The Clarkses' desert homes
Bay Cities' transit system

SINGULAR NOUNS

4.55 The possessive of singular nouns not ending in *s* is formed by adding *apostrophe and s.*

student**'s** record
secretary**'s** typewriter
Poe**'s** "The Raven"
salesman**'s** territory

4.56 The possessive of singular nouns ending in *s* is formed by adding an *apostrophe.*

Roths' supervisor
Sara Hawkins' project

4.57 If another syllable is sounded when the possessive is formed, add an *apostrophe and s.*

my boss**'s** report
Thomas**'s** new job

TROUBLESOME POSSESSIVES

4.58 The possessive forms of pronouns are often confused with contractions because they are sounded alike.

Possessives	*Contractions*
its	it's (for *it is* or *it has*)
their	they're (for *they are* or *they were*)
theirs	there's (for *there is* or *there has*)
whose	who's (for *who is* or *who was*)
your	you're (for *you are* or *you were*)

Prefixes

4.59 Learning the meanings of prefixes makes it easier to spell and define prefixed words.

ante before or in front of
antedate, anteroom, antecedent

anti against
antibiotic, antifreeze, anti-European

bi two or occurring every two time periods
biannual, bicycle

co with or together
coordinate, copartnership

com, con with or together
company, companion; confer, connect

counter against
counterbalance, counter check (n), countercheck (v)

dis apart
disburse, disassemble, discard

ex out of or from
exchange, exemption, exit

inter between or among
interoffice, interstate

mis badly or wrongly
misdeed, mismanage, misspell

multi much or many
multimillionaire, multiplicity

non not or absence of
nonparallel, nonsupport, non-Government

post after or subsequent
postdate, postpaid

pre before or prior
prepay, presell, preclude

pro in favor of or prior to
probate, proceed, pro-German

super over and above, exceeding
superabundance, superhighway

trans across or beyond
transatlantic, transcontinental, trans-Mexico

un not or none
unanswered, uncared for, unpopular

Word Division Rules

4.60 At the end of a line, divide a word between syllables. A dictionary or other reference source should be consulted when in doubt about syllabication. Type a hyphen at the end of the line to indicate the division and type the remainder of the word on the succeeding line.

RULES TO FOLLOW ALWAYS

4.61 The rules below must be observed in deciding how, or whether, to divide a word.

1. A word that has five or fewer letters or that is pronounced as one syllable should not be divided.

allot	could	fuel	rotor
change	echo	length	though

2. A one-letter syllable at the beginning of a word should not be separated from the syllable that follows.

achieve	**e**clipse
again	**o**blige

3. A two-letter syllable at the end of a word should not be separated from the other letters.

hang**er**	live**ly**
heav**en**	moth**er**

4. Root words ending in double letters are divided between the double letters.

bag-gage	ship-per
get-ting	swim-ming

5. Compound words should be divided at the hyphens.

mother-in-law	self-confidence
Mexican-American	Winston-Salem

6. The following word endings should be kept as a single unit:

-able	-cion	-icle	-tial
-cial	-ible	-sion	-tion
-cient	-ical	-sive	-tive

7. Contractions should not be divided.

can't	(for *cannot*)
don't	(for *do not*)

8. Abbreviations should not be divided.

a.m.	Dr.	p.m.
D.C.	KJIV	S & K

9. Proper names should not be divided. However, compound names may be separated between the words.

Annie	Mary / Louise
Kennedy	Thomas / William

10. Amounts and numbers should not be divided.

$15,750.36	4,673,550
25 cents	$23 million

11. Information that is read as one unit should not be divided.

Article IV	page 13
chapter 6	Section IA

12. A word with a one-letter syllable in the middle should be divided after the single-letter syllable.

mani-fest	particu-lar
melo-dy	sepa-rate

13. A word with two single-letter accented vowels written together should be divided between the vowels.

abbrevi-ate	medi-ocre
continu-ally	recre-ation

RULES TO FOLLOW WHENEVER POSSIBLE

4.62 1. Retain the prefixes by dividing after the prefix.

circum-stances	**post**-pone
con-venience	**pur**-chase

2. Retain the suffixes by dividing before the suffix.

atten-**tion**	offi-**cial**
glad-**ness**	promis-**ing**

3. Do not divide more than two lines in succession.

4. Do not divide a word at the end of the first line of a paragraph.

5. Do not divide the last word on the page.

6. Words that might be misread by the reader or otherwise confused should not be divided.

cooperation	readminister
demonstration	superfluous

Glossary of Words That Sound Alike

4.63 The sound of words does not necessarily conform to their spelling. Some words with the same or almost the same pronunciation are spelled and/or used differently; those most commonly confused are paired and defined below.

4.64 **accept** (v) to receive

The store was willing to **accept** a small down payment.

except (v) to leave out
(prep) with the exclusion of

Jane **excepted,** no one in the class really enjoys studying.

Everyone went to the movies **except** John.

4.65 **access** (n) admittance or approach

In his position as vice president, he had **access** to all the files.

excess (n) more than necessary

There was an **excess** of onions in the sauce.

4.66 **ad** (n) advertisement

The Smiths put an **ad** in the local paper when they decided to sell their second car.

add (v) to total

Although Mr. Roberts was a successful businessman, he could not **add** a long column of figures.

4.67 **adapt** (v) to make suitable

Ramos Industries will **adapt** the machine to suit the customer's specific needs.

adept (adj) skilled or proficient

John Luciero is an **adept** keypunch operator.

4.68 **addition** (n) an increase

We expect an **addition** of three assistants to our paramedical staff.

edition (n) a copy or version

The *Prudential Operations Manual* is in its third **edition.**

4.69 **advice** (n) recommendation(s)

The **advice** that Mr. Smith gave his son was excellent.

advise (v) to counsel

Her uncle will **advise** her to attend college.

4.70 **affect** (v) to influence

The quality of the food might **affect** his stomach.

effect (v) to bring about
(n) a result

As hard as the new manager tried, he could not **effect** any changes.

One **effect** of inflation is higher prices for most goods and services.

4.71 **all ready** (adv) prepared

The corporation's executive secretary was **all ready** to leave on a week's vacation when he received a call to return for a conference.

already (adv) previously

James was **already** gone when Fred reached the hotel.

4.72 **allude** (v) to make indirect reference

One should not **allude** to an event that might be misunderstood by others.

elude (v) to avoid skillfully; to evade

The burglars were able to **elude** their pursuers for only a few minutes.

4.73 **allusion** (n) an indirect reference

The mayor's **allusion** to the cost of mass transit was not ignored by reporters.

illusion (n) a misleading image or idea

The heavy fog strengthened his **illusion** that the house was shrouded in mystery.

Before the guests arrived, Mary had been under the **illusion** that only two were coming.

4.74 **all ways** (n) every respect

He is in **all ways** an understanding and a fair executive.

always (adv) at all times, without exception

Fred has many interests and is **always** going somewhere.

4.75 **allowed** (v) permitted

The company **allowed** him to take two weeks' vacation.

aloud (adv) a manner of speaking

Since Frank enjoys talking, he presented the entire report **aloud.**

4.76 **altar** (n) a raised structure as a center of religious worship

The couple took their vows before the **altar.**

alter (v) to change

It is against the law to **alter** the reading on an automobile odometer.

4.77 **any way** (n) any manner or fashion

Local industries were forbidden to pollute the river in **any way.**

anyway (adv) nevertheless, in any case

Anyway, she made every effort to win the contest.

4.78 **appraise** (v) to estimate the value of

He requested the assessor to **appraise** the property.

apprise (v) to inform

Be sure to **apprise** the buyers of the exact closing fees.

4.79 **are** (v) plural present tense of verb *to be*

The Greens **are** leaving the state and will settle in Arizona.

hour (n) time of day

The party broke up at a late **hour.**

our (pron) possessive pronoun, first person plural

Our home was not destroyed by the flood.

4.80 **assistance** (n) help or support

Please call us whenever you need **assistance** in making your household purchases.

assistants (n) helpers

My **assistants,** Joan de la Cruz and George Retana, are experienced interior designers.

4.81 **attendance** (n) the fact of, or number, attending

The seminar had 350 professors in **attendance.**

attendants (n) persons who wait on others

Ambassadors usually travel with a large group of **attendants.**

4.82 **biannual** (adj) twice a year

The **biannual** report is published on March 15 and September 15.

biennial (adj) every other year

Since the statistical material is not published annually, the **biennial** report is important.

4.83 **canvas** (n) closely woven cloth

Covering the boat with **canvas** will protect it from the elements.

canvass (v) to examine or solicit

Volunteers will **canvass** their neighborhoods for charitable contributions.

4.84 **capital** (adj) important; punishable by death; excellent
(n) wealth; seat of government (city)

The **capital** point of his paper was the need for energy conservation.

In some states, premeditated murder is still a **capital** crime.

Moby Dick is a **capital** novel.

James Smith had $50,000 in **capital** to expand his business.

Trenton is the **capital** of New Jersey.

capitol (n) buildings in which state government functions

The state legislature meets on the second floor of the **capitol.**

Capitol (n) building in which Congress meets

As a U.S. senator, Mr. Schweiker spends much time at the **Capitol.**

4.85 **cease** (v) to discontinue

Because of increasing costs, we will have to **cease** publishing a weekly newsletter.

seize (v) to confiscate or capture

The police **seized** the suspect's gun collection after his arrest.

4.86 **censor** (n) official who removes objectionable written material

The **censor's** job is important in totalitarian societies.

censure (n) a judgment involving condemnation

(v) to criticize adversely; to disapprove of or dispraise

Several academy members used their power of **censure** during the demonstration.

Members of the reviewing committee have the authority to **censure** textbooks not suitable for use in schools.

4.87 **cite** (v) to quote

You may **cite** the encyclopedia as your source of reference.

sight (n) vision

Although he was over ninety years old, his **sight** was excellent.

site (n) location

The **site** chosen for the summer cottage was perfect in every respect.

4.88 **complement** (n) that which completes

Now that a new vice president has been named, the executive staff has a full **complement** of personnel.

compliment (n) praise

(v) to praise

His immediate superior gave John a well-deserved **compliment** on his presentation.

Robin was **complimented** several times after she won the steeplechase.

4.89 **conscience** (n) one's awareness of moral implications

The jurors, with clear **consciences,** found the defendants not guilty on all counts.

conscious (adj) aware

McGee's supervisors had been **conscious** of his absenteeism for the past two months.

4.90 **consul** (n) representative for a nation's commercial interests

The French **consul** was asked to discuss several Common Market problems with the prime minister.

council (n) group of elected or appointed advisers

The city **council,** which meets every two weeks, gave the mayor some good suggestions.

counsel (n) advice

(v) advise

After receiving the letter, he went to his attorney for **counsel.**

The personnel director's job was to **counsel** new employees.

4.91 **correspondence** (n) letters or other communications

Please return these documents to the **correspondence** files.

correspondents (n) letter writers; distant news reporters

Our foreign **correspondents** are scattered throughout the world.

4.92 **decent** (adj) adequate

Without a high school education, no one can expect to earn a **decent** living.

descent (n) a downward step; one's derivation from an ancestor

The politician's **descent** into corruption was slow but steady.

Pierre Gant is an Englishman of French **descent.**

dissent (v) to differ in opinion
(n) difference of opinion

Their intention was to **dissent** from the majority opinion.

There was much **dissent** among the three candidates.

4.93 **depositary** (n) person entrusted with something

The executor of the estate was named **depositary** of the funds.

depository (n) place of safekeeping

Use the bank's night **depository** for your cash and checks.

4.94 **desert** (n) dry area
(v) to abandon

A number of camels were seen on the **desert.**

He was the type of man who would not **desert** a friend.

dessert (n) final course in a meal

They served ice cream and cake for **dessert.**

4.95 **device** (n) instrument; plan

That tool is a good **device** to use in fixing the kitchen table.

The animated toys in the window served as an effective **device** to draw people into the store.

devise (v) to contrive

The car is so old that the mechanic will have to **devise** a new part to repair it.

4.96 **disapprove** (v) to pass unfavorable judgment upon

That committee, led by its chairperson, was the first to **disapprove** our newest proposal.

disprove (v) to prove something false

The attorney successfully **disproved** the allegations submitted in the complaint.

4.97 **disburse** (v) to pay out

The company had to **disburse** $350 for reprographic supplies.

disperse (v) to spread or scatter

The advertising department will **disperse** fliers to the appropriate markets.

4.98 **dual** (adj) double

The actor played a **dual** role—both father and son.

duel (n) a conflict or combat

Aaron Burr and Alexander Hamilton used pistols in their 1804 **duel.**

4.99 **elicit** (v) to draw forth

Let the mediators try to **elicit** the facts from the union officials.

illicit (adj) unlawful

There was speculation that the merger was **illicit.**

4.100 **emigrate** (v) to leave a country

Will more U.S. citizens **emigrate** to other countries?

immigrate (v) to enter a country

In the past several decades, relatively few people have been allowed to **immigrate** to the U.S.

4.101 **eminent** (adj) conspicuous; famous

Stone walls are an **eminent** feature of the New England landscape.

His mother was an **eminent** surgeon who had saved many lives.

imminent (adj) threatening or impending

Gasoline and oil price increases are **imminent.**

4.102 **envelop** (v) to enclose

The fire had begun to **envelop** the firefighters on top of the hill.

envelope (n) container for letters

The quality of the **envelope** should match that of the stationery.

4.103 **exceed** (v) to extend outside of or enlarge beyond; to surpass

Automobile drivers should not **exceed** the posted 55 m.p.h. limits.

accede (v) to express approval or give consent

The minority group had to **accede** to the wishes of the majority in budget allocations for the fiscal year.

4.104 **expand** (v) to spread out, open wide; to unfold; to increase

We should **expand** the width of the freeway to allow more lanes of through traffic.

expend (v) to spend, pay out, or distribute; to consume by use

Efficient office workers should not have to **expend** much physical energy in performing their work.

4.105 **farther** (adj) at a greater distance

The planet Neptune is **farther** from the sun than Jupiter.

further (adv) in addition, moreover
(adj) additional, extending beyond
(v) to promote or advance

It is **further** understood that a $1,000 deposit will be paid by the tenth.

If our competitors expand their market **further** west, they will soon have the entire district.

Successful executives are those who continue their educations to **further** their careers.

4.106 **foreword** (n) preface

The **foreword** to the book was well written.

forward (adj) situated in advance
(adv) toward what is before or in front
(v) to advance or transmit

He chose a **forward** seat on the plane.

The troops moved **forward** at the command of General Smith.

Please **forward** three copies of the book.

4.107 **formally** (adv) in a formal manner

The new senator **formally** assumes office on January 20.

formerly (adv) before

She was **formerly** the mayor of a large city.

4.108 **forth** (adv) forward

The troops showed their bravery when they went **forth** in battle.

fourth (adj) number

Fred was the **fourth** member of his family to attend Stanford University.

4.109 **incidence** (n) rate of occurrence

The **incidence** of drug use among young people is alarming.

incidents (n) events

Several unfortunate **incidents** involving alcohol preceded his dismissal from the job.

4.110 **ingenious** (adj) clever

The self-correcting typewriter is an **ingenious** device.

ingenuous (adj) natural, naive

He was remarkably **ingenuous** in his assumption that car salesmen were always truthful.

4.111 **interstate** (adj) between states

Regulations of **interstate** commerce is one of Congress's major functions.

intrastate (adj) within a state

The governor's main responsibility is to concentrate on **intrastate** affairs.

4.112 **its** (pron) possessive pronoun

The car's old battery is **its** main problem.

it's (contraction) it is

It's a great day to go swimming.

4.113 **knew** (v) past tense of the verb *to know*

He **knew** Paul Smith for a period of many years.

new (adj) recent

They buy a **new** car every fall.

4.114 **later** (adv) after a particular time; at another time

John Chow-Kim was seen **later** in the Information Systems Center.

Enroll in the accounting course now or **later.**

latter (adj) relating to the second of two items

The Cincinnati and Dayton representatives will plan the conference; the **latter** group will host the dinner meeting.

4.115 **lay** (v) to set or put down

Please **lay** the report on my desk.

lie (v) to recline

Lie with your feet above your head for improved circulation.

4.116 **leased** (v) granted or held for a term

The Al Turnbull family **leased** the condominium for a three-month period.

least (adj) lowest, smallest

The orchestra seats were the most expensive in the theater; the balcony seats were the **least** expensive.

We were **least** impressed with the manner in which the lecturer presented her ideas.

4.117 **lessen** (v) to minimize or decrease

Receipt of a new government contract would **lessen** the chances of worker layoffs next year.

lesson (n) a unit of instruction

The **lesson** for the day was on caring for indoor plants.

4.118 **liable** (adj) responsible or susceptible

The company was held **liable** for the accident because of its negligence in providing safety precautions.

libel (n) a defamatory statement in writing

The employer's negative report was presented as evidence of **libel.**

4.119 **local** (adj) nearby, neighborhood

Brogan's Drugs has been in the **local** area for many years.

locale (n) location, site, situation

The **locale** for next year's convention is San Francisco.

4.120 **loose** (adj) not tightly bound

The front porch has a **loose** board, and John tripped over it.

lose (v) to suffer loss or deprivation

Though John always tries to be careful, he managed to **lose** his watch.

If Peter is not more alert, the team will **lose** another game.

4.121 **maybe** (adv) perhaps

Maybe he'll make a trip to New York.

may be (v) [auxiliary verb plus verb]

John **may be** able to make the trip to Denver.

4.122 **overdo** (v) to do something to excess

Some actors have a tendency to **overdo** their gestures.

overdue (adj) past due

John's **overdue** phone bill caused him much embarrassment.

4.123 **passed** (v) moved or transferred

He **passed** the book along to his best friend.

past (adj) former; recently elapsed
(prep) beyond
(n) time gone by
(adv) so as to reach and go beyond a point

Dorothy is the **past** president of the faculty club.
Carla could see **past** the pier to the boats moored in the bay.
Each nation celebrates great events from its **past.**
Do not drive **past** the detour sign ahead.

4.124 **personal** (adj) private

He had a **personal** problem that he refused to discuss with anyone.

personnel (n) employees

The bank **personnel** were delighted with the increase in salary.

4.125 **postcard** (n) card on which a message may be written

Richard received a picture **postcard** of the campus.

postal card (n) a postcard with an imprinted postage stamp

Jean bought six **postal cards** at the post office.

4.126 **principal** (adj) most important
(n) school administrator; capital placed at interest

The double indemnity clause was the **principal** article they quoted.

Mr. Jones, formerly an English teacher, is the high school **principal.**

John borrowed money from the bank, and he pays 7 percent interest on the **principal.**

principle (n) rule

In making a decision of this type, one should consider the **principle** of probability.

4.127 **residence** (n) structure that serves as a home

The Smiths have a beautiful **residence** in the country.

residents (n) individuals living in a particular place

The apartment house was large enough to accommodate several hundred **residents.**

4.128 **respectfully** (adv) with reverence or respect

I **respectfully** request a one-month leave of absence.

respectively (adv) each in the order given

John and Bill are from New York and Des Moines, **respectively.**

4.129 **role** (n) part in a play

John is a natural actor; therefore, he had a leading **role** in the play.

roll (n) list

The **roll** named outstanding graduates from the local college.

4.130 **set** (v) to place

She **set** the briefcase on the desk.

sit (v) to rest in a seated position

He was so tired that he decided to **sit** on the floor.

4.131 **stationary** (adj) still, not moving

The bird dog remained **stationary** until the hunters flushed their quarry.

stationery (n) writing paper

Company policy requires the use of white **stationery** only.

4.132 **suit** (n) a court action
(v) to adapt or to agree

The lawyer filed a **suit** on behalf of his client.

Our present plant facilities should **suit** our needs in the future.

4.133 **than** (conj) used with the second member of a comparison
(prep) in comparison with

Developing a new set of blueprints is more expensive today **than** it was several years ago.

An electric typewriter is faster **than** a manual.

then (adv) at that time; as a necessary consequence
(n) that time

I would prefer to attend at 8 a.m. if a seat is available **then.**

Check these figures; **then** you can vouch for their accuracy.

The authors decided to submit the manuscript on May 1; publication would be scheduled a year from **then.**

4.134 **their** (pron) [possessive, third person plural]

Their blazers certainly are well-tailored.

there (adv) in or at that place
(n) that point

John was sitting over **there.**

"You take it from **there,** Dan," suggested the coach.

they're (contraction) they are

They're going to face some stiff competition.

4.135 **therefor** (adv) for or in return for that

The sum of $450 will be paid to the contractor by the owner; in consideration **therefor** the contractor will begin construction by January 10.

therefore (adv) consequently

The trucking company went on a three-week strike; **therefore,** all shipments are on backlog.

4.136 **to** (prep) direction
(adv) indicates direction toward

Invite students from nearby schools **to** the bank for field trips.

The children ran **to** and fro in the field.

too (adv) excessively; also

Some employees use their coffee-break time **too** freely.

I, **too,** believe that a certified public accounting firm should be called in immediately.

two (adj) a given number

Two men were looking at the accident.

4.137 **weak** (adj) lack of skill or strength

John was in the hospital for two months, and he was indeed **weak** when he came home.

week (n) period of seven days

Fran spent one **week** of her vacation in Canada.

4.138 **weather** (n) atmosphere or climate

The **weather** was so beautiful that the family went swimming.

whether (conj) if

Because of a recent illness, John couldn't decide **whether** to make the trip.

4.139 **whose** (pron) [possessive]

Whose pencil are you using?

who's (contraction) who is

Who's going to the bank to make the deposit?

4.140 **your** (pron) [possessive, second person singular and plural]

Your desk always looks so neat.

you're (contraction) you are

You're going to the store, aren't you?

SPELLING DEMONS

4.141 The list below includes words that are often misspelled. Familiarize yourself with the correct spellings of these common words.

A
abbreviate
absence
absolutely
abundance
accept
acceptable
accessories
accidentally
accommodate
accompanying
accountant
accumulate
accustom
achievement
acknowledge
acknowledgment
acquaintance
actually
addition
addressed
adequate
adjustable
adjustment
admirable
advertisement
advice
advisable
advise
advocate
aggravate
agreeable
alignment
all ready
all right
allotted
allowance
already
aluminum
always
amendment
amount
analysis
analyze
announcement
apologies
apologize
apology
appearance
appointment
appraisal
appreciation
appropriate
approval
arctic
arguing
argument
arrangement
article
aspirant
assistance
assume
assurance
athletics
attendance
attention
audience
auditor
auditorium
authoritarian
authoritative
authorization
authorize
automatic
auxiliary

B
balance
bargain
beginning
belief
believe
believing
beneficial
benefited
benevolent
bookkeeper
budgeting
bulletin
bureau
business

C
calendar
campaign
canceled
cancellation
candidate
canvas
canvass
capacity
capital
capitol
carburetor
career
carrying
carton
cartoon
censure
ceremony
certificate
changeable
characteristic
chargeable
chiefly
choice
choose
choosing
chose
Cincinnati
clientele
collaborate
collectible
collision
collusion
column
command
commend
commission
commitment
committed
committee
commodities
communicate
comparative
compelled
competence
competent
competitive
complementary
complimentary
comptroller
concede
conceivable
concession
concur
conductive
conference
conferred
confidential
confidently
confirm
congratulate
conscientious
conscious
consensus
consul
contribute
controlled
convenience
conviction
correspondence
correspondents
corridor
corroborate
council
counsel
counterfeit
courteous
courtesy
creditor
criticism
criticize
currency
customary

D
deceive
decision
deductible
default
defendant
deferred
deficient
deficit
definite
definitely
definition
departure
dependent
depository
describe
description
desirable
desolate
despite
destination
deteriorate
determination
devastate
develop
development
diagram
dialect
dictionary
difference
difficulty
dilemma
diligent
diminish
diplomatic
disappearance
disappointment
disastrous
disbursement
discipline
discrepancy
diseases
dismissal
disposition
dissatisfied
distinction
division
doesn't
dominant
dropping
durable

E
earlier
earnest
eccentric
economical
effect
efficiency
eighth
electric
eligible
eliminate
embarrassment
emergency
eminent
emphasis
employee
encouragement
endowment
enforceable
engagement
enlightenment
envelope
environment
equally
equation
equilibrium
equipped
equitable
equity
equivalent
erroneous

especially
essence
essential
eventually
evidently
exaggerated
examination
exceed
excellent
except
exceptionally
excessive
exchangeable
excusable
executing
exemption
exhaust
exhilarate
existence
existent
exorbitant
expenditure
expenses
experience
explanation
expression
extant
extension
extent
extraordinary
extremely

F

familiar
fascinate
favorable
feasible
financial
fiscal
flexible
fluorescent
forcible
foreign
forfeit
formally
formerly
fortunate
fourth
fragile
franchise
frantically
frequently
fulfill
fundamental
futurity

G

gauge
generalize
generally
genuine
gesture
government
grammar
grateful
grievance
guarantee
guaranty
guidance

H

hackneyed
handicapped
handsome
harass
hazard
headache
headquarters
height
helpful
hesitancy
hindrance
homogeneous
honorary
humiliate
humorous
hurriedly
hypothetical

I

illegal
illegible
illicit
illiterate
illustrative
immaterial
immigrant
imminent
implement
impracticable
inaccessible
inadequate
inaugurate
incidentally
incomparable
inconvenienced
independent
indispensable
inducement
inexhaustible
infinite
inherent
initiative
innocence
innocent
inoculate
inquiries
insignificant
installment
institution
intercede
interfered
invalidate
irresistible
itinerary

J

jealousy
jeopardize
journeyman
judgment
judicial
justifiable
juvenile

K

kernel
knowledge
know-nothing

L

labeled
laboratory
latter
layout
legible
leisure
leniency
letterhead
liable
library
license
lightening
lightning
liquidation
livelihood
loneliness
loose
lose
losing
luxurious
lying

M

magnificent
maintain
maintenance
manageable
maneuver
mankind
manufacturer
Massachusetts
maturity
meant
medal
medicine
medieval
mediocre
mercantile
merchandise
miniature
minute
miscellaneous
mischievous
misinterpreted
misspell
monotonous
morale
mortgage
motivation
municipal

N

naturally
necessarily
necessary
negligible
negotiable
neighbor
nevertheless
niece
nineteenth
ninety
nominal
nonessential
noticeable
notoriety
numerous

O

obliged
obsolete
obstacle
occasionally
occur
occurred
occurrence
occurring
o'clock
offered
official
often
omission
omitted
operate
opinion
opportunities
optimistic
ordinarily
ordnance
organization
orientation
originate
outrageous

P

paid
pamphlet
panel
parallel
paralyze
paraphernalia
parcel post
parliamentary
participate
particularly
passbook
pastime
patience
peaceable
peculiar
perceive
perforated
perform
performance
permanent
permissible
permission
permitting
perpetrate
perpetuate
perseverance
persistence
personal
personnel
perspiration
persuade
pertinent
pessimistic
phenomenon
physical
piece
plagiarism
planned
plausible
pleasant
plebeian
policyholder
possession
postdated
potentiality
practicable
practically
precarious
precede
precedence
predominant
preferable
preference
preferred
prejudice
preparation
prerequisite
presence
preservation
pretentious

4.141

prevalent
principal
principle
privilege
probability
probably
procedure
proceed
proceedings
proficient
profited
prohibitive
prominent
promissory
pronunciation
propaganda
prophecy
prophesy
prosecute
prove
pseudonym
psychiatry
psychology
purchasable
purchasing
pursue
pursuing

Q

qualification
qualitative
quantitative
quantity
quarantine
quarreled
quarterly
questionnaire
quiet
quite

R

readily
readjustment
realize
rearrange
reasonable
receipt
receivable
receive
receiving
recipe
recipient
reciprocal
recognize
recommend
reconcile
recruitment
recuperate
reducible
refer
referable
reference
referred
register
regrettable
reimbursement
reinstate
reliable
relief
relieve
reluctance
remember
remembrance
remittance
remnant
remunerate
rendezvous
renewable
repetition
representative
requisition
reservation
resistance
restaurant
retroactive
reversible
rhythm
ridiculous
roofs
royalty

S

sailable
salable
salaries
satisfactorily
satisfactory
scarcity
schedule
scholastic
scrupulous
secretary
seize
self-confidence
separate
separation
sergeant
serviceable
severely
shelves
shining
siege
significance
similar
simultaneous
sincerely
specifically
spontaneous
stationary
stationery
statistical
stature
statute
stereotype
studying
subsequent
subsidiary
subsistence
substantially
substantiate
substitute
substitution
subterfuge
subtle
succeed
success
successful
succession
succinct
sufficiently
superficial
superfluous
superintendent
supersede
supervisory
supplementary
surprise
susceptible
suspicious
sympathize
synonym
systematic
systematize

T

tactfulness
taxable
technician
technique
tedious
temperament
temporarily
tenacious
tendency
testimonies
their
themselves
then
there
they're
thorough
through
throughout
to
together
too
tournament
tragedy
transact
transcribe
transcription
transfer
transferable
transferred
transmission
treasurer
tremendous
triumph
truly
twelfth
two
typewriting
typical

U

ultimately
umbrella
unanimity
unanimous
unavoidable
unbelievable
unconscious
uncontrollable
underrate
undoubtedly
unforeseen
unmarketable
unnecessary
unprecedented
unprofitable
until
usable
usage
use
useful
using
usually
utility
utilize

V

vacancies
vacancy
vacillate
vacuum
vague
validity
valuable
valuation
variety
various
vehicle
venturesome
verbatim
versus
vetoes
vicious
vigilant
vigorous
vivacious
voluntary

W

waive
warehouse
warranted
weakness
weather
Wednesday
weekday
weighed
weird
welfare
where
whether
wholly
whose
withdrawal
witnessed
woman
women
won't
write
writer
writing
written

Y

yield
your
you're
yourself

Z

zero
zigzag
zinc
zoning
zoology

Five

Abbreviations

Introduction

5.1 Basic guidelines for the use of abbreviations are:

1. Use the generally accepted forms of abbreviations as listed in the dictionary or other reference.

2. Be consistent in using an abbreviation. Some abbreviations may be written in different ways, but the same form should be used throughout a typewritten document.

3. Space once after the periods used within or at the end of an abbreviation, except as noted.

Academic Degrees

5.2 The more common academic degrees are abbreviated as follows.

A.A.	Associate in Arts
A.A.S.	Associate in Applied Science
B.A. or A.B.	Bachelor of Arts
B.B.A.	Bachelor of Business Administration
B.S.	Bachelor of Science
D.A.	Doctor of Arts
D.B.A.	Doctor of Business Administration
D.D.	Doctor of Divinity
D.D.S.	Doctor of Dental Surgery, Doctor of Dental Science
Ed.D.	Doctor of Education
Ed.M.	Master of Education
Ed.S.	Specialist in Education
J.D.	Doctor of Jurisprudence
J.M.	Master of Jurisprudence
J.S.D.	Doctor of the Science of Laws
LL.B.	Bachelor of Laws
M.A. or A.M.	Master of Arts
M.B.A.	Master of Business Administration
M.D.	Doctor of Medicine
M.Div.	Master of Divinity
M.S.	Master of Science
Ph.D.	Doctor of Philosophy
Th.D.	Doctor of Theology

Broadcasting Stations

5.3 Radio and television broadcasting stations are known by their call letters. These call letters are written in capital letters with no periods or spaces between them.

BBC (British Broadcasting Corporation)	KPOL-AM/FM
Station KBRT	FM-104
KNBC News Service	KCET

Organized Groups

5.4 Many businesses, professional organizations, associations, and other organized groups are known by their abbreviated names. In such cases, all letters in the abbreviated name are capitalized. Generally, no periods or spaces are used within the abbreviation. Refer to the dictionary for a complete listing of abbreviations.

AAA	American Automobile Association
ABA	American Bankers Association American Bar Association
AFL-CIO	American Federation of Labor and Congress of Industrial Organizations
AIB	American Institute of Banking
AMA	American Medical Association
AMS	Administrative Management Society
API	American Petroleum Institute
ARMA	Association of Records Managers and Administrators
ASA	American Standards Association American Statistical Association
ASCAP	American Society of Composers, Authors, and Publishers
ASCE	American Society of Civil Engineers
ASME	American Society of Mechanical Engineers
ASTA	American Society of Travel Agents, Inc.
BBB	Better Business Bureau
FBLA	Future Business Leaders of America
IBM	International Business Machines
NAACP	National Association for the Advancement of Colored People
NAM	National Association of Manufacturers
NANA	North American Newspaper Alliance, Inc.
NAS	National Academy of Sciences
NEA	National Education Association National Editorial Association
NMA	National Microfilm Association
NSA	National Secretaries Association
PTA	Parent-Teachers Association
RCA	Radio Corporation of America
UPI	United Press International
YWCA	Young Women's Christian Association

Calendar Dates

5.5 Months of the year and days of the week should not be abbreviated except within tables, financial documents, or where space is limited. If abbreviations must be used, follow the guidelines below.

DAYS

5.6 When necessary, the days of the week may be abbreviated as follows:

Sun.		S.
Mon.		M.
Tues.		Tu.
Wed.	or	W.
Thur.		Th.
Fri.		F.
Sat.		Sa.

In tables and financial reports, the days may be abbreviated without periods, as follows:

Sun Mon Tue Wed Thr Fri Sat

MONTHS

5.7 With the exception of the months of May, June, and July, the months may be abbreviated, as follows:

Jan.	Apr.	Oct.
Feb.	Aug.	Nov.
Mar.	Sept.	Dec.

In tables and financial reports, the months may be abbreviated without periods, as follows. (June and July are abbreviated here to conform with the other three-letter abbreviations.)

Jan	Apr	Jly	Oct
Feb	May	Aug	Nov
Mar	Jun	Sep	Dec

Compass Points

5.8 Compass points written within sentences as adjectives and nouns should be spelled in full.

The aircraft made an emergency landing somewhere in the **northwest.**

Our new site will be the **southeast** corner of Sierra Madre and Del Mar.

BEFORE A STREET ADDRESS

5.9 Compass points *preceding* a street name in an address are spelled in full.

1570 **East** Colorado Boulevard

AFTER A STREET ADDRESS

5.10 When compass points *follow* the street name in addresses, use the abbreviated forms. A comma is written after the street name to separate it from the compass point. Capitalize each letter and use periods after each letter.

1401 Sixteenth Street, N.W.

Data Processing Terminology

5.11 Specialized data processing terms and their abbreviations include the following.

ADP	automatic data processing
ALGOL	algorithmic oriented language
ARP	audio-response unit
COBOL	common business oriented language
CRT	cathode ray tube
EAM	electrical accounting machine
EDP	electronic data processing
EDST	electric diaphragm switch technology
EDVAC	electronic discrete variable automatic computer
ENIAC	electronic numeral integrator and computer
EOF	end of file
FORTRAN	formula translation system
IDP	integrated data processing
I/O	input-output
MICR	magnetic ink character recognition
OCR	optical character recognition

Foreign Expressions

5.12 The following are abbreviations for some foreign expressions used in business. Because these expressions are common enough to appear in the dictionary, they are not underscored.

ad hoc	"for a particular purpose"
a.m., A.M.	ante meridian; "before noon"
A/V	ad valorem; "according to value"
e.g.	exempli gratia; "for example"
et al.	et alii; "and others"
et seq.	et sequens; "and the following" et sequentes; "those that follow"
etc.	et cetera; "and so forth"
ibid.	ibidem; "in the same place"
idem	"the same"
i.e.	id est; "that is"
LS	locus sigilli; "in place of the seal"
loc. cit.	loco citato; "in the place cited"
N.B.	nota bene; "note well"
op. cit.	opere citato; "in the work cited"
P.S.	postscriptum; "postscript"
q.v.	quod vide; "which see"
R.S.V.P.	réspondez s'il vous plait; "please reply"
re, in re	"regarding" or "in the matter of"
s.s.	scilicet; "namely"
viz.	videlicet; "namely"
vs., v.	versus

Geographic Names

5.13 Geographic names are generally abbreviated by using the first letter of each word in the name, capitalized. Each letter may be followed by a period (without spaces), or the periods may be omitted; one practice or the other should be followed consistently. (Note that for address purposes, slightly different abbreviations have been adopted by the postal service; see 5.14 and 5.15.)

U.S.A. or USA	United States of America
U.A.R. or UAR	United Arab Republic

5.14 Names of **states, districts,** and **territories** of the United States are abbreviated as follows. (The two-letter Postal Service abbreviations must appear on all envelope addresses.)

States, District, and Territories	*Abbreviations*	
	STANDARD	*TWO-LETTER*
Alabama	Ala.	AL
Alaska	Alaska	AK
Arizona	Ariz.	AZ
Arkansas	Ark.	AR
California	Calif.	CA
Canal Zone	C.Z.	CZ
Colorado	Colo.	CO
Connecticut	Conn.	CT
Delaware	Del.	DE
District of Columbia	D.C.	DC
Florida	Fla.	FL
Georgia	Ga.	GA
Guam	Guam	GU
Hawaii	Hawaii	HI
Idaho	Idaho	ID
Illinois	Ill.	IL
Indiana	Ind.	IN
Iowa	Iowa	IA
Kansas	Kans.	KS
Kentucky	Ky.	KY
Louisiana	La.	LA
Maine	Maine	ME
Maryland	Md.	MD
Massachusetts	Mass.	MA
Michigan	Mich.	MI
Minnesota	Minn.	MN
Mississippi	Miss.	MS
Missouri	Mo.	MO
Montana	Mont.	MT
Nebraska	Nebr.	NE

Nevada	Nev.	NV
New Hampshire	N.H.	NH
New Jersey	N.J.	NJ
New Mexico	N. Mex.	NM
New York	N.Y.	NY
North Carolina	N.C.	NC
North Dakota	N. Dak.	ND
Ohio	Ohio	OH
Oklahoma	Okla.	OK
Oregon	Oreg.	OR
Pennsylvania	Pa.	PA
Puerto Rico	P.R.	PR
Rhode Island	R.I.	RI
South Carolina	S.C.	SC
South Dakota	S. Dak.	SD
Tennessee	Tenn.	TN
Texas	Tex.	TX
Utah	Utah	UT
Vermont	Vt.	VT
Virgin Islands	V.I.	VI
Virginia	Va.	VA
Washington	Wash.	WA
West Virginia	W. Va.	WV
Wisconsin	Wis.	WI
Wyoming	Wyo.	WY

5.15 Names of Canadian provinces are abbreviated as follows.

	Abbreviations	
Province	***STANDARD***	***TWO-LETTER***
Alberta	Alta.	AB
British Columbia	B.C.	BC
Labrador	Lab.	LB
Manitoba	Man.	MB
New Brunswick	N.B.	NB
Newfoundland	Newf./Nfld.	NF
Northwest Territories	N.W.Ter.	NT
Nova Scotia	N.S.	NS
Ontario	Ont.	ON
Prince Edward Island	P.E.I.	PE
Quebec	Que.	PQ
Saskatchewan	Sask.	SK
Yukon Territory		YT

Government Agencies

5.16 Abbreviations for the more common government agencies are listed below. These abbreviations are usually written in capital letters with neither periods nor spaces after the letters.

AEC	Atomic Energy Commission
BIA	Bureau of Indian Affairs
CIA	Central Intelligence Agency
CSC	Civil Service Commission
FBI	Federal Bureau of Investigation
FDA	Food and Drug Administration
FDIC	Federal Deposit Insurance Corporation
FHA	Federal Housing Administration; Farmers Home Administration
FICA	Federal Insurance Contributions Act
FR, F.R.	Federal Reserve
FRB, F.R.B.	Federal Reserve Bank, Federal Reserve Board
FTC	Federal Trade Commission
ICC	Interstate Commerce Commission; Indian Claims Commission
IRS	Internal Revenue Service
NASA	National Aeronautics and Space Administration
NATO	North Atlantic Treaty Organization
NBS	National Bureau of Standards
NLRB	National Labor Relations Board
PHA	Public Housing Administration
SBA	Small Business Administration
SEC	Securities and Exchange Commission
SSA	Social Security Administration
TVA	Tennessee Valley Authority
USIA	United States Information Agency
VA	Veterans Administration

Personal Names

5.17 Some people prefer to use the **abbreviated forms** of their given names in correspondence and in their signatures. Space once after the period before typing the last name.

Chas.	Charles	Jos.	Joseph
Edw.	Edward or Edwin	Robt.	Robert
Geo.	George	Thos.	Thomas
Jas.	James	Wm.	William

5.18 Some people use **initials** in place of their first and/or middle names. Space once after each period after an initial.

J. G. Muha
Nancy P. Lee
J. Donald Curry

Personal Titles

5.19 A personal title written before a complete name is written in its abbreviated form. One space follows the period after the abbreviation.

Mr. Norman Rittgers	Ms. Kathy Tyner
Mrs. Rosalba Salinas	Dr. Kenneth Zimmer

5.20 Except for the titles Mr., Mrs., Ms., Messrs., and Mmes., personal titles written before a surname only are spelled out.

Reverend Bingham
Doctor Bray
Father Monaghan

Units of Measure

5.21 Units of measure (length, weight, volume, temperature, and so on) are generally abbreviated when they appear in technical and scientific contexts and spelled out in others. (See chapter 11 for abbreviations.)

Six

Numbers & Symbols

Introduction

6.1 Guidelines are provided in this section for typing numbers (as words and as numerals) and various symbols used in documents office workers frequently encounter.

Numbers

6.2 In general, numbers between one and ten and those that can be written as one word are spelled out in full. The rules that follow indicate when to spell out numbers and when to use numerals.

WITH ABBREVIATIONS AND/OR SYMBOLS

6.3 Numbers written with abbreviations or symbols should be indicated in figures.

```
5 doz.      $14      @ $1.02      1 lb.      #2
```

IN STREET ADDRESSES

6.4 Use figures for house and building numbers except the number *one,* which should be spelled out. Use figures for numbered streets, beginning with 13. A hyphen should be placed between a house or building number and a numbered street. Do not use "-th" and "-st" after numerals.

```
One East Twelfth Street     2 East 13 Street
2 West Twelfth Street       751 - 34 Street
```

ZIP CODES

6.5 ZIP (Zone Improvement Plan) code numbers are written in figures, beginning one space after the state name or its two-letter abbreviation.

```
Washington, DC 20022
Dallas, Texas 75204
```

TO BEGIN SENTENCES

6.6 When a sentence starts with a number, spell the number out—regardless of the number of words it takes. If possible, however, avoid beginning a sentence with a number.

```
Thirty-eight people were invited to the party at
the Joneses, and everyone attended.
The Joneses invited 38 people to their party, and
everyone attended.
```

WITH COMMAS

6.7 A comma should be placed between each set of three figures in whole numbers, counting from right to left.

```
1,942        10,926,367
682,745      $2,345.74
```

6.8 Some exceptions to this rule are:

```
Catalog No. 46321
Checking Account No. 653 021 1194
Credit Card No. 045 382 715 4 236
Invoice No. 46528
Social Security No. 199-24-3806
```

DATES

6.9 When the day follows the month, use numerals only. When the day precedes the month, use numerals and the *st, nd, rd,* or *th* endings.

February 22 22nd of February

6.10 When a date consists of a month and year, do not use a comma after the month. When the day is included, use a comma.

The December 1975 issue of that magazine is out of print.

John gloomily mailed his income tax check on April 16, 1977.

DECIMALS

6.11 Decimal amounts should be written in figures, using the period for the decimal point. Do not add any extra zeros to the right of any decimal figures except when the numbers are aligned in columns.

3.75 inches	12.040
.075 inch	1.000
specific gravity of 0.6241	3.875
325.085	

FRACTIONS

6.12 Fractions written with whole numbers are expressed in figures. Fractions used without whole numbers are spelled out except in a series. When whole numbers are typed with fractions made on the typewriter, a space separates the whole number from the fraction so the number is read correctly. A hyphen may also be used to separate the whole number from the fraction.

8 4/5
three-fourths of a mile
1/4 = 3/12

6.13 Most typewriters have the fractions ¼ and ½ on the keyboard. When only these two fractions occur within business communications and reports, the typewriter fractions may be used. However, when these fractions are used with other fractions, all fractions should be made with the figures and diagonal for consistency of form.

Incorrect: 7/8 + 2/3 + 5½ = ?

Correct: 7/8 + 2/3 + 5 1/2 = ?

HYPHENATED NUMBERS

6.14 Numbers from 21 to 99 are hyphenated when written out, as is any number that is part of an adjective compound.

twenty-one	forty-two thousand
one hundred eighty-three	a ten-cent stamp

6.15 Use hyphens to connect figures representing a continuous sequence, as in calendar dates and page numbers. Do not space before or after the hyphen. The hyphen takes the place of the word *to* in the sequence.

```
the years 1975-1980
pages 11-18
```

6.16 The second number of a hyphenated number may be abbreviated if the main number of the second item is the same as the first.

1970-78 instead of 1970-1978
pages 204-11 instead of pages 204-211

6.17 Do not, however, abbreviate the second number of the sequence if the first number contains two zeros or if the second number begins with a new series of digits.

```
1970-2001     pages 200-264
```

DOLLARS

6.18 Type the dollar sign immediately before the amount. Do not use a decimal point or ciphers after an even dollar amount unless a high degree of exactness is required.

```
$15
$278
```

```
John has a balance of $2,836 in his savings account.
```

```
. . . monthly payments of three hundred ninety-five dollars ($395.00) each.
```

6.19 When dollar amounts are written **in a series,** repeat the dollar sign before each amount.

```
The quarterly dividends for the past year have been $1.05, $1.15, $1.04, and $1.02.
```

6.20 When typing **tables or columns of amounts,** use the decimal point and ciphers after even dollar amounts if there are mixed amounts within the columns. The dollar sign is written next to the first amount, positioned in front of the largest amount in the column. The dollar sign would also be written in the total.

```
$ 15.00      $128.95     $390
 207.06        40.00       30
$222.06        15.30      198
```

6.21 The dollar sign should not be used with an amount less than one dollar unless the amount is in a series or a table with amounts greater than one dollar. Instead of the cent symbol, the dollar sign is used, followed by a decimal point.

John's earnings for shoveling snow were $.95, $1.50, $.75, $2.25, and $1.85.

6.22 Whenever amounts are written out, the word dollars is written after the amount.

thirty-five dollars
sixteen and 50/100 dollars

CENTS

6.23 Write out the word *cents* (see exceptions below) with numerals or with spelled out numbers (those between one and ten and those that can be written in one word).

three cents
98 cents

6.24 Use the cents symbol (¢) and numerals on invoices, purchase orders, and other business forms.

39¢
14¢

ORDINAL

6.25 Ordinal numbers that can be written in one or two words should be spelled out; otherwise, the figures are used with the ordinal endings.

first	tenth	350th
hundredth	twenty-fifth	three thousandth

PERCENTAGES

6.26 Percentages are written in figures (unless they begin a sentence), and the word *percent* is spelled out.

The credit manager approved a 5 percent discount for us.

Ten percent of the students had never taken typewriting in high school.

Fractional

6.27 Percentages of **less than one percent** should be written out or converted into decimal equivalents.

```
three-fourths of a percent    .75 percent
one-half of 1 percent         .5 percent
```

6.28 Fractional percentages of **more than one percent** are expressed in figures, either with the whole number and the fraction or as the decimal equivalent.

```
9½ percent          9.5 percent
10 3/4 percent      10.75 percent
```

Sequential

6.29 When hyphens are used to connect percentages representing a continuous sequence or a range, the word *percent* is written after the last percentage. If, however, the percent symbol (%) is used with the percentages, it must be used with each percentage figure.

```
15–20 percent
15% to 20%
returns of up to 15, 20, and 25 percent
returns of up to 15%, 20%, and 25%
```

RATIOS AND PROPORTIONS

6.30 Numbers indicating ratios and proportions are written in figures.

```
5 to 1 ratio or 5:1 ratio
odds of 1,000 to 1
```

ROMAN NUMERALS

6.31 Roman numerals are formed as follows:

1	I	50	L
2	II	60	LX
4	IV	90	XC
5	V	100	C
6	VI	400	CD
9	IX	500	D
10	X	600	DC
11	XI	800	DCCC
14	XIV	900	CM
30	XXX	1,000	M
40	XL	1975	MCMLXXV
41	XLI	2,000	MM

6.32 Roman numerals used to indicate major divisions in outlines are written with a period and two spaces after them. Roman numbers in outlines and in columns of information are aligned at the right.

```
  I.
 II.
III.
```

6.33 Roman numerals are also sometimes used to indicate chapter numbers, volumes of books, years, and family heritage of names.

I. Philosophy [first major division in an outline]
Chapter III
Volume VI
ii [small numerals for prefatory pages]
MCMLXXI [1971]
Charles L. Steel, III

ROUND NUMBERS

6.34 Use words rather than figures to indicate round numbers.

Never in a million years will this happen again.

Approximately five hundred men work in this plant.

SUCCESSIVE NUMBERS

6.35 When two numbers are used successively in a sentence, write out the smaller number and use figures for the larger number, if possible. Otherwise, try to write the sentence so a comma may be inserted between the numbers.

John bought 8 two-cent stamps at the post office.

Of the eight, three men were experienced in telephone technician work.

TIME

6.36 Time periods are usually expressed in words.

ten seconds	five days
three minutes	six months

6.37 When precise units of time must be expressed, use **figures.**

30-day overdue obligation
2 years, 6 months, 5 days

6.38 Use figures when the abbreviation **a.m.** or **p.m.** is used.

7:55 a.m.
10:45 p.m.

6.39 When **o'clock** is used, the time may be expressed either in figures or words.

```
8 o'clock       eight o'clock
12 o'clock      twelve o'clock
```

6.40 When time on the hours is expressed with either **p.m., a.m.,** or **o'clock,** do not add the ciphers for minutes.

```
6 a.m.      6 o'clock
11 p.m.     11 o'clock
```

This rule is followed when time on the hour is included in a series of times, even though it may appear inconsistent.

```
The departure times are 6:15 a.m., 10 a.m., and
1:10 p.m.
```

6.41 Use the word **noon** or **midnight** to indicate the 12 o'clock hour.

```
12 noon          12 o'clock noon
12 midnight      12 o'clock midnight
```

UNITS OF MEASUREMENT

6.42 Use figures to indicate capacities, dimensions, distances, measures, temperature, and weights in technical or scientific contexts. Numbers less than ten may be written out in nontechnical measurements.

```
1 pint or one pint           120 horsepower
3 miles or three miles       4' x 6' or 4 by 6 feet
20° or twenty degrees        8 1/2-x-11-inch paper
45 pounds                    10 feet 6 inches
```

6.43 No comma is used to separate the parts of a measurement unit within a sentence.

```
At age 21, he stands 6 feet 2 inches tall.
```

Symbols

6.44 Like abbreviations, symbols reduce the time and effort needed to write or type out a given word. This section presents guidelines for using business symbols, mathematics symbols, and proofreader's marks; and instructions for typing some of these symbols.

BUSINESS SYMBOLS

6.45 Common business symbols include the following.

Symbol	Definition	Example
'	accent	Busche'
&	ampersand (*and* sign)	Merrick & Poore
*	asterisk	1975*
@	at, each	@ 12 cents
( ) ( ) ( )	braces	January) February) $395.00 March)
[ ]	brackets	[Exhibit B]
¢	cent, cents	75¢
c	Copyright	c Glencoe Press, 1976
°	degree, degrees	69°
/	diagonal	and/or, either/or 3/4, 15/16, 3 1/4
$	dollar, dollars	$15.00
'	feet, minutes	6'
"	inches, seconds, ditto	10"
:	is to, ratio	5:1
#	number	#402
%	percent	100%
#	pound	20#
R	registered	R. or R U.S. Patent Office
§	section	USC §1104

MATHEMATICAL SYMBOLS

6.46 Common mathematical symbols include the following.

Symbol	Definition	Example
+	plus	5 + 5
−	minus	10 − 7
±	plus or minus	±6
∓	minus or plus	∓8
x or •	multiply by	10 x 10 10 • 10

Symbol	Definition	Example
÷	divided by	10 ÷ 4 = 2.5
=	equal to	10 x 10 = 100
>	greater than	12 > 11
⊅	not greater than	11 ⊅ 12
<	less than	10 < 11
≮	not less than	11 ≮ 10
‖	parallel	Line AB ‖ line CDE.
⊥	perpendicular	Line BD ⊥ line MN.
∟	right angle	90 degrees = ∟
△	triangle	△ ABC is an isoceles
□	square	Line QR intersects □ ABCD.
▭	rectangle	In ▭ HIJK, HI = 10.
○	circle	○A>○B
Ⓢ	circles	Ⓢ A, B, and C
√	radical, root, square root	$\sqrt{4} = 2$
∛	cube root	$\sqrt[3]{16} = 2$
π	pi	The area of a circle is πr^2).
⬡	hexagon	⬡ABCDEF

PROOFREADERS' MARKS

6.47 Proofreaders' marks are symbols used to indicate any changes in rough draft copy—handwritten or typewritten—before final typing is done.

Symbol	Definition	Example
cl or ⁐	close up the space	no s pace here
tr or ∿	transpose	out of odrer
⊐	move to right	⊐indent one space
5⊐	indent 5 spaces	5⊐Make a paragraph
⊏	move to left	⊏uneven margin
cap or ≡	capitalize	proper noun
═	all caps	report title
∨ or ∧	insert	make cor^ection here
ℯ	delete, take out	exxtra letter

#	add space	make aspace here
l.c. or /	lower case; small letters	not Capitalized
___ or ital	underline (or italics)	book title
( )	insert parentheses	(by the way)
⊙	insert period	end of sentence⊙
¶	paragraph	¶ Make a paragraph here
no ¶	no paragraph	no ¶ Do not make a paragraph here
~~word~~	delete the word	extra ~~extra~~ word
word	delete the letter	extra lettter
stet	let it stand; leave it as it was	stet this correction is a mistake–ignore it

INSTRUCTIONS FOR TYPING SYMBOLS

6.48 If the typewriter contains the appropriate combination of keys to type symbols that are not included on the keyboard, use these keys to make the symbols. To save time when symbols cannot be made quickly on the typewriter, leave extra spaces so symbols can be handwritten when the typing has been completed.

Subscripts

6.49 Subscripts are numbers or letters typed slightly below the line of typing. Subscripts are used in mathematical and scientific formulas and equations.

In chemical equations:

H_2O $NaClO_3$ $C_{12}H_{22}O_{11}$ CH_4

In mathematical equations:

$\sin^{\theta}{}_{12}$

6.50 Subscripts are placed immediately after a letter, word, or figure and are typed as follows:

1. Engage the ratchet release lever of the typewriter.
2. Roll the cylinder knob slightly, turning the cylinder away from you.
3. Type the subscript.
4. Disengage the ratchet release lever.
5. Return the cylinder to the original line of typing.

Superscripts

6.51 Superscripts are numbers or lowercase letters typed slightly above the line of typing. Superscripts are used for footnote numbers in the body of the text or table, for mathematical formulas, and for equations.

Footnotes in text:	Ralph S. Spanswick states:[4] $14 million deficit[10]
Footnotes in tables:	14.2 3.5[a] 11.0[b]
Mathematical formula:	The area of a square is equal to S^2.
Mathematical equation:	$14\ (x^2 - y^2)\ 56 =$

6.52 A superscript is placed immediately after a word, letter, or figure and is typed as follows:

1. Engage the ratchet release lever of the typewriter.
2. Roll the cylinder knob slightly toward you.
3. Type the superscript.
4. Disengage the ratchet release lever.
5. Return the cylinder to the original line of typing.

Seven

Business Correspondence

Letters

7.1 Letters are the most common means of business communication. Thus, letter preparation is a major office expense in terms of stationery, envelopes, postage, dictator's time, the time of the typist/secretary, and office overhead. Accuracy, neatness, and efficiency in turning out each day's quota of letters are crucial secretarial skills.

LETTER STYLES

7.2 Most business letters fall into one of three categories: the **individual** (**or personalized**) **letter,** the **guide letter,** or the **form letter.** Each style is defined below.

Individual Letters

7.3 All correspondence that cannot suitably be answered by using a form or guide letter requires an individual response. This response may be conveyed by dictation to a secretary or on a machine; by writing, for the stenographer or typist to transcribe; or as a verbal idea or group of ideas for the secretary to compose into a letter.

7.4 A carefully written personalized letter builds goodwill and creates a favorable impression of the writer and the company. To determine whether you have written an effective letter, ask yourself the following questions.

Checklist for Effective Letters

1. **Organization.** Have you determined the purpose of the letter? Is it to sell, to inform, to persuade, to entertain? Defining the purpose helps you organize your thoughts.

2. **Conciseness.** Have you used the words and expressions that will best convey your thoughts to the reader? Are only the essential facts included? Information that is irrelevant or too wordy tends to confuse the reader and to reduce comprehension of the message.

3. **Clarity.** Has your purpose been set forth clearly? Does your choice of words help the reader understand what is being said? Are ideas presented in logical sequence?

4. **Completeness.** Did you include all the facts, figures, dates, names, and addresses? Are all possible questions answered that might be raised? Stating the facts helps prevent any misunderstandings and helps the reader interpret the message. Insufficient information leaves the reader in doubt and may generate additional correspondence.

5. **Tone.** Does the tone of your letter indicate friendliness, warmth, and cooperation? The manner in which ideas are conveyed will influence the reader's response.

6. **Correctness.** Are the dates, facts, and figures correct? Incorrect information may lead to misunderstandings and will necessitate additional communications to clarify the situation.

Guide Letters

7.5 A guide letter makes use of **prepared paragraphs** written in advance to meet most of the situations encountered in daily correspondence. Such letters are practical when a company receives many similar inquiries requiring fairly routine responses.

7.6 The prepared material usually includes standard opening and closing paragraphs phrased in general terms that apply to all such routine correspondence. Several more specific paragraphs, designed to suit a variety of common queries or problems, are also supplied—with blank spaces left for the insertion of dates, amounts, numbers, names, addresses, and other variable information (see Figure 7-1). These paragraphs are used individually or in different combinations for the body of each routine letter.

Each guide paragraph is coded with a number. To prepare a letter, the writer selects the paragraphs that are most appropriate to the situation and lists their numbers in the desired sequence. The secretary or typist can then refer to the paragraphs identified by these numbers and type the letter quickly and easily.

Form Letters

7.7 A form letter is a standard communication that is printed and used for large volumes of routine correspondence where a form reply is both appropriate and necessary. Such letters contain specific information carefully tailored to fit numerous similar or identical circumstances that are anticipated in daily correspondence (see Figures 7-2 and 7-3).

As in guide letter paragraphs, blank spaces are usually provided for such variable information as dates, amounts, numbers, names, and addresses. The typist inserts the form letter into the typewriter and types only the date, the inside address, and any other variable information for that particular letter.

7.8 Offices that handle a large volume of routine correspondence often use word processing equipment to expedite form letters. All the form letter paragraphs are recorded on these special machines by means of such media as punched paper tape, magnetic tape, magnetic discs, or magnetic cards. When a letter is to be typed, the typist refers to the specific reference code, the machine "selects" the desired paragraphs, and the letter is typed automatically. (For more information on word processing, see 13.2–13.25.)

LETTER APPEARANCE

7.9 The physical appearance of a letter is as important as its contents. If the letter is not attractively typed, the reader will be distracted from the message. The typist has a variety of formats

1 (opening)

I am concerned to learn of the disappointment you experienced in connection with your recent trip to _____. Thank you for bringing the matter to our attention.

2 (opening)

Thank you for taking the time and trouble to write us in detail about your recent experience with us. You are due our apology, of course; and I want to be prompt in extending it.

3

Your comments are disturbing, for you certainly did not receive the kind of service we want to extend to our passengers. Please accept our apologies. Your experience has, of course, been brought to the attention of our Flight Service Manager, who will review the matter in very serious terms with the flight crew concerned and will take other measures to ensure better performance in the future.

4

We strive for on-time performance of all our flights. However, in view of the fact that no transportation company can guarantee its schedules, we must decline reimbursement for any extra expenses incurred as a consequence of the late arrival.

5

I am very sorry about the problem you had with your excess baggage, and I can well understand your disappointment. Although it is difficult to account for the difference in weight you mentioned, unfortunately there is little we can do in an after-the-fact investigation. As you know, we are a highly regulated industry and have to follow certain rules from which we cannot deviate. Under these rules, the excess baggage receipt accepted by the traveler at check-in must be considered as the correct record of the weight of the baggage presented at the time, and an adjustment of an excess charge is possible only when a computation error has been made.

FIGURE 7-1. SAMPLE GUIDE LETTER PARAGRAPH

6

Under the circumstances, there appears to be no way that the charge you paid can be adjusted. I realize that this will be disappointing to you, but we hope that you will understand our position.

7

While we have done little on this occasion to merit your goodwill, I hope that we may have another opportunity to demonstrate that we can provide a fine service.

8

Thank you for taking the time to commend _____. It is always reassuring to learn that our people have done an especially good job. _____, I am sure, was only too pleased to be of assistance and will join us in looking forward to serving you again soon.

If there is anything we can do for you on future trips, _____, please call on us.

9

This is to certify that _____ is an employee in good standing with Dixie Celestial Airlines and is eligible to participate in the Universal Airlines Interline Tour program.

10 (closing)

Thank you for writing, _____. It is our policy to offer the finest service in every respect, and we hope that this policy will be more evident when you travel with us again.

ZEST Magazine, Inc.

300 So. Sanders Court • Los Angeles, CA 90054

CABLE ZESTLA
PHONE 659-2300

Thank you for submitting your manuscript entitled _____ to ZEST. It has been read with interest.

However, because of previous commitments in the same subject area, we are returning the manuscript to you for publication elsewhere.

Please do not hesitate to submit other articles you have authored, as we would like to see more of your work.

Thank you again for thinking of publishing in ZEST.

Sincerely yours,

John J. Richardson
Editor, ZEST

FIGURE 7-2. SAMPLE REJECTION LETTER

ZEST Magazine, Inc.

300 So. Sanders Court • Los Angeles, CA 90054

CABLE ZESTLA
PHONE 659-2300

Thank you for your manuscript entitled _____. We would like to publish it in a forthcoming issue of ZEST. Current rates of remuneration are $25 for an article of this length, payable on publication.

Please confirm that this rate is satisfactory and that the manuscript has not been published elsewhere in its present form. We ask for editorial privileges in printing the article in our magazine.

Along with a check for $25, we will be pleased to send a complimentary copy of the issue of ZEST that contains your article.

Keep on looking at the unusual people around you, and help us tell their story in ZEST.

Cordially yours,

John J. Richardson
Editor, ZEST

FIGURE 7-3. SAMPLE ACCEPTANCE LETTER

from which to choose in arranging the different parts of the business letter on the page. To achieve an attractive, uncluttered appearance, the letter should conform to a standard business letter style.

7.10 The standard parts of a business letter (discussed in 7.12–7.54) are the letterhead, date, inside address, salutation, body, complimentary closing, typed name, official title, and reference initials. Figures 7-4 through 7-11 illustrate several acceptable arrangements for these parts. Special letter parts, such as enclosure, copy, and blind copy notations, postscript and post-postscript, mailing and addressee notations, and page headings, are discussed in sections 7.55 through 7.70.

7.11 The terms **mixed** and **open punctuation** refer to the inclusion or omission of punctuation marks after the salutation and complimentary closing. With mixed punctuation (generally used in modified block letters; see Figure 7-6) a colon follows the salutation and a comma follows the closing. With open punctuation (generally used in full block letters; see Figure 7-4), no punctuation mark follows either salutation or closing.

Regardless of format or punctuation style, the letter must be attractively centered on the page. Table 7–1 illustrates guidelines for line length and spacing of business letters.

Letter Classification	*Number of Words*	*Line Length (Inches)*	*Spaces (Pica)**	*Margins (Pica)**	*Spaces (Elite)**	*Margins (Elite)**	*Lines (Date to Address)*
Short	Under 100	5	50	17–67	50	25–75	12
Average	101–200	5	50	17–67	60	20–80	8
Long	201–300	6	60	12–72	70	15–85	6
Two-Page	Over 301	6	60	12–72	70	15–85	6

TABLE 7-1. LETTER PLACEMENT GUIDE (STANDARD SIZE STATIONERY)

*Does not include allowance for bell at right margin.

LETTER ELEMENTS

7.12 Every part of a business letter has a specific purpose. When the correct form is observed in typing these elements, the message will be conveyed more quickly.

Letterhead

7.13 Letterhead refers both to the high-grade paper used for business letters and to the company insignia, trade name, or product name printed at the top of each sheet. The printed information also includes the company name, address, and telephone number. More detailed letterheads may list the name and title of an executive officer, the name of a department, or the company's cable address. Several examples are illustrated in Figures 7-4 through 7-11.

Letterhead

Treasures From 'Round The World

800 Sansome Street
San Francisco, California 94111

Date

February 7, 1979

Inside Address

Mr. Leonard J. Adams
Executive Secretary
Montgomery Corporation
4421 Roosevelt Avenue
Dayton, OH 45426

Salutation

Dear Mr. Adams

Body

This is an illustration of a letter prepared in the full block style. Every line of the letter begins at the left margin.

The full block style is frequently used by office employees because it is easy to set up and letters can be typed more quickly. This form is preferred by office executives because the production rate of stenographers and typists is increased when this format is used.

Because of its simplicity and distinctiveness, the full block style has become one of the more popular letter styles in business.

To further increase efficiency in typing letters, open punctuation is usually used with the full block style letter. There is no punctuation after the salutation nor after the complimentary closing.

Complimentary Closing

Sincerely yours

Typed Name
Official Title

Peter L. Starkey
Office Manager

Reference Initials

jh

FIGURE 7-4. FULL BLOCK STYLE (OPEN PUNCTUATION)

Return Address

7.14 When business letters are written on plain paper (Figure 7-11), the writer's address must be typed in place of the printed letterhead. The return address includes the writer's street address, city, state, and ZIP code. This information is typed immediately above the date of the letter in block style, single space.

street address	371 Woodbine Boulevard
city, state, ZIP code	Spokane, Washington 99212
date	October 10, 1979

The placement of the return address depends on the letter style used. If the full block style is used, these lines are typed at the left margin (Figure 7-4). If the modified block style or hanging indented style is used, these lines are typed beginning at the center of the page (Figures 7-6 and 7-9).

Letterhead	EXECUTIVES' CONSULTANTS, INC. International Building/190 North Michigan Avenue/Chicago, IL 60601 ECI — Area Code 312 657-7830
Date	February 3, 1979
Inside Address	Mrs. Janet K. LaCroix 1427 North Broadway Cedar Falls, IA 56613
Salutation	Dear Mrs. LaCroix:
Subject Line	SUBJECT: Account No. 14701-K
Body	This letter illustrates the use of a subject line in the full block style. The subject line is typed a double space below the salutation and a double space before the body of the letter. Since all lines in the full block style of letter begin at the left margin, the subject line must also be typed in that position. However, the subject line in the modified block style is usually centered on the page to call attention to the content of the letter. The use of a subject line in business correspondence helps the reader focus on the main topic of the letter, and it is also an aid for the person filing correspondence.
Complimentary Closing	Yours very truly,
Typed Name Official Title	Ruth P. Collins General Manager
Reference Initials	cm

FIGURE 7-5. FULL BLOCK STYLE (MIXED PUNCTUATION)

Date

7.15 The date the letter is written may be typed (1) at the left margin (in the full block style letter), (2) beginning at the center point of the page (in the modified block and hanging indented styles), or (3) centered on the page (modified block style and hanging indented styles) to match the arrangement and design of the company letterhead.

The date is typed three to five lines below the last line of the letterhead. The month is always spelled out, with the day of the month and the year written in full.

```
October 10, 1979
```

7.16 The Armed Forces prefer the inverted method of writing dates: the day of the month, the month, and the year. No punctuation is used between the parts of the date:

```
10 October 1979
```

Letterhead

SUPERIOR STEEL CORPORATION

260 South Broad Street / Philadelphia, PA 19102 / Area Code (215) 387-9000

Charles Rowland
President

Date

December 3, 1979

Inside Address

Mr. Edward H. Whitton
2129 Westfield Avenue
Cedar Falls, IA 56613

Salutation

Dear Mr. Whitton:

Body

This letter is typed in the modified block style with mixed punctuation. When mixed punctuation is used, a colon is typed after the salutation, and a comma is typed after the complimentary closing.

The date and the closing lines begin at the center of the page. The closing lines may also be typed beginning five spaces to the left of the center and blocked in that position.

Most typists like to place the date to begin at the same point as the closing lines because only one tabulator stop has to be set. Some letter writers, however, prefer to type the date to end even with the right margin. The date should be positioned where it looks best in conjunction with the design of the letterhead.

The modified block style is one of the most popular because it is easy to set up and gives a balanced appearance.

Complimentary Closing

Sincerely yours,

Typed Name

Ellen A. McConnell

Reference Initials

chs

FIGURE 7-6. MODIFIED BLOCK STYLE (MIXED PUNCTUATION)

7.17 Dates in business letters should not be typed entirely in figures, such as 10/2/79, because the figures may be misinterpreted. For example, in the Armed Forces **10/2/79** would be read as February 10—written **10 February 1979.** Others would interpret these figures as **October 2, 1979.** Using figures for months makes more work for the reader and increases the likelihood of transposition errors in typing.

Inside Address

7.18 The complete name and address of the intended recipient is called the **inside address.** It is typed at the left margin approximately four to eight lines below the date. When a window envelope is used (see Figure 7-19), the inside address also serves as the envelope address.

Letterhead	**BARRY, LORD & DYKES, INC.**
	72 Northpark Avenue Dallas, Texas 75280
	Raymond Lewis *Registered Representative*
Date	December 3, 1979
Inside Address	Consolidated Chemicals Corporation 24605 Bundy Drive West Suite 1401 Albuquerque, NM 87101
Attention Line	Attention: Mrs. Sara Hawkins
Salutation (see 7.28)	Gentlemen:
Body	Please note the arrangement of information in the inside address of this letter typed in the modified block style with five-space paragraph indentions. The letter is addressed to the company but is to be directed to the attention of the individual named. The attention line is always typed at the left margin a double space below the inside address and a double space before the salutation. It is considered part of the inside address. Notice that although the letter is addressed to the attention of a woman, the salutation is "Gentlemen." The attention line may contain the name of an individual or the name of a particular department or section of the business. Including an attention line in a letter helps expedite delivery of correspondence to the person or department concerned.
Complimentary Closing	Yours truly,
Typed Name Official Title	Raymond L. Lewis Registered Representative
Reference Initials	fjk

FIGURE 7-7. MODIFIED BLOCK STYLE WITH ATTENTION LINE (MIXED PUNCTUATION)

7.19 A complete inside address for letters written to **individuals** includes either of the following:

name of individual	Mr. James C. Garven
title or department	Vice President
name of company	Fairchild Business Products
street address	82303 West Kensington Road
city, state, ZIP code	Tacoma, WA 98412

or

name of individual	Miss Naomi Sugimoto
street address	906-B Easy Street
city, state, ZIP code	Tempe, AZ 85281

An appropriate title, such as Dr., Miss, Mr., Mrs., or Ms., should precede the names of individuals. **Ms.** should be used when the marital status of a woman is not known or when she indicates

Letterhead

SOUTHERN FEDERAL SAVINGS AND LOAN ASSOCIATION
SOUTHERN FEDERAL TOWER
3326 Hollywood Boulevard
Hollywood, FL 33020

Date

March 17, 1979

Inside Address

Miss Jane K. Williams
4013 Camden Boulevard
Topeka, KS 66612

Subject Line

AMS SIMPLIFIED LETTER STYLE

Body

This letter is an example, Miss Williams, of the simplified letter style recommended by the Administrative Management Society. It incorporates the following features:

1. Full block style

2. No salutation or complimentary closing

3. A subject line typed in all capitals

4. Frequent use of enumerated items, always typed at the left margin

5. The writer's name and official title typed in capital letters

This letter style is designed for maximum efficiency, saving time for both the typist and the recipient. To maintain a businesslike yet personalized tone, the addressee's name is usually included in the opening sentence of the letter.

Typed Name and Official Title

DAVID X. GONZALES, CASHIER

Reference Initials

loy

FIGURE 7-8. ADMINISTRATIVE MANAGEMENT SOCIETY SIMPLIFIED STYLE

that she prefers it, as by signing a letter (Ms.) Jane Thomas. **Mr.** should be used when the addressee's name could be that of a man or woman.

7.20 A complete inside address for letters written to **companies** includes either of the following:

name of company	International Biscuits Corp.
department name	Advertising Department
street address	201 North Main Street
city, state, ZIP code	Baton Rouge, LA 70807

or

name of company	Crystal Springs Stationers
street address	59–61 North Collins Road
city, state, ZIP code	Norwalk, CT 06850

Letterhead	***Unique* Office Supplies** **909 EMERYVILLE HIGHWAY • OAKLAND, CALIFORNIA 94608**
Date	March 15, 1979
Inside Address	Mr. Robert C. Wolfinger 52 Center Street Blacksburg, VA 24061
Salutation	Dear Mr. Wolfinger:
Body	This letter illustrates the format of the hanging-indented style letter with mixed punctuation. The hanging-indented style is a variation on the modified block style. You will agree that it has an attention-getting format. That is why this style is used in advertising letters. The paragraphs begin with the first line blocked at the left margin, and the second and succeeding lines are indented five spaces. The date and the complimentary closing are typed beginning at the center of the page. The hanging-indented style is not used for most business correspondence because of the additional time involved in setting up and typing correspondence. Please note the use of mixed punctuation in this particular letter-a colon after the salutation and a comma after the complimentary closing.
Complimentary Closing	Yours very truly,
Typed Name	Randal B. Parks, Jr.
Reference Initials	dlm

FIGURE 7-9. HANGING INDENTED STYLE (MIXED PUNCTUATION)

7.21 A full address, or **long address,** on the letter and the envelope insures that the letter will reach its destination without delay. An address should consist of not more than six lines.

name of individual	Mr. Oscar B. Levitz
official title	Vice President, Finance
department name	Executive Offices
name of company	Minnesota Publishing Corp.
street address	397 West Arlington Avenue
city, state, ZIP code	New Duluth, MN 55816

7.22 In some cases a street address may not be necessary, as with letters to a large organization or an individual residing in a small community. A three-line inside address, or **short address,** should then be used, with the city and state names typed on separate lines.

Letterhead

Cartier Manufacturing Company
300 Park Avenue
New York, New York 10021

Executive's Name/Title

Reginald C. Keating
Vice President

Date

June 21, 1979

Inside Address

Mr. Russell A. Freeman
General Counsel
Security Life Insurance Company
1210 Forest Rivers Road
Des Moines, IA 50322

Salutation

Dear Russ:

Body

Please note the use of executive-size stationery by a high-ranking officer in an organization. The name and position of the executive officer is usually imprinted on executive-size stationery.

Executive stationery (also known as monarch stationery) measures 7 1/4 × 10 1/2 inches; its matching envelope measures 7 1/4 x 3 7/8 inches.

This size stationery is used most often for informal business and social correspondence. Letters are usually brief so that a second page is not necessary. One-inch side margins are usually sufficient for an attractively placed letter. The date should be typed so that it balances the information in the letterhead. In this example, it is placed slightly to the right of center across from the executive's title.

Correspondence typed on executive or monarch stationery should reflect the prestige and integrity of the office held by the writer.

Complimentary Closing

Sincerely yours,

Reginald C. Keating

FIGURE 7-10. MODIFIED BLOCK STYLE, EXECUTIVE STATIONERY

name of company	Lockwood Trust Company
city	Lexington
state, ZIP code	KY 40504

7.23 The **state name** should be written using the two-letter abbreviation adopted by the United States Postal Service (see section 5.14 for complete list).

```
Jones, Katz & Bloom
Attorneys at Law
3181 Marvin Road
Dayton, OH 45431
```

7.24 The five-digit **Zone Improvement Plan (ZIP) code,** used on all correspondence, is typed one space after the state abbreviation (see 14.30 for additional ZIP code information).

```
Jones, Katz & Bloom
Attorneys at Law
3181 Marvin Road
Dayton, OH 45431
```

Return Address
Date

Inside Address

Salutation

Body

Complimentary Closing

Typed Name

```
                                    2241 Lansdowne Street
                                    Los Angeles, CA 90032
                                    July 18, 1979

Ms. Jeri Grassmueck
16 Sycamore Drive
Ridley Park, PA 19078

Dear Ms. Grassmueck:

This is an illustration of the letter style used for personal
and business correspondence typed on plain paper.

Because letterhead stationery is not used, the return address
of the writer must be typewritten at the top of the page for
identification.  The return address is typed in single spacing
above the date approximately 2 1/2 inches from the top edge of
the page.  It consists of the writer's street address, city,
state, and ZIP Code.  The state name may be spelled out, or the
two-letter abbreviation may be used.

The return address and date lines begin at the center point of
the page in this modified block style letter.  They would be
typed at the left margin if the full block style were used.

In personal letters, the writer's typed name and/or official
title may be omitted, as may reference initials.

                                    Sincerely yours,



                                    Michael Dieson, Jr.
```

FIGURE 7-11. MODIFIED BLOCK STYLE, PLAIN PAPER

Attention Line

7.25 An attention line is used when a letter is addressed to a company but directed to a specific individual or department for processing. The attention line, part of the inside address, is typed at the left margin a double space below the inside address and a double space before the salutation. If typed in capital and lowercase letters, the word "Attention" is followed by a colon; if it is typed all in capitals, no colon is used. (See 7.28 for a discussion of salutations to follow the attention line.)

```
Consolidated Chemicals Corporation
24605 Bundy Drive West
Suite 1401
Albuquerque, NM 87101

Attention:  Mrs. Sara Hawkins

Pacific Southwest Radio Corp.
5107 Avenue of the Stars
Los Angeles, CA 90067

ATTENTION Accounting Department
```

Salutation

7.26 The salutation, or greeting, is typed at the left margin a double space below the inside address or attention line, if one is used. If mixed punctuation is used in the letter, a colon follows the salutation. If open punctuation is used, no punctuation follows the salutation.

```
Mrs. Janet K. LaCroix
1427 North Broadway
Lincoln, NE 68529

Dear Mrs. LaCroix:
```

7.27 The following salutations meet the majority of letter-writing needs (see 7.80 for other forms of address).

Gentlemen	To a company or group of people
Dear Madam Dear Sir	To an individual; impersonal business form
Dear Miss Dear Mr. Dear Mrs. Dear Ms.	To an individual; preferred business form
Dear Mr. and Mrs. or Dear Dr. and Mrs.	To a husband and wife
Dear Chadwick Dear Virginia	To an individual; informal business and social form
Dear Mr. Jackson and Mr. Ruiz or Dear Messrs. Jackson and Ruiz	To two men with different names
Dear Mrs. Busche and Mrs. Fargo or Dear Mmes. Busche and Fargo	To two married women with different surnames
Dear Miss Rozowski and Miss Fung or Dear Misses Rozowski and Fung	To two single women with different surnames
Dear Ms. Irvine and Ms. Iwahashi	To two women whose marital status is unknown and/or who prefer the title
Dear Messrs. Freeman	To two or more men with the same surname

Dear Mmes. Johnson	To two or more married women with the same surname
Dear Misses Dionisio	To two or more single women with the same surname
Dear Professor Clark and Professor Casey or Dear Professors Clark and Casey	To two persons with different surnames

7.28 The salutation **Gentlemen** is used when a letter is addressed to a company with an attention line to an individual or department. (See Fig. 7-7 for illustration.) If *Gentlemen* seems awkward or inappropriate because a letter is addressed to the attention of a woman, it is best to eliminate the attention line and address the letter to the woman, rather than the company:

```
Mrs. Sara Hawkins
Consolidated Chemicals Corporation
24605 Bundy Drive West
Suite 1401
Albuquerque, NM 87101

Dear Mrs. Hawkins:
```

The following alternative salutations may also be used for correspondence addressed to companies whenever questions arise as to the appropriateness of the salutation *Gentlemen*.

Greetings
Dear [name of company]
Dear Customer [if appropriate]

Subject Line

7.29 The subject line refers to the topic of the letter and is considered part of the body. It is typed a double space below the salutation and a double space before the body. It may be centered on the page in the modified block and hanging indented styles, but it must be typed at the left margin in the full block style. Including an account number or case title within the subject line helps the reader focus on the main subject. **SUBJECT** or **RE** may be typed before the subject and followed by a colon.

Dear Mrs. LaCroix:	Dear Mrs. LaCroix:
SUBJECT: Account No. 14701-K	RE: Account No. 14701-K

SUBJECT or RE is not essential in the subject line, however, since the placement of information below the salutation indicates that it is the subject.

```
Dear Mrs. LaCroix:

Account No. 14701-K
```

Body

7.30 The body of the letter, which contains the message, is typed single spaced with double spacing between paragraphs. The style of the letter determines whether paragraphs are blocked, indented, or hanging (see Figures 7-4 through 7-11). One-paragraph letters may be typed double spaced.

Numbered List

7.31 A list is used to set off specific items the writer wishes to call to the reader's attention. Each item is introduced either by Arabic numbers (1, 2, 3, etc.) or by letters (A, B, C, or a, b, c, etc.). The sentence immediately preceding—or introducing—the list must be a complete thought. No punctuation is used after each item unless each is stated as a complete sentence.

7.32 **Short lists** may be typed **within a sentence** as a series, with the items separated by commas (if there are commas within items, separate items with semicolons). Arabic numerals or lowercase letters, written in parentheses, identify each item. Items may consist of either phrases or complete sentences, but they always begin with a lowercase letter.

```
The guidelines for typing lists within sentences
are:  (1) use Arabic numbers or lowercase letters
within parentheses to introduce each item, (2) use
commas to separate the items from each other,
(3) maintain parallel construction in writing each
item, and (4) word each item as concisely as
possible.

A list may be used to (a) draw the reader's eye to
important information, (b) present key ideas in
condensed form, or (c) indicate the correct order
of steps in a procedure.
```

7.33 A short list may also be placed **outside** the paragraph to which it refers, and **long lists** must be typed this way. Very short items may be written as phrases, but longer items should be written in sentence form.

```
Lists in a block style letter are typed as follows:

1. Each item begins at the left margin.

2. The second and succeeding lines are also typed
beginning at the left margin.

3. Individual items are single-spaced with a
double space between each item and the next.
```

Complimentary Closing

7.34 The complimentary, or formal, closing of a letter is typed a double space below the last line of the body. It is typed at the left margin in a full block letter or beginning at the center of the page in modified block and hanging indented letters. (See also Figures 7-4 through 7-11).

7.35 The following closings are customarily used in business correspondence.

```
Cordially                 Very sincerely yours
Cordially yours           Very truly yours
Respectfully              Yours sincerely
Respectfully yours        Yours truly
Sincerely                 Yours very truly
Sincerely yours
```

7.36 More personal closings such as the following may take the place of formal closings at the writer's discretion.

```
As always            Regards
As ever              Warmest regards
Best wishes          With regards
Kindest regards
```

7.37 The punctuation after the complimentary closing depends on whether mixed or open punctuation is used in the letter. If mixed punctuation is used, a comma follows the closing; if open punctuation is used, no punctuation mark follows the closing.

Typed Company Name

7.38 Although the company name appears in the letterhead, some companies like to highlight the name by including it in the closing as well. The name should be typed as it appears in the letterhead, a double space below the complimentary closing in solid capital letters.

```
Yours very truly,

BARRY, LORD & DYKES, INC.
```

Signature Line

7.39 Sufficient space should be left after the complimentary closing or typed company name to allow for the writer's signature. Three or four blank lines is usually ample space, but more space can be left if the writer has a large handwriting.

```
Yours very truly
Raymond L. Lewis
Raymond L. Lewis
```

```
Yours very truly,

BARRY, LORD & DYKES, INC.

Raymond L. Lewis
Raymond L. Lewis
```

7.40 The **formal signature** includes the writer's (1) first name, middle initial, and surname; (2) first initial, middle name, and surname; or (3) first and middle initials and surname. Titles such as Miss, Mrs., and Ms. may be written in parentheses before the signature or the typewritten name below. Professional titles or degrees may be included with the typewritten name but should not be written as part of the signature.

Randal B. Parks, Jr.

(Ms.) D. Claire Almeida

Randal B. Parks, Jr.

7.41 When business or social correspondence is signed in an informal manner, the writer's first name alone may be used, but the typed signature includes the full name.

Randal B. Parks, Jr.

Signing for Another

7.42 When a secretary signs correspondence in the absence of or on behalf of the employer, the employer's name is written with the secretary's initials just below.

CIN

Jackson P. Collins
General Manager

7.43 When the secretary writes a letter, the secretary's name is typed as the writer. His or her capacity is indicated on the next line as an official title.

Jean Harris
Secretary to Mr. Starkey

Jean Harris
For Mr. Starkey

For Peter L. Starkey
Advertising Department

Writer's Typed Name

7.44 The writer's name should be typed in full as it appears on all business correspondence, regardless of how the letter is signed. A typed name helps the reader identify the writer easily, especially when the writer's signature is difficult to read. The name is typed three or four lines below the complimentary closing or typed company's name.

```
Sincerely yours,
CONSULTANTS, INC.

Jackson P. Collins
Jackson P. Collins
```

```
Yours truly,

M. Clifford Kajiwara
M. Clifford Kajiwara
```

7.45 **Woman's marital status.** It is desirable to indicate a woman's preferred designation within the typed signature line for the convenience of business correspondents. The title **Miss, Mrs.,** or **Ms.** is typed in parentheses before the woman's name or may be written in parentheses before the signature.

```
Dorothy Higashi
(Miss) Dorothy Higashi

Teresa Reyes
(Mrs.) Teresa Reyes

Cynthia S. Miller
(Mrs.) Cynthia S. Miller
```

```
(Miss) Dorothy Higashi
Dorothy Higashi

Teresa Reyes
(Ms.) Teresa Reyes

Mrs. Cynthia S. Miller
Cynthia S. Miller
```

7.46 A woman may wish to be addressed by her husband's first name for business and/or social correspondence. The typed name is her husband's full name preceded by the title **Mrs.**

```
Beverly Warwick
Mrs. Dana D. Warwick
```

7.47 A **widow** may use her first name, middle name or initial, and surname in business correspondence but her husband's full name for social correspondence.

```
Bonita C. Kennedy
Mrs. Bonita C. Kennedy
```

```
Bonita C. Kennedy
Mrs. Bryan F. Kennedy
```

7.48 A **divorced woman** may use her first name and maiden name with her former husband's surname unless she reverts to her maiden name. She may also use her first name and her former husband's surname.

```
Isabella Garcia Lopez
Mrs. Isabella Garcia Lopez
```

```
Isabella Lopez
Mrs. Isabella Lopez
```

7.49 A **professional woman** who is married may wish to use her maiden name for business purposes. The title preceding her typewritten name in business correspondence is **Miss** or **Ms.;** or her typewritten name is followed by her professional title or degree. Socially, however, she uses her husband's surname preceded by the title **Mrs.** or **Ms.** If a woman has married *without* taking her husband's name, her maiden name preceded by **Miss** or **Ms.** is used for both business and social correspondence.

Maiden name for business purposes: Ms. Janice Engel or Janice Engel, M.D.

Husband's name used socially: Mrs. Janice Engel Dalton or Ms. Janice Engel Dalton

Married without taking husband's name: Miss or Ms. Janice Engel [business and social]

Title, Degree, and Department Name

7.50 The writer's official title or capacity should follow the typewritten name, either on the same line or the next depending on the length of name and the title. When both name and title are typed on one line, a comma separates them.

```
David X. Gonzales, Cashier          Peter L. Starkey
                                    Office Manager
```

Also, when both name and title are typed on one line, the line should not extend beyond the right margin of the letter. A long title may be divided as follows:

```
(Miss) Marcella Avakian
Assistant Vice President
  and Cashier
```

7.51 When both a professional degree and an official title are included as part of the typewritten name, only the degree is typed on the same line as the name. When a degree is included, no other designation, such as Dr. or Ms. is used.

```
Janice Engel, M.D.
Chief Resident
```

7.52 When a department or section name is to be included in the closing lines, it is typed on a separate line below the typewritten name or official title.

```
James D. Curry               Eugene Pinchuk, CPA
Assistant Professor          Accounting Department
Department of Business
```

Reference Initials

7.53 Reference initials are used to identify the typist and/or dictator of a letter. These initials are typed at the left margin a double space below the last line of the signature block. Lowercase letters are used, with no periods or spaces separating them.

```
Sincerely yours,

Norman Rittgers
Norman Rittgers
Operations Manager

csm
```

7.54 The initials of the writer or dictator are not usually included in the reference initials. However, if the person who dictates or initiates correspondence is different from the person who signs letters, his or her initials or last name may be included within the reference lines. The dictator's initials are typed in capital letters with no spaces or periods between the letters, or the first and middle initials are typed with the surname immediately following. A colon or diagonal separates the initials of the dictator from those of the typist.

```
LCH:csm      LCHenning:csm
LCH/csm      LCHenning/csm
```

Enclosure Notation

7.55 When documents or other papers are to be enclosed with or attached to correspondence, an enclosure notation should be typed a single or double space below the reference initials at the left margin.

Single Enclosure	*Multiple Enclosures*
Enc.	Encs.
Encl.	Encls.
Enclosure	Enclosures

Enclosures may be itemized for the reader's convenience, also, when there is more than one enclosure, the number may be indicated.

```
Enclosures:  Release Form Contract

Enclosures:  2   or   Enclosures (2)
```

Copy Notation

7.56 When an extra copy of correspondence is prepared—either by making a carbon copy or by photocopying—and distributed to another person, this fact should be noted on all copies for the addressee's information, when appropriate. The copy notation is typed at the left margin a double space below the last reference line.

```
cc: William McDaniels
CC: William McDaniels
Copy to William McDaniels
```

7.57 The expressions **cc** and **Carbon copy** are still used even though copies are commonly made by various photocopying methods.

7.58 The complete name and address of the copy recipient may also be indicated on the letter, again if appropriate.

```
cc:  William McDaniels
     Rutherford and Jones
     17 Robbins Building
     New Haven, CT 06518

Copy to:  Bob Sarkisian,
          Controller's Dept.
```

7.59 When several copies of one letter are to be made and distributed, all names should be indicated in the notation.

```
cc:  John Fitzhugh
     William Hartford
     Elena C. Castagna

Copies to:  John Fitzhugh
            William Hartford
            Elena C. Castagna
```

Blind Copy Notation

7.60 When an extra copy of a letter is prepared for another person—by making a carbon copy or by photocopying—but the addressee is not to be informed, a blind copy notation is indicated on all but the original letter (hence "blind"). The original and first carbon sheet are removed from the typewriter so the notation can be typed on all copies. This notation is typed a double space below the last reference line at the left margin.

```
Bcc:  Gloria Fielding

bcc:  Gloria Fielding

BCC:  Gloria Fielding

 BC:  Gloria Fielding

 Bc:  Michael Ramirez
      John C. Carroll
```

Postscript

7.61 A postscript is an afterthought, sometimes used for emphasis at the very end of the letter. The postscript is typed a double space below the last reference or notation line. It should be typed in the same style as the body of the letter—with blocked, indented, or inverted paragraphs.

7.62 The position at the end of the letter identifies the addition as a postscript; therefore, the letters P.S. are omitted.

Post-Postscript

7.63 When a writer wishes to add still another afterthought, a separate paragraph or **post-postscript** is typed a double space below the postscript and follows the same paragraph style as the letter. The letters **P.P.S.** are typed to separate it from the postscript.

```
P.P.S.  Dave Williams is planning to show his
movies of the Annual Sales Conference in Topeka, so
the June meeting should be an interesting one for
all.

     P.P.S.  Dave Williams is planning to show his
movies of the Annual Sales Conference in Topeka, so
the June meeting should be an interesting one for
all.

P.P.S.  Dave Williams is planning to show his
        movies of the Annual Sales Conference in
        Topeka, so the June meeting should be an
        interesting one for all.
```

A post-postscript eliminates the need to retype the letter in order to insert additional information.

Mailing Notations

7.64 Mailing notations such as **AIRMAIL, SPECIAL DELIVERY, REGISTERED MAIL,** and **CERTIFIED MAIL** tell the Postal Service that special processing is desired. Such notations are typed in solid capital letters at the left margin a double or triple space above the inside address.

```
REGISTERED MAIL

Miss Leona J. Adams
Executive Secretary
Montogomery Corporation
4421 Roosevelt Avenue
Dayton, OH 45426
```

```
AIR MAIL

Mr. Robert C. Wolfinger
52 Center Street
Blacksburg, VA 24061
```

7.65 On the **envelope,** the mailing notation is typed in the upper right corner below the postage stamp in solid capital letters.

Addressee Notation

7.66 Addressee notations indicate how mail is to be handled when received. These special notations include **PERSONAL, CONFIDENTIAL, PLEASE HOLD FOR ARRIVAL, PLEASE FORWARD,** and **PERSONAL AND CONFIDENTIAL.** Addressee notations are typed above the inside address of the letter at the left margin. On the envelope, they appear in the upper left corner below the return address.

```
CONFIDENTIAL

United Press Services
81 Huntington Drive
Billings, MT 59102
```

```
PERSONAL

Ms. Elizabeth Chang
Personnel Services
Acme Employment Agency
9350 North Brooklyn Road
Newport, KY 41073
```

Second and Subsequent Pages

7.67 The second and subsequent pages of business letters are typed on plain paper of the same quality as the letterhead. To identify each additional page, a heading is typed at the top of each page, which includes the following information:

individual's name	Mr. Allen Robair
page number	Page 2
date	January 5, 1979
company's name	Jurgenson Brothers
attention line, if used	Attention: Mr. Jason Myers
page number	Page 2
date	January 17, 1979

7.68 The **block style** of heading is typed in single spacing one inch from the top of the page at the left margin. This style must be used with full block letters and may be used with modified block and hanging indented letters.

```
Mr. Allen Robair          Jurgenson Brothers
Page 2                    Attention Mr. Jason Myers
January 5, 1979           Page 3
                          March 21, 1979
```

7.69 The **horizontal style** heading is typed across the top of the page one inch from the top. This style is used with either modified block or hanging indented letters. The name of the individual or company is typed beginning at the left margin. The page number is typed at the center of the page by itself, and the date is typed so it ends close to the right margin.

```
Mr. Allen Robair                  2    January 5, 1979

Jurgenson Brothers                2    January 5, 1979
Attention:  Mr. Jason Myers
```

7.70 On the second and subsequent pages the body of the letter is continued **three to four lines below** the heading and is typed in the same form as the first page.

```
Mr. Allen Robair          2            January 5, 1979


Continue the body of the letter approximately
three to four lines below the heading. More space
may be left if the letter is not going to fill the
entire page.
```

ADDRESSING ENVELOPES

7.71 The envelope address ensures that the carefully written message will be received by the addressee. The use of optical character readers (OCR) by the U.S. Postal Service to scan addresses for delivery has encouraged more efficient mail distribution.

Return Address

7.72 Most companies have their return addresses preprinted on all company envelopes to match the design of the letterhead stationery.

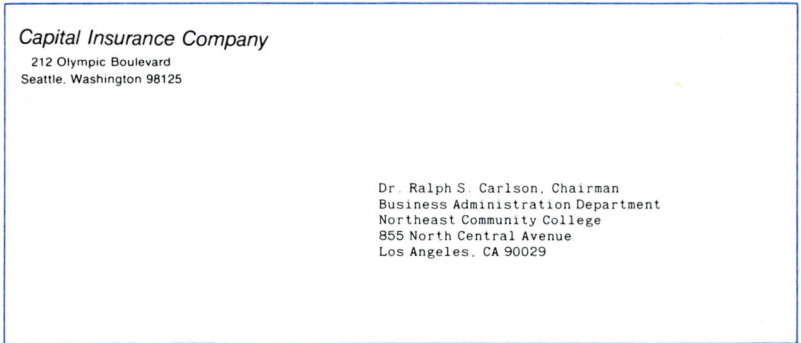

Capital Insurance Company
212 Olympic Boulevard
Seattle, Washington 98125

Dr. Ralph S. Carlson, Chairman
Business Administration Department
Northeast Community College
855 North Central Avenue
Los Angeles, CA 90029

FIGURE 7-12. ENVELOPE WITH PREPRINTED RETURN ADDRESS

7.73 If **plain envelopes** are used, the complete return address should be typed in the upper left corner of the envelope, approximately two lines from the top edge and two or three spaces from the left edge. The single-spaced address is typed in block style.

Name of writer
Name of company
Street address
City, state, ZIP

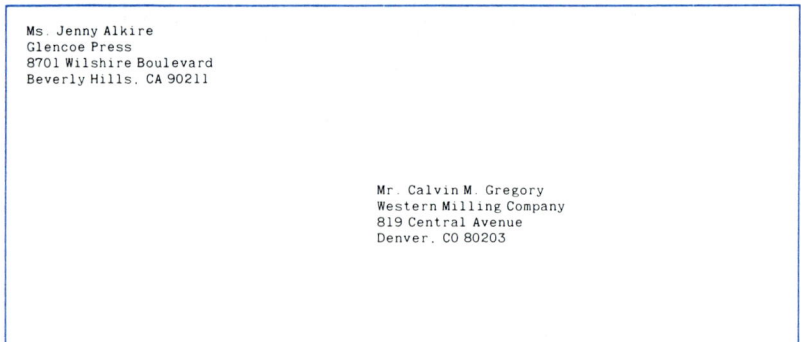

Ms. Jenny Alkire
Glencoe Press
8701 Wilshire Boulevard
Beverly Hills, CA 90211

Mr. Calvin M. Gregory
Western Milling Company
819 Central Avenue
Denver, CO 80203

FIGURE 7-13. ENVELOPE WITH TYPED RETURN ADDRESS

7.74 The return address should include the two-letter **state abbreviation** and the **ZIP code.** Also, the writer's name should be typed above the company name so mail can be redirected to this person if necessary.

7.75 The titles **Mr.** and **Miss** are omitted in the typed return address; however, the titles Dr., Mrs., and Ms. may be typed before the writer's name.

Ann Downs
Unique Office Supplies
909 EMORYVILLE • OAKLAND, CALIFORNIA 94608

Mr. James C. Garven
Vice President
Fairchild Business Products
82303 West Kensington Road
Tacoma, WA 98412

Unique Office Supplies
909 EMORYVILLE • OAKLAND, CALIFORNIA 94608

October 4, 1979

Mr. James C. Garven
Vice President
Fairchild Business Products
82303 West Kensington Road
Tacoma, WA 98412

Dear Mr. Garven:

Sincerely,

(Ms.) Ann Downs
Vice President

FIGURE 7-14. INSIDE ADDRESS AND ENVELOPE ADDRESS

Envelope Address

7.76 The envelope address should be identical to the inside address.

An envelope address must contain at least three typed lines. When a street address is not necessary for delivery of mail, such as to a large organization or to an individual in a small community, the city and state names may be separated. The city is typed on the second line by itself. The two-letter state abbreviation adopted by the U.S. Postal Service is typed on the third line together with the five-digit ZIP code. Leave one space between the state abbreviation and the ZIP code, as this information is processed by the optical character scanning devices.

```
Mrs. Jean N. Harris          Lockwood Trust Company
Rockwood                     Lexington
PA 15557                     KY 40504
```

Postal Notations

7.77 Postal notations such as AIRMAIL, SPECIAL DELIVERY, CERTIFIED MAIL, REGISTERED MAIL, and RETURN RECEIPT REQUESTED are typed in solid capital letters in the upper right corner of the envelope below the postage stamp (see 14.51–14.60 for class distinctions).

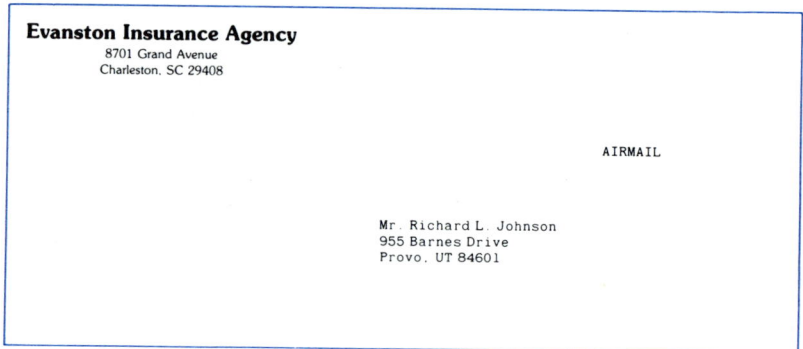

Evanston Insurance Agency
8701 Grand Avenue
Charleston, SC 29408

AIRMAIL

Mr. Richard L. Johnson
955 Barnes Drive
Provo, UT 84601

FIGURE 7-15. ENVELOPE WITH POSTAL NOTATION

Addressee Notations

7.78 Addressee notations are typed in solid capital letters in the upper left part of the envelope below the return address. They request special handling by the recipient. Examples include:

ATTENTION	When correspondence is to be directed to the attention of a specific person or department of an organization.
CONFIDENTIAL	When correspondence contains information that is privileged and is to be seen only by those persons authorized to receive and handle such matters.

HOLD FOR ARRIVAL	When correspondence is mailed to arrive before the individual addressee; arrival date included in the notation.
PERSONAL	When correspondence is intended only for the addressee's eyes and/or is of a personal nature.
PLEASE FORWARD	When correspondence is sent to an individual whose address may since have changed; notation includes addressee's new address, if available.

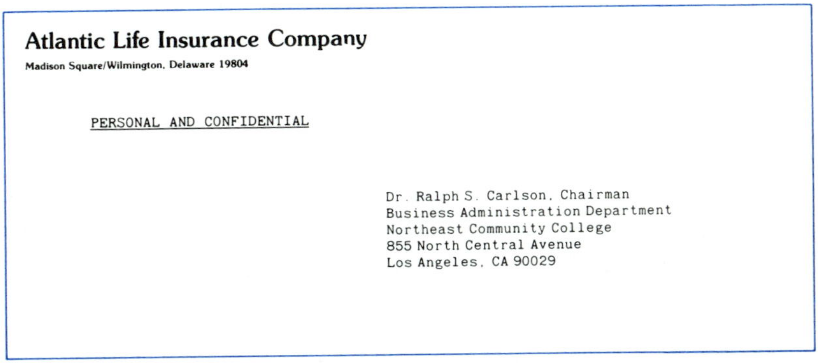

Atlantic Life Insurance Company
Madison Square/Wilmington, Delaware 19804

PERSONAL AND CONFIDENTIAL

Dr. Ralph S. Carlson, Chairman
Business Administration Department
Northeast Community College
855 North Central Avenue
Los Angeles, CA 90029

FIGURE 7-16. ENVELOPE WITH ADDRESSEE NOTATION

Envelope Sizes

7.79 Business stationery comes in a variety of sizes, and envelopes of corresponding sizes accompany them. The different sizes and appropriate uses for each are illustrated in Table 7-2 and Figures 7-17 through 7-22.

Size of Stationery	Envelope Sizes	When To Use
Half Sheet or Baronial (5½ by 8½ inches)	No. 6 (6½ by 3⅝ inches)	One- or two-page letter or memorandum
Standard (8½ by 11 inches)	No. 6 (6½ by 3⅝ inches)	One-page letter or memorandum
	No. 10 (9½ by 4⅛ inches)	One-page letter or memorandum with enclosures Two-page or longer letter or memoranda
	Manila (9 by 12 inches) Manila (10 by 12 inches)	One- or two-page letter (unfolded) with many enclosures
Executive or Monarch (7¼ by 10½ inches)	No. 7 (7½ by 3⅞ inches)	One- or two-page letter
Government (8 by 10½ inches)	No. 10 (9½ by 4⅛ inches)	One- or two-page letter

TABLE 7-2. ENVELOPES FOR LETTERS AND MEMORANDA

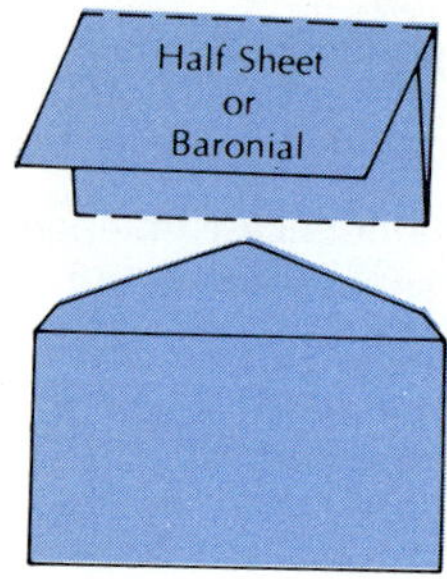

Fold bottom of letter up approximately one-third of the page; fold top of letter down to about one-half inch from bottom crease.

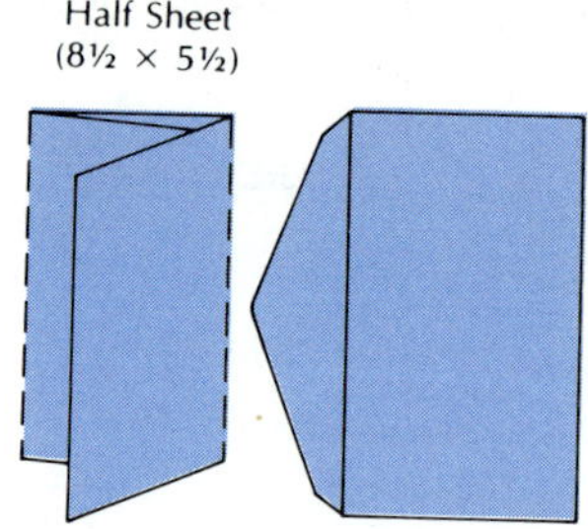

Fold left side of letter approximately one-third of the page to the right; fold right side over to left about one-half inch from the left crease.

FIGURE 7-17. USING NO. 6 ENVELOPE FOR HALF SHEET STATIONERY

If an address is written or typed as shown above, the same envelope may be used several times.

FIGURE 7-18. ADDRESSING INTEROFFICE ENVELOPE

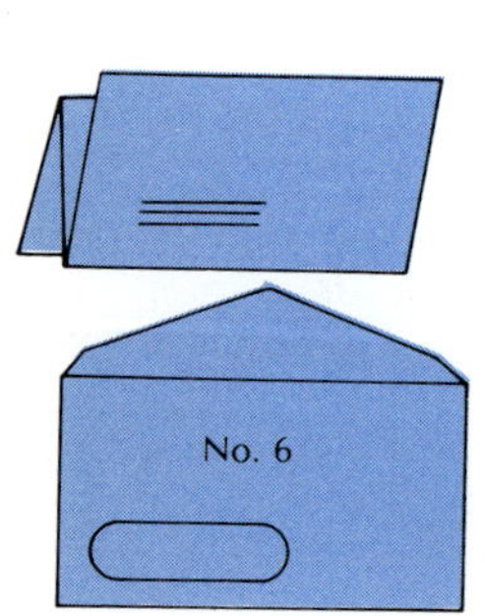

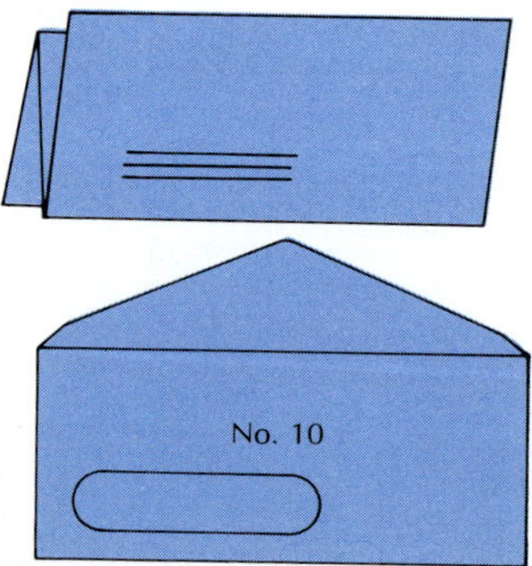

The inside address on correspondence for window envelopes must be typed so it can be properly aligned with the window. Fold bottom of letter up approximately one third of the page; fold top edge backwards and down to about one-half inch from bottom fold.

FIGURE 7-19. WINDOW ENVELOPES FOR HALF SHEET AND STANDARD STATIONERY

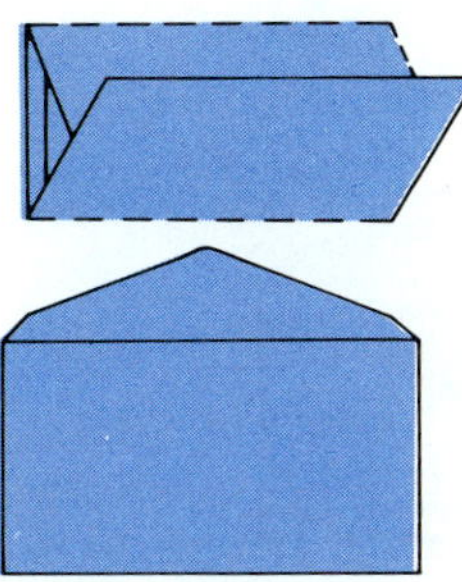

No. 6: Fold bottom edge up to within one-half inch of top of page; fold right side of letter about one third to the left; fold left side over to right about one-half inch from the right crease. (Or start with the left side, if you are left-handed.)

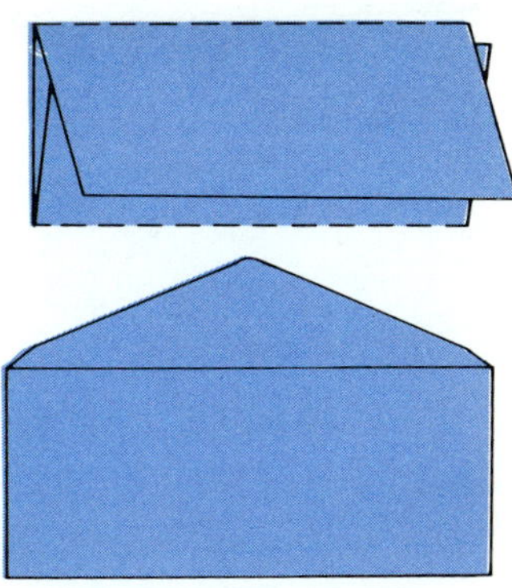

No. 10: Fold bottom edge up about one third of the page; fold top of letter down to about one-half inch from bottom fold. Note: some no. 10 envelopes are marked with boxed sections for multiple use.

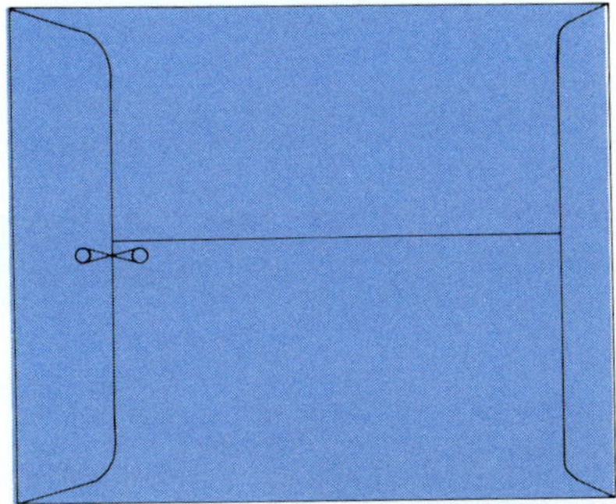

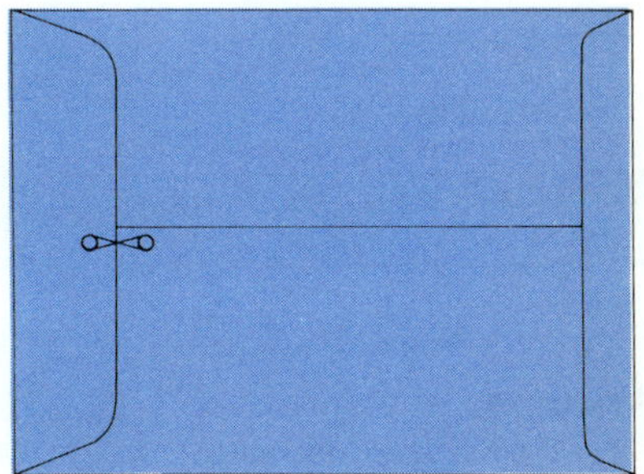

Manila: No folding is needed for memoranda and enclosures sent in larger envelopes. Illustration shows string-and-button fastener; envelope may also have glued flap. Note that enclosures accompanying a memorandum should be securely attached with a paper clip, staple, or rubber band.

FIGURE 7-20. ENVELOPES FOR STANDARD STATIONERY

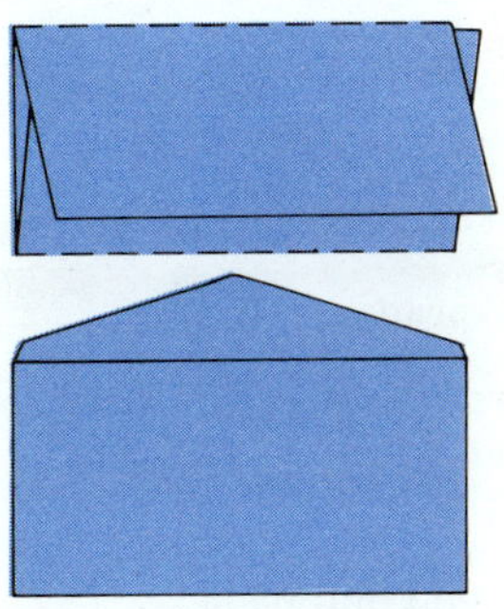

Fold bottom edge of letter up approximately one third of the page; fold top of letter down to about one-half inch from bottom fold.

FIGURE 7-21. ENVELOPE FOR EXECUTIVE OR MONARCH STATIONERY

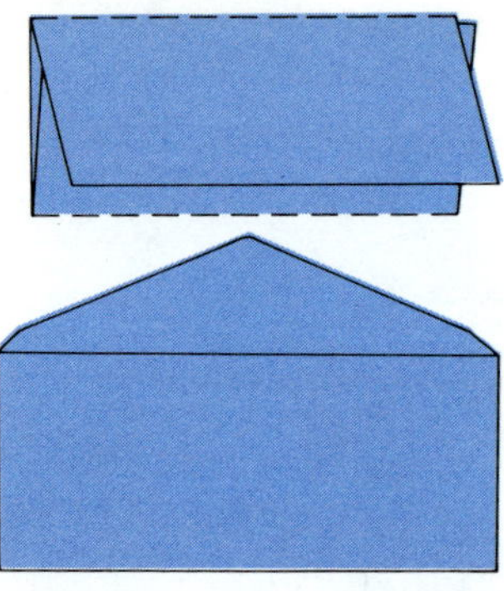

Fold bottom edge of letter up approximately one third of the page; fold top of letter down to about one-half inch from bottom fold.

FIGURE 7-22. ENVELOPE FOR GOVERNMENT STATIONERY

Forms of Address

7.80

Titles and Inside Address	*Salutation and Complimentary Close*
Alderman	
Alderman (full name)	Dear Alderman (surname) Dear Mr. (surname)
The Honorable (full name) Alderman, City of ________	Yours very truly Sincerely yours
Ambassador	
The Honorable (full name) American Ambassador (city, country)	Sir Dear Mr. Ambassador Dear Madam Ambassador
The Honorable (full name) The Ambassador of the United States (city, country)	Very truly yours Sincerely yours
American Consul	
Mr. (full name) United States Consul (city, country)	Sir Dear Mr. (surname) Very truly yours Sincerely yours
Archbishop	
The Most Reverend (full name) Archbishop of (diocese)	Your Excellency Dear Archbishop (surname) Sincerely yours Very truly yours

Armed Forces Officers

General (full name), USA Admiral (full name), USN General (full name), USMC Colonel (full name), USAF Captain (full name), USCG	Dear (Rank) (Surname) Very truly yours Sincerely yours
Chaplain: Lieutenant (full name) (Ch.C.) USN	Dear Chaplain (surname) Sincerely yours

Associate Justice of the Supreme Court

Mr. Justice (surname) The Supreme Court of the United States Washington, DC 20543	Dear Mr. Justice Dear Mr. Justice (surname) Very truly yours Sincerely yours

Bishop (Catholic)

The Most Reverend (surname) Bishop of (diocese)	Your Excellency Dear Bishop (surname) Sincerely Very truly yours

Bishop (Protestant)

The Reverend (full name) Bishop of ________	Dear Reverend Dear Mr. (surname)
The Right Reverend (surname)	Very truly yours Sincerely yours

Cabinet Member

The Honorable (full name) Secretary of (name of department) Washington, DC 20520	Dear Mr. Secretary Dear Madam Secretary Very truly yours Sincerely yours

Cardinal (Catholic)

His Eminence, (given name), Cardinal (surname) Archbishop of (diocese)	Your Eminence Dear Cardinal (surname) Sincerely yours

Chief Justice of the Supreme Court

The Chief Justice The Supreme Court Washington, DC 20543	Dear Mr. Chief Justice Very truly yours Sincerely yours
The Honorable (full name) Chief Justice of the United States Washington, DC 20543	

City Attorney

Honorable (full name) City Attorney	Dear Mr. (surname)
Mr. (full name) City Attorney	Very truly yours Sincerely yours

Titles and Inside Address	Salutation and Complimentary Close
Commissioner, Director, or Chief of Government Bureau	
The Honorable (full name) (Commissioner, Director, Chief), (Name of Government Bureau)	Dear Mr. (surname) Very truly yours Sincerely yours
Congressional Representatives	
The Honorable (full name) House of Representatives Washington, DC 20515 The Honorable (full name) Representative in Congress (local address) (city, state, ZIP code)	Dear Representative (surname) Dear Mr. (surname) Dear Mrs. (surname) Very truly yours Sincerely yours
Councilman	
Councilman (full name) The Honorable (full name) Councilman, City of ________	Dear Councilman (surname) Dear Mr. (surname) Very truly yours Sincerely yours
County Officials	
Honorable (full name) Supervisor, (county)	Dear Mr. (surname) Dear Supervisor (surname) Very truly yours Sincerely yours
Dean of a School	
Dean (full name) School of Fine Arts Dr. (full name) Assistant Dean	Dear Dean (surname) Dear Doctor (surname) Sincerely yours
District Attorney	
The Honorable (full name) District Attorney County Courthouse	Dear Mr. (surname) Very truly yours Sincerely yours
Foreign Officials	
His Excellency (surname) Ambassador of (country) Washington, DC 20035 His Excellency Mr. (full name) Minister of (country) Washington, DC 20046	Excellency Dear Mr. Ambassador Very truly yours Sincerely yours
Governor	
The Honorable (full name) Governor of (state) (state capitol) (state, ZIP code)	Dear Governor (surname) Very truly yours Sincerely yours

Judge

The Honorable (full name)
Judge of the (name of court)

Dear Judge (surname)

Very truly yours
Sincerely yours

Lieutenant Governor

The Honorable (full name)
Lieutenant Governor of (state)
(state capitol)
(state, ZIP code)

Dear Mr. (surname)

Very truly yours
Sincerely yours

Mayor

The Honorable (full name)
Mayor of (city)
(city, state, ZIP code)

Dear Mayor (surname)
Dear Mr. Mayor
Dear Madam Mayor
Very truly yours
Sincerely yours

Minister

The Reverend (full name)
Title
Name of church

Reverend Sir
Dear Reverend (surname)

The Very Reverend (full name) D.D.
Dean of (name of church)

Very Reverend Sir
Dear Dean (surname)

Respectfully yours
Sincerely yours

President of a College or University

Dr. (full name)
President, (name of school)

Dear Dr. (surname)
Dear President (surname)

Very truly yours
Sincerely yours

President of a Catholic College or University

The Very Reverend (full name),
(initials of religious order)
President, (name of college or
university)

Dear Father (surname)

Very truly yours
Sincerely yours

President of the United States

The President
The White House
Washington, DC 20500

Dear Mr. President
Mr. President

or

The President of the United States
The White House
Washington, DC 20500

Respectfully

Priest

The Reverend (full name)
(name of church)

Dear Reverend Father (surname)
Dear Father (surname)

The Reverend (full name), Ph.D.
(name of college or university)

Dear Doctor (surname)

Sincerely yours

Professor

Professor (full name)
(department)
(name of institution)

Dear Mr. (surname)
Dear Professor (surname)
Dear Doctor (surname)

Dr. (full name), (title)
(name of institution)

Very truly yours
Sincerely yours

Titles and Inside Address	*Salutation and Complimentary Close*
Rabbi Rabbi (full name) Temple (name) Dr. (full name)	Dear Rabbi (surname) Dear Doctor (surname) Sincerely yours
Secretary or Assistant to the President of the United States The Honorable (full name) Secretary to the President The White House Washington, DC 20500	Dear Mr. (surname) Very truly yours Sincerely yours
Senator The Honorable (full name) United States Senate Washington, DC 20510 The Honorable (full name) State Senate (state capitol, state, ZIP code)	Dear Mr. (surname) Dear Senator (surname) Very truly yours Sincerely yours
Sister Sister (full name or religious name), (initials of order)	Dear Sister (full name or religious name) Dear Sister Sincerely yours Very truly yours
Speaker of the House The Honorable (full name) Speaker of the House of Representatives Washington, DC 20515	Dear Mr. Speaker Sincerely yours Respectfully
State Legislators The Honorable (full name) The House of Representatives (state capitol, state, ZIP code) The Honorable (full name) The State Assembly (state capitol, state, ZIP code)	Dear Mr. (surname) Dear Representative (surname) Dear Assemblyman (surname) Sincerely yours Very truly yours
State Officials The Honorable (full name) Secretary of the State of California Sacramento, CA 95800	Dear Mr. Secretary Dear Mr. (surname) Dear Madam Secretary Sincerely yours Very truly yours
United Nations His Excellency (full name) Secretary General of the United Nations United Nations, NY 10021	Dear Mr. Secretary General Sincerely yours Very truly yours

Vice-President of the United States

The Vice President United States Senate Washington, DC 20501	Dear Mr. Vice-President
	Very truly yours Sincerely yours
or	
The Honorable (full name) Vice President of the United States Washington, DC 20501	

Adapted from J. Harold Janis and Margaret H. Thompson, *New Standard Reference for Secretaries and Administrative Assistants* (New York: Macmillan Pub. Co., Inc., 1972).

Interoffice Correspondence (Memoranda)

7.81 Interoffice correspondence—called an interoffice memorandum or memo—conveys information among company employees and is seldom seen by outsiders. Memos communicate the ideas, suggestions, facts, and requests for data that are the basis of company decisions; these decisions, in turn, generate correspondence to people outside the company.

7.82 Formal memoranda are generally typed on printed **memorandum** or **interoffice communication forms** (see Figures 7-23 and 7-24). These forms come in two sizes—8½ × 11 (standard size) and 8½ × 5½ (half sheet). The standard size forms are preferable to ensure that all correspondence placed in the files will be of uniform size.

7.83 Less formal memos may consist simply of a handwritten note on regular memo form or on a sheet of note paper. When an inquiry requires a quick response and the exchange of information need not be filed, the handwritten note (or a telephone call) provides an efficient means of soliciting and obtaining information.

WRITING EFFECTIVE MEMOS

7.84 Just as effective letters project a positive impression to people outside the company, carefully prepared memos will build goodwill and create a favorable impression within the company. To determine the effectiveness of your memos, ask yourself these questions:

Checklist for Effective Memoranda

7.85 1. **Purpose.** Have you determined the purpose of the interoffice correspondence? While the main purpose of such communications is to inform, memoranda must often sell an idea, persuade others to accept or adopt a point of view, or inquire about specific facts.

2. **Conciseness.** Have you used the words and expressions that will best convey your thoughts to the reader? Interoffice communications are usually written in less formal language than letters. Stating your thoughts or needs as directly as possible is the most expedient approach.

3. **Clarity.** Has your purpose been set forth clearly? Ideas should be presented in logical sequence to help the reader interpret and act upon your message.

4. **Completeness.** Did you include all the necessary facts, figures, dates, names, and addresses? Without the essential information, the reader may have to backtrack and ask you the relevant questions before taking action.

5. **Tone.** Does the tone of your memo indicate friendliness, warmth, and cooperation? Each correspondent within the company is a representative for his or her particular department or section. If the company is to operate smoothly and efficiently, consideration for the time and problems of all employees is essential in requesting information or assistance.

6. **Correctness.** Are the facts and figures correct? The accuracy of information conveyed outside the company depends on the accuracy of information conveyed within it.

MEMORANDUM STYLES

7.86 Figures 7-23 and 7-24 illustrate two forms of printed memoranda. Note the variation in the printed headings and placement of information within each illustration and the use of a subject line in Figure 7-23.

MEMORANDUM ELEMENTS

7.87 Note that the procedures for setting up a memo do not always correspond to those for typing a letter.

Letterhead

7.88 The letterhead of a memorandum usually consists of the company's name. Large organizations with several branch offices or departments may have the branch or department name imprinted below the company name for identification purposes. The printed form is usually labeled **INTEROFFICE MEMORANDUM** or **MEMORANDUM.** Since interoffice communications do not go outside the company, a company address is not necessary.

Heading

7.89 The memorandum heading is usually printed with the words **TO, FROM, SUBJECT,** and **DATE,** to save typing time. Headings may be arranged in different ways.

Addressee and Writer

7.90 The addressee's name, title (if space allows), and department name or number are typed after TO. The same information for

SONOMA CITY COLLEGE
SONOMA, CALIFORNIA

MEMORANDUM

TO	Patsy P. Mark, Interviewer Personnel Department	DATE	December 21, 1978
FROM	Janice Jackson, Assistant Legal Department		
SUBJECT	BRADBURY WILLS v. ATLANTIC INSURANCE CO.		

This memorandum form illustrates the block style of typing both the heading and the body. All information except the date is typed at the same point. Although the words TO, FROM, and SUBJECT in the printed heading are staggered, the blocked heading gives a more balanced appearance.

The subject line aids the reader in focusing his attention on the topic of the communication and is a valuable aid for the typist or secretary in filing and retrieving correspondence. The subject line may be typed in solid capital letters, or the first letter of important words may be capitalized.

An important factor in creating an attractive communication is that of properly aligning each item of information with the printed words in the heading. The variable line spacer on the typewriter will help in proper alignment.

sml

FIGURE 7-23. BLOCK STYLE MEMORANDUM WITH SUBJECT LINE

Aero-Tech Corporation

TO:	Ronald Messinger Advertising Department	DATE:	August 19, 1978
FROM:	Alicia Gonzales Personnel Department		

This memorandum illustrates the block style of typing the heading. All information except the date is typed at the same point--two or three spaces after the colon. This facilitates the typing of information and is easier to read because all information within the heading begins at the same place.

The body of the memorandum begins three or four lines after the last line of the heading. The left margin in this illustration is set even with the longest line in the heading. Memoranda are usually typed in single spacing with double spacing between paragraphs and are typed in the block style with no paragraph indentions. A short memorandum may be typed in double spacing.

Because memoranda are internal correspondence, the salutation and complimentary closing are omitted. The writer may simply write his or her initials next to the typed name or at the end of the memorandum.

khl

FIGURE 7-24. BLOCK STYLE, HEADING ONLY

the writer is typed after FROM. Such words as "Department," "Section," "Building," and "Number" may be abbreviated. The designations Dr., Miss, Mr., Mrs., and Ms. are not used. The identifying information may be arranged in various ways depending on the printed memorandum form.

Addressee

TO: Patsy P. Mark, Interviewer
Personnel Department (*or:* Personnel Dept.)

TO: Patsy P. Mark, Interviewer
Department 102 (*or:* Dept. 102)

Writer

FROM: Ellen C. Fong, Attorney
Legal Department (*or:* Legal Dept.)

FROM: Ellen C. Fong, Attorney
Department 107 (*or:* Dept. 107)

Subject

7.91 "Subject" (often the caption under which related correspondence is filed) may be typed with initial or solid capital letters. When "Subject" is printed below "From," the subject should be typed across the page; a long subject can be typed on two lines.

FROM: Glenda Baldwin

SUBJECT: Bradbury Wills v. Atlantic Insurance Co.

When "Subject" is printed below "Date" near the right margin, two lines are used:

DATE: September 13, 1979

SUBJECT: Bradbury Wills v.
Atlantic Insurance Co.

The subject line should be as brief as possible yet include sufficient information for the reader to focus on the topic of the communication.

Date

7.92 The date of the communication is typed with the month spelled out, unless space is limited:

DATE: November 30, 1979

DATE: Nov. 30, 1979

Body

7.93 The body of the memorandum, which contains the typed message, begins three to four lines below the last line of the heading. It is usually typed in single spaced block style paragraphs with double spacing between them.

SUBJECT: Bradbury Wills v. Atlantic Insurance Co.

Begin the message three to four lines below the last line of the heading. This is generally sufficient space between the heading and the body of the memo.

Margin Settings

7.94 The margin settings for interoffice correspondence depend on the format of the printed heading.

TO: Arthur B. Segal
Operations and Planning
FROM: Cynthia Wong
Personnel Services
SUBJECT: MARGINS FOR INTEROFFICE MEMOS

When the words in the printed heading of the memorandum end at the same point, set the left margin two or three spaces after each line in the heading. This format is easy for the reader to follow because all information begins at the same place on the page.

This form is especially attractive when there is a narrow margin at the left because of the placement of the lines in the heading.

ehs

TO: Arthur B. Segal
Operations and Planning
FROM: Cynthia Wong
Personnel Services
SUBJECT: MARGINS FOR INTEROFFICE MEMOS

When the words in the printed heading of the memorandum end at the same point, the left margin may be set even with the longest word of the heading. This format is pleasing to the eye because it provides a balanced appearance of information on the page.

This format should be used when there is a wide enough left margin before the printed heading.

ehs

TO: Arthur B. Segal
Operations and Planning
FROM: Cynthia Wong
Personnel Services
SUBJECT: MARGINS FOR INTEROFFICE MEMOS

When the words in the heading of the memorandum begin at the same point and are staggered, the left margin for the message may be set either where the printed words begin or it may be set beginning with the typewritten words.

ehs

Reference Initials

7.95 Reference initials, which identify the typist, are typed in lowercase letters at the left margin a double space below the last line of the memorandum. No periods or spaces appear between the letters, as shown under 7.94.

Signature

7.96 Memoranda are not generally signed by the writer, but the memo may be initialed next to the typed name in the heading or at the end of the memorandum.

TO:	Legal Department
FROM:	Ellen C. Fong **ECF**
SUBJECT:	Bradbury Wills v. Atlantic Insurance Co.

Enclosure or Attachment Notation

7.97 When one or more papers will be enclosed with or attached to the memorandum, this fact should be noted a double space below the reference initials at the left margin.

Enc.	or	Encs.
Encl.	or	Encls.
Enclosure	or	Enclosures
Attachment	or	Attachments

The enclosure(s) or attachment(s) may also be itemized, or the number of enclosures may be indicated.

```
Enclosures:  ACV Letter, Dec. 10, 1979
             Escrow Instructions
             Deposit Slip

Enclosures:  3   or   Enclosures (3)
```

Second and Subsequent Pages

7.98 The second and subsequent pages of a memorandum are typed on plain white paper of the same quality as the first page. A blocked or horizontal heading is typed one inch from the top of each additional page, starting at the left margin, that lists addressee's name and department, the page number, and the date.

```
Gerald Manning
Real Estate Dept.
Page 2
February 4, 1979

Gerald Manning          2        February 4, 1979
Real Estate Dept.
```

7.99 The body of the memorandum is continued three to four lines below the heading and is typed in the same form as the first page.

Eight

Business Reports

Report Writing Guidelines

8.1 A business report is prepared to present factual information to persons within or outside the company, based on a study or investigation of a given subject. Information is conveyed to those concerned with the business operations of the company —stockholders, employees, customers, prospective customers, and the public. Reports provide the bases for determining progress and shaping decisions within the organization.

WRITING EFFECTIVE REPORTS

8.2 Report writing may be divided into three tasks: defining the objective(s) of the report, gathering information and constructing an outline (see 8.6 through 8.21), and writing the actual report. The list below includes questions you should ask as the report is being prepared.

Business Report Checklist

1. **Purpose.** Has the purpose of the report been determined? Is there a problem to be solved? Is certain information needed to keep a department running smoothly or to serve as the basis for a decision? Ideally, to simplify the writer's task, the report purpose should be stated as a series of specific objectives.

2. **Scope.** Has the scope of the report been defined? What limitations, if any, will determine the writer's approach to the subject? Is an in-depth analysis called for, or will a brief factual summary do?

3. **Conciseness.** Is all pertinent information presented as briefly, yet completely, as possible? Business reports should contain the minimum number of words needed to accomplish the intended goals.

4. **Completeness.** Does the report include all facts, figures, and supporting information that relate to the topic?

5. **Tone.** Does the tone of the report reflect a consistent, businesslike point of view? It is the writer's responsibility to present various aspects of the topic to the reader based on the data gathered; it is up to the reader to interpret the facts and decide on subsequent courses of action.

6. **Accuracy.** Are all facts cited in the report accurate? Do the data substantiate the conclusions? Incorrect information is worse than no information at all because it may lead to misunderstandings and can involve additional time in obtaining the correct data.

A NOTE ON STYLE

8.3 The way a report is written determines its effectiveness. Unless facts and ideas are communicated in the proper order and in direct, simple language, the report will fail to meet its objectives. One important aspect of good writing style is avoiding such awkward, redundant expressions as those indicated on the following page.

Avoid	Use	Avoid	Use
above listed	those	in the very near future	soon
above mentioned	those	in this day and age	today
absolutely complete	complete	in view of the fact that	because, since
actual experience	experience	inasmuch as	since
along these lines	similar to, like this	inside of the	inside the
arrived at the conclusion	concluded	later on	later
articulate	explain	might possibly	might
as per	as, according	my personal opinion	my opinion
assemble together	assemble	necessary requisite	requisite
at a cost of	at	party	person
at a later date	later	past experience	experience
at all times	always	previous to	before
at the present time	now	prior to the	before
attached please find	attached is	reason is because	the reason is
basic fundamentals	fundamentals	remembering the fact that	remembering that
by means of	by	repeat again	repeat
circumstances surrounding	circumstances	revert back	revert to
close proximity	close	same identical	same, identical
consensus of opinion	consensus	significant	important
continue on	continue	small in size	small
disseminate	distribute	square in shape	square
due to the fact that	because, since	still persists	persists
during the course of the day	during the day	subsequent to	after
during the time that	while	the reason is due to	because
each and every one of us	each of us	thrust	direction, emphasis
enclosed please find	enclosed is	under date of	on
entirely completed	completed	under separate cover	separately
for the purpose of	for, to	uniformly consistent	consistent
for the reason that	because, since	unique	somewhat different
held at meeting	met	until such time	until
if it is possible	if possible	up until	until
in accordance with your request	as you requested	utilize	use
in connection with	about	whether or not	whether
in order that	so	will you be kind enough	please
in regard to	regarding, about	with a view to	to
in the event that	if	with regard to	about
in the neighborhood of	about	with respect to	about
in the normal course of our procedures	normally	with the result that	so that
		without further delay	now, immediately

8.4 Avoid using two words that mean the same thing. In the list below, either word would be adequate by itself.

agreeable and satisfactory
anxious and eager
courteous and polite
first and foremost
full and complete
hope and trust
if and when

8.5 Eliminate such trite expressions as the following; they have been used so often that they are meaningless.

along these lines	for your information
as a matter of fact	I have your letter
beg to acknowledge	permit me to say
beg to inform	replying to yours
contents duly noted	this letter is for the purpose of

Outlines

8.6 The outline, or organization plan for the report, enables the writer to formulate the structure of the report as a whole before starting to write. An outline indicates the major points of the report, the secondary topics to be discussed, and substantiating information. The number of divisions in an outline varies, depending on the length and detail of the report; but there should be no more than five divisions.

8.7 An outline may be arranged in either the **standard**or **decimal** format. In standard outlines, Roman numerals, Arabic numerals, and letters of the alphabet are combined to identify different heading levels. In decimal outlines, Arabic numerals are used with decimal points to represent each division.

```
I.  PURPOSE OF STUDY

    A.  Scope

    B.  Limitations
        1.  Time
        2.  Money
        3.  Personnel
            a.  Existing employees
                (1)  Full-time
                (2)  Part-time
            b.  Outside consultants

II. DEFINITION OF STUDY
```

FIGURE 8-1. STRUCTURE OF A STANDARD OUTLINE

```
1.  PURPOSE OF STUDY

    1.1  Scope

    1.2  Limitations

         1.2.1 Time
         1.2.2 Money
         1.2.3 Personnel
               1.2.3.1 Existing employees
                       1.2.3.1.1 Full-time
                       1.2.3.1.2 Part-time
               1.2.3.2 Outside consultants

2.  DEFINITION OF STUDY
```

FIGURE 8-2. STRUCTURE OF A DECIMAL OUTLINE

Regardless of the format, a new heading level is introduced *only* if it will be used more than once. In a standard outline, for example, an "A" must be followed by a "B," a "1" by a "2," and so on.

TYPING A STANDARD OUTLINE (Figure 8-1)

8.8 Roman numeral I, which identifies the first major division heading, is typed at the left margin, followed by a period and two spaces. Subsequent Roman numerals are aligned at the right, as follows:

1. Return the carriage or the carrier to the left margin.
2. Depress the margin release key.
3. Backspace the desired number of spaces outside the left margin setting. (For example, to type Roman numeral II, backspace *once;* to type III, backspace *twice*.)

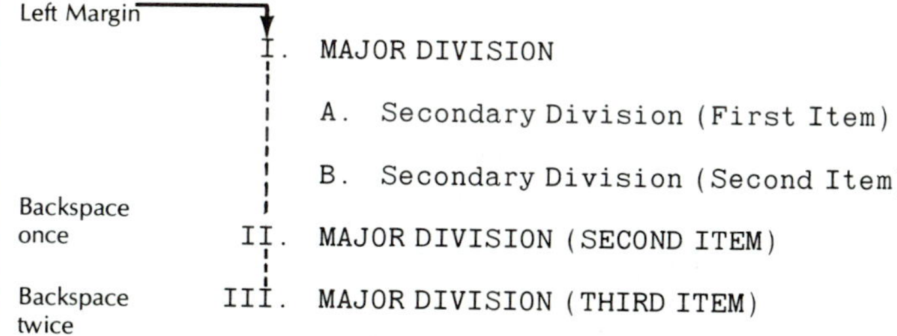

Left Margin
I. MAJOR DIVISION
A. Secondary Division (First Item)
B. Secondary Division (Second Item)
Backspace once
II. MAJOR DIVISION (SECOND ITEM)
Backspace twice
III. MAJOR DIVISION (THIRD ITEM)

8.9 The **capital letters** that identify secondary headings are typed at the first tabulator stop, set four spaces from the left margin, followed by a period and two spaces. Each secondary heading begins a double space below the major division heading. If the secondary heading is followed by an Arabic numeral subdivision, single-space before the next item. If it is followed by another secondary heading, single-space or double-space, depending on the length of the outline.

8.10 The **Arabic numerals** that identify the third division are typed at the second tabulator stop, set four spaces from the first stop, followed by a period and two spaces. These items are single-spaced, except in very short outlines.

8.11 The **lowercase letters** that identify the fourth division are typed at the third tabulator stop, set four spaces from the second stop, followed by a period and two spaces. These items are always single-spaced.

8.12 Use of **Arabic numerals in parentheses** (identifying the fifth division) should be kept to a minimum. A fourth tabulator stop is set four spaces from the third stop. One or two spaces follow the right parenthesis before the item is typed.

8.13 To continue an outline on a **second or subsequent page,** follow these guidelines.

1. Maintain a minimum one-inch bottom margin. A slightly wider margin is better than a narrow one.

2. Begin the second or subsequent page with a secondary subdivision (identified by a capital letter).

3. Start a new page with items beginning with Arabic numerals if:
   a. at least two Arabic numeral items are carried over to the page, and

   b. the outline does not end with these items.

4. Do not start a new page with items beginning with lowercase letters and Arabic numerals in parentheses.

5. Complete an entire section at the bottom of a page, if possible.

6. Do not type only one line of any division at the bottom of the page.

7. Do not type only one line of any division at the top of the next page.

8. Follow the margin settings, spacing, and tabulator stops used on the first page; begin second and subsequent pages at the appropriate tabulator stop to continue the outline.

TYPING A DECIMAL OUTLINE
(Figure 8-2)

8.14 The **whole numbers** that identify major topics are typed at the left margin, followed by a decimal point (period) and two spaces before the major heading. If an outline contains more than nine major topics, the tenth and subsequent major headings are aligned at the right in the same way as Roman numerals with two or more digits.

8.15 **Secondary divisions** are identified by the *whole number plus a decimal figure* to the right of the decimal point, followed by one space. They are typed at a tabulator stop set four spaces from the left margin. The first secondary division begins a double space below the major division heading. If it is followed by another subdivision, single-space before the next item. If it is followed by another secondary heading, double-space.

To create **further divisions,** add a decimal point and another digit to the right of the decimal figure and set tabulator stops accordingly. The total number of digits identifies the level of a particular division.

8.16 To continue an outline on a second or subsequent page, follow the guidelines for standard outlines (8.13).

OUTLINE STYLES

8.17 The headings and subdivisions in an outline may follow one of three styles: **topic, descriptive,** or **full caption.**

Topic Outline

8.18 In a topic outline, the items consist of one-, two-, or three-word phrases. The first letter of each important word is capitalized.

noun	I. Purpose
verb phrase	A. Solve Problem
verb phrase	B. Seek Information
noun	II. Definition
verb phrase	A. Determine Scope
verb phrase	B. Determine Limitation
noun	1. Time
noun	2. Money

Descriptive Outline

8.19 In a descriptive outline, the major headings and subdivisions are written in phrases or clauses (known also as "talking captions") to provide more details about the information in each section. In major and secondary headings, the first letter of each important word is capitalized; in lesser headings, only the first letter of the first word and the first letters of proper names are capitalized.

noun phrases used throughout	I. Description of the Study
	A. Attempt to Solve a Problem
	B. Attempt to Seek Information
	II. Definition of the Extent of the Study
	A. Scope or Range of the Study
	B. Limitations of the Study
	1. Time not of the essence
	2. Money critical factor

Full Caption Outline

8.20 A full outline may be written in complete sentences (see Figure 8-3), it may combine sentences and noun phrases, or it may combine sentences and verb phrases. Capitalize the first letter of each sentence, proper names, and each important word in the phrases.

noun phrase	I. Purpose of the Study
sentence (question)	A. Is it to solve a problem?
sentence (question)	B. Is it to obtain information?
noun phrase	II. Definition of the Study
sentence (question)	A. What is the scope or range of the study?
sentence (question)	B. What limitations are there?
noun	1. Time?
noun	2. Money?

TYPING A SENTENCE OUTLINE

I. Placement

A. Center the outline attractively on the page.
B. Set margins.
1. Use a 60-space line for most outlines.
2. Begin outline 1½ to 2 inches from the top of the first page.
3. Continue outline 1 to 2½ inches on succeeding pages.
4. Allow approximately 1 inch for bottom margin on all pages.

II. Capitalization

A. Center the main heading (outline title) in all capitals.
B. Capitalize the first letter of each important word in all roman numeral headings.
C. Capitalize only the first letter of the first word in the secondary headings (those beginning with A, B, C, etc.) and any proper names in the sentence.
D. Capitalize only the first letter of the first word in the following subheadings.
1. The second subdivision (which begins with Arabic numerals).
2. The third subdivision (which begins with lowercase letters).
3. The fourth subdivision items (which begin with Arabic numerals in parentheses).

III. Spacing

A. Follow these rules for line spacing.
1. Triple-space after the main heading.
2. Double-space before and after main divisions.
3. Single-space all subdivision items.
4. Double-space very short outlines.

B. Follow these rules for indentions.
1. Align Roman numerals at the left margin.
2. Set tabulator stops for four-space indentions for each division in the outline.
3. Begin the second line of an item directly under the first letter of the first line.

C. Follow these rules for punctuation.
1. Use a period after numerals and letters.
2. Space twice after the period.
3. Use a period after an item if a complete thought is expressed.
4. Do not use a period after single words or phrases.

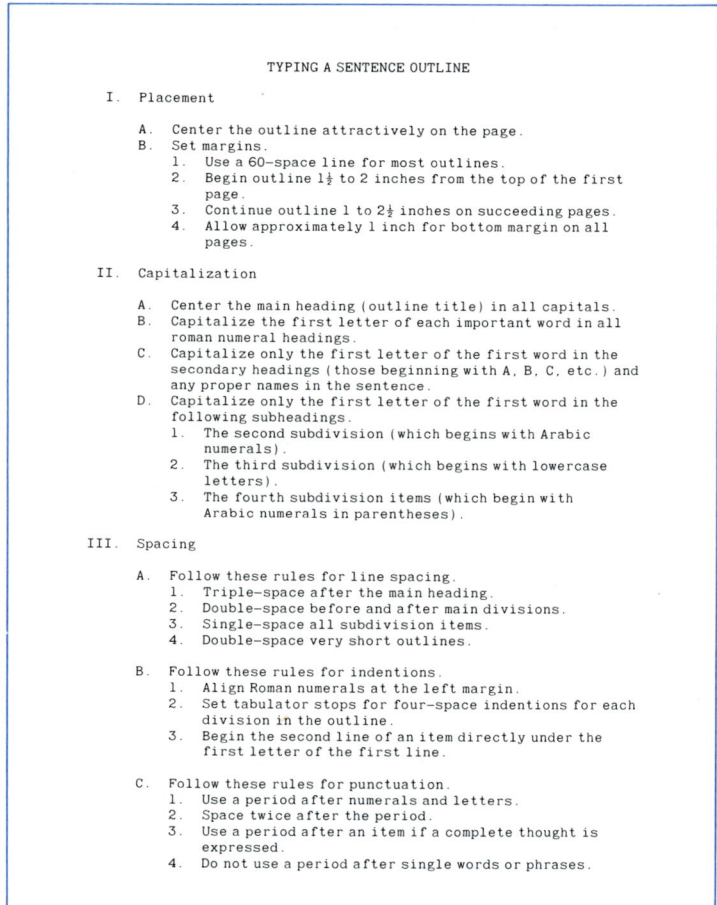

FIGURE 8-3. SENTENCE OUTLINE

8.21 If a full outline is not written entirely in complete sentences, care must be taken to construct all divisions of equal importance in **parallel form.** If heading I is written in sentence form, for example, all other Roman numeral headings must be in the same form. Similarly, if one secondary division (identified by capital letters) is written as a noun phrase, all secondary divisions must be written the same way. Parallelism can be achieved by consistently following one pattern throughout: complete sentences, noun clauses or phrases, or verb clauses or phrases.

Informal Reports

8.22 Brief reports written in the form of a letter or memorandum are appropriate when information must be distributed on a periodic or routine basis or when a special situation demands a quick, concise response.

8.23 **Periodic or routine reports** (also known as serial reports) are written on a fairly regular basis—daily, weekly, monthly, semiannually, or annually. They include sales reports, progress reports, and financial statements.

8.24 **Special reports** include justification reports, written specifically to substantiate a point of view or recommendation, and professional reports prepared by outside consultants. (When a special situation calls for a longer report, however, formal report style should be observed; see 8.43–8.91).

LETTER REPORT

8.25 When an informal report (periodic or special) is to be distributed outside the company, it is prepared in the form of a business letter on company letterhead stationery (see Figure 8-4). Letter reports are usually three to four pages long. While the elements of a letter report are similar to those in business letters (see 7.12–7.70), there are a few minor distinctions, as explained below.

Report Style

8.26 The letter report may be prepared either in the modified block or full block style (see Figures 7-4–7-7).

Date

8.27 Because the date indicates when the report data were presented, it should be written in full on each page of the letter report.

Inside Address

8.28 The report is addressed to the person or organization that requested or authorized it; it may also be addressed to the person responsible for taking action based on the report findings. The elements of the inside address for an individual or a company correspond to those in a business letter.

Subject Line

8.29 When a subject line is used in a letter report, it is typed a double space below the salutation, preceded by **SUBJECT** or **RE.**

Body

8.30 The body of the letter contains the text of the report: **introductory paragraph, description and analysis** of the facts, and **recommendations or conclusions.** It is typed single-spaced with double spacing between paragraphs.

8.31 The introductory paragraph identifies the request or authorization for the report (the purpose) and summarizes the method of investigation and the conclusions or recommendations.

Central Valley Bank
6500 Ventura Boulevard
Glendale, California 91403

September 19, 1978

Fifth Avenue Cleaners
2031 Fifth Avenue
Concord, CA 94520

Gentlemen:

This is an illustration of a letter report prepared and distributed to persons outside the company. Letter reports generally follow the same format used for other business correspondence. This letter is typed in the modified block style with blocked paragraphs and mixed punctuation.

Use of Side Headings

The use of side headings, especially in lengthy letter reports, helps divide information into smaller pieces for the reader's comprehension. Side headings are typed at the left margin and are underscored. A double space precedes and follows each side heading.

Body of the Report

The body of the report is the report itself, the facts, analyses, recommendations, or conclusions. The report should be written briefly, yet completely.

Recommendation or Conclusion

The closing paragraph(s) should contain some recommendation or conclusion based on the facts presented within the report. Information must therefore be correct and logically presented.

Very truly yours,

Manfred J. Mielke

ftv

FIGURE 8-4. SAMPLE LETTER REPORT WITH SIDE HEADINGS

8.32 If the report is lengthy or detailed, use **side headings** to divide it into sections (see Figure 8-4). Type each side heading at the left margin, underscored; side headings should not be more than a few words long. Double-space before and after each heading. Capitalize the first letter of each important word. No punctuation follows a heading.

8.33 If side headings are used, at least two must be included within the report; one should be used to set off the recommendation or conclusion paragraph(s).

Complimentary Closing

8.34 The complimentary closing for a letter report is more formal than that used in other business correspondence. Type the complimentary closing a double space below the last line of the body of the letter report.

```
Respectfully                Yours truly
Respectfully submitted      Yours very truly
Respectfully yours          Very truly yours
```

Typed Company Name

8.35 If the company name is typed as part of the closing lines in other business correspondence, it should be included in letter reports. As in business letters, it is typed a double space below the closing in solid capital letters above the writer's signature (see 7.38 and 7.39).

Other Closing Elements

8.36 The writer's signature, typed name, and full title, as well as the reference initials, are included in letter reports as in business correspondence (see 7.39–7.44).

Enclosures or Attachments

8.37 When documents such as charts, illustrations, or other information are to be sent with the letter report, this fact is indicated by typing an enclosure notation at the left margin a double space below the reference initials. The word "Enclosure" or "Enclosures" is sufficient, but if there are numerous enclosures it may be desirable to list them (see 7.55).

MEMORANDUM REPORT

8.38 When an informal report (periodic or special) is to be distributed within the company, it may be organized as an interoffice memorandum and typed on a company memorandum form. The elements in memorandum reports correspond to those in standard memoranda (see 7.87–7.99). A few differences are explained below.

Addressee

8.39 The report is addressed to the person(s) within the organization who requested or authorized the report; it may also be addressed to those who will take action based on the report findings. The addressee's official title and/or department name or number are typed after "To" on the memorandum form.

Writer

8.40 The "From" heading usually consists of the name, title, and/or department name or number of the person preparing the report. When the report will be transmitted by someone other than the writer, however, that person's name is typed after "From."

Subject

8.41 The "Subject" heading consists of the full title of the report or study, typed in solid capital letters or with the first letter of each important word capitalized.

Body

8.42 The body of the memorandum contains the same kinds of information and is typed the same way as the body of a letter report (see 8.30–8.32 and Figure 8-4). If side headings are used, they are typed as in a letter report.

Formal Reports

8.43 When a brief, informal report is not sufficient to provide the necessary data, a more comprehensive, formal report is prepared. This longer report is the result of a study or investigation of all aspects of a particular topic.

ELEMENTS OF A FORMAL REPORT

8.44 Formal reports usually contain the following elements, assembled in the sequence shown below.

Introductory Pages (8.58–8.69)
- Cover
- Title Page
- Letter or Memorandum of Transmittal
- Preface or Foreword
- Acknowledgments
- Table of Contents
- List of Illustrations
- Abstract

Body of the Report (8.70–8.86)
- Introduction
- Discussion
- Concluding Pages
- Quoted Material
- Ellipses
- Lists
- Statistical Data

Supplementary Pages (8.87–8.91)
- Appendix
- Bibliography
- Index

APPEARANCE

8.45 The neat and attractive appearance of a well-written report helps convey the intended message more effectively. The use of proper spacing and margin settings and the arrangement of section headings and parts of the report contribute to a more impressive presentation.

Margins

8.46 Margin settings depend on the binding style selected for the report: left-bound, top-bound, or unbound (see Table 8-1, Placement of Report Margins). If the report is to be unbound, the pages should be held together with a paper clip or rubber band and the report placed in a folder.

Spacing

8.47 The text of the report is typed double-spaced, although lengthy quotations and lists are typed single-spaced to make them stand out. Five-space paragraph indentions are used.

Headings

8.48 The headings within the report usually correspond to the major and secondary headings in the preliminary outline. They are

	Type of Report		
	UNBOUND	***LEFTBOUND***	***TOPBOUND***
Top Margin, First Page	2 inches	2 inches	2½ inches
Top Margin, Succeeding pages	1 inch	1 inch	1½ inches
Left Margin	1 inch	1½ inches	1 inch
Right Margin	1 inch	1 inch	1 inch
Bottom Margin	1 inch	1 inch	1 inch
Page Numbers	Bottom or right corner	Right corner	Bottom

TABLE 8-1. PLACEMENT OF REPORT MARGINS

useful to the reader in both locating and understanding information. Each level of heading is typed and arranged somewhat differently than other levels (see Figure 8-5) so the importance of a particular topic will be evident to the reader at a glance.

8.49 **Title or Main Heading.** The title of the report may be stated in topic form or may describe the nature of the report. It is centered and typed in solid capitals 2 to 2½ inches from the top of the first page, depending on which report format is used. Depending on its length, the title may be typed in one, two, or possibly three lines, with each line centered on the page.

```
MICROFILM--AN EFFECTIVE RECORDS MANAGEMENT TOOL

     RECOMMENDATIONS FOR THE ACQUISITION
 AND IMPLEMENTATION OF A WORD PROCESSING CENTER
```

Triple-space after the main heading before beginning the report, unless a secondary heading follows the main heading. In that case, double-space after the main heading.

8.50 **Subtitle.** A subtitle may accompany a one- or two-line title to identify the report topic more specifically. The subtitle is centered and typed a double space below the main heading. Only the first letters of important words are capitalized.

```
MICROFILM--AN EFFECTIVE RECORDS MANAGEMENT TOOL

      A Study of Its Applications and Uses
            in the Banking Industry
```

Since the subtitle is part of the main heading, a triple space follows it.

8.51 **Centered heading.** Centered headings, used to introduce major divisions or topics, correspond to Roman numeral headings in the outline and may be preceded by Roman numerals.

A centered heading is typed a triple space below the line above. It may be typed in solid capital letters, or it may be underlined with only the first letter of each important word capitalized.

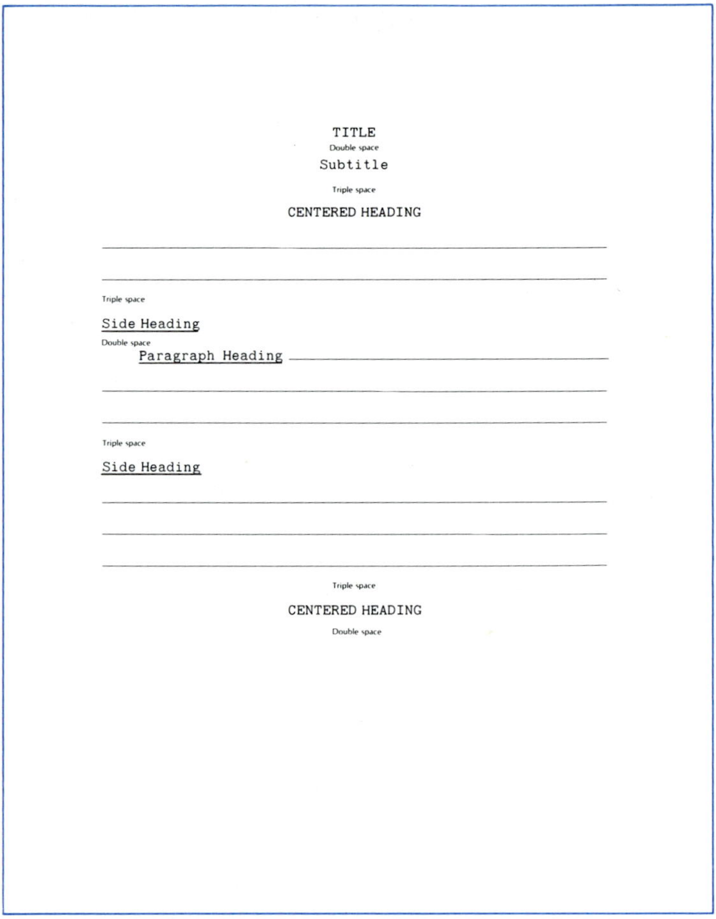

TITLE
Double space
Subtitle
Triple space
CENTERED HEADING

Triple space
Side Heading
Double space
Paragraph Heading

Triple space
Side Heading

Triple space
CENTERED HEADING
Double space

FIGURE 8-5. HEADING ARRANGEMENT

Double-space after the heading before typing the information under it.

```
(I. Purpose of the Report)

                    Purpose of the Report
```

8.52 **Side or marginal heading.** Side or marginal headings, which correspond to "capital" letter heads in the outline (those preceded by "A," "B," and so on), are typed beginning at the left margin. A triple space precedes each side or marginal heading, and a double space follows it. Capitalize only the first letters of important words, and underline the entire heading. No punctuation is used after the heading.

```
Side Heading

     Side headings are typed at the left margin to
introduce subdivisions within the report.
```

8.53 **Paragraph or run-in heading.** Paragraph or run-in headings correspond to items preceded by Arabic numerals in the report outline. These headings, typed at the paragraph indention, introduce the information within the paragraph. Only the first letter of the first word is capitalized unless a proper name appears within the heading. Underline the heading and type a period after it. Leave two spaces after the period before beginning the paragraph.

```
     Paragraph heading. A paragraph heading intro-
duces the information typed within the paragraph.
This heading begins at the paragraph indention and
is underscored.
```

Page Numbers

8.54 Every page of the report except the cover and title page is numbered consecutively. The introductory pages are numbered in small Roman numerals; the body of the report and the supplementary pages are numbered in Arabic numerals.

8.55 **Introductory pages.** Beginning with Roman numeral ii centered and typed at the bottom of the page following the title page (usually the transmittal letter), continue to type small Roman numerals by using a combination of lowercase letters. The page number on all introductory pages (transmittal letter, preface, acknowledgments, table of contents, list of illustrations, and summary) is centered and typed approximately one-half inch from the bottom edge.

8.56 **Report pages.** Arabic numerals are used for all pages within the body of the report beginning with page 1. The number of the first page of each new division, section, or chapter is centered and typed approximately one-half inch from the bottom edge. With the exception of topbound reports, other report pages are numbered in the upper right corner at the margin approximately one-half inch from the top edge. In topbound reports, page numbers appear at the bottom of each page, centered approximately one-half inch from the edge.

8.57 **Supplementary pages.** Supplementary pages (such as the appendix, bibliography, and index) are numbered consecutively, starting with the number following that on the last body page.

INTRODUCTORY PAGES

8.58 Introductory pages include the cover, title page, letter or memorandum of transmittal, preface, acknowledgments, table of contents, list of illustrations, and summary. These pages are prepared after the report has been typed and page numbers assigned.

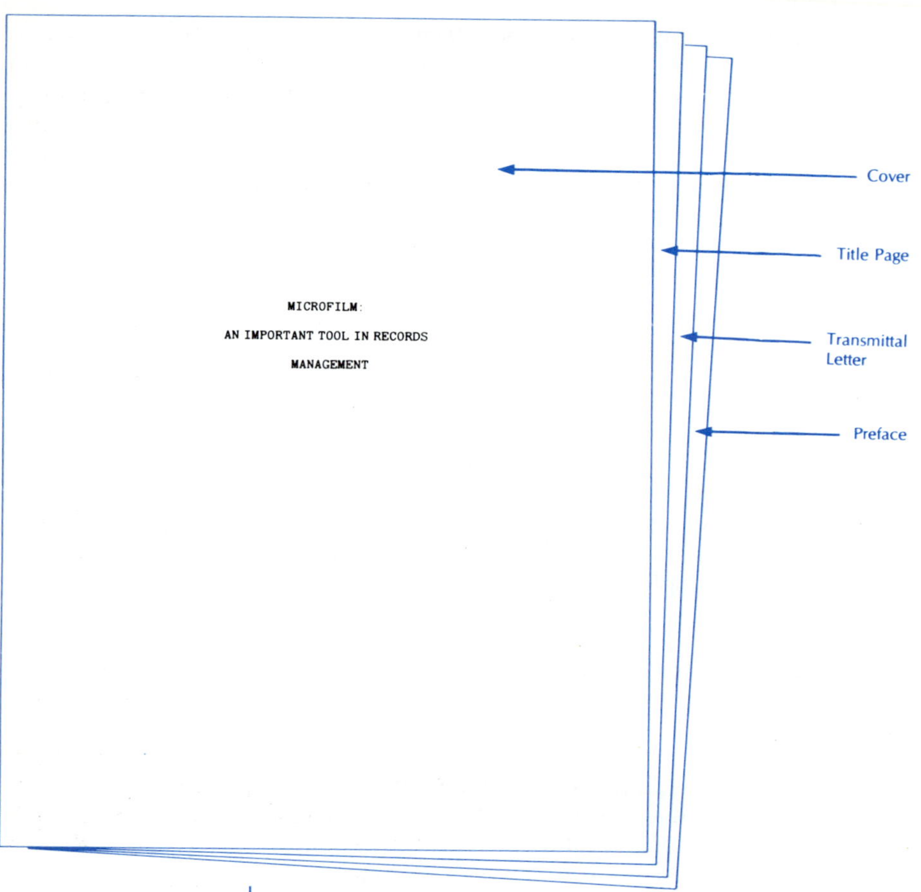

FIGURE 8-6. INTRODUCTORY PAGES

Cover

8.59 The report cover is a typewritten or printed sheet, on paper of the same quality as the report. It contains only the report title, centered and typed in solid capitals. A title of two or more lines is double- or triple-spaced.

Title Page

8.60 The title page contains the report title, the writer's name, title, and/or department, and the date the report is submitted. Each piece of information is centered horizontally across the page, and all information is spread over the page to provide a balanced appearance.

8.61 The **name** of the person who prepared—or is transmitting—the report is centered and typed about midway between the report title and the bottom of the page. If the writer has a title, such as Doctor or Professor, it should precede the name. An official title and department or company name may be typed below the writer's name.

Dorothy Linton
Managing Editor

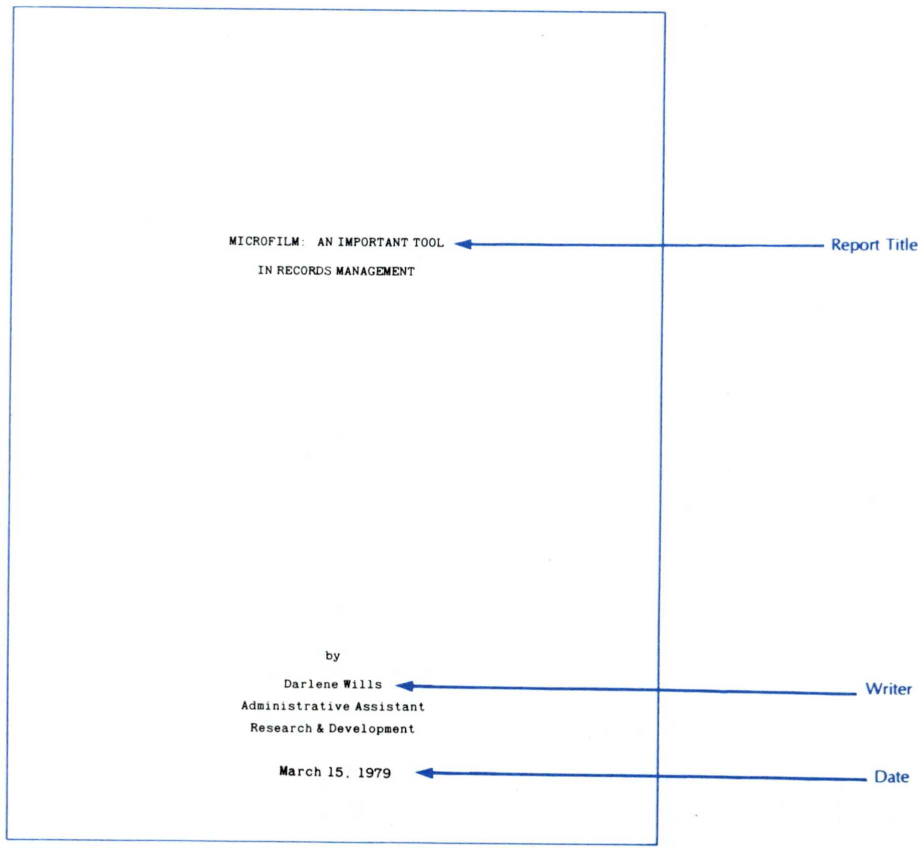

MICROFILM: AN IMPORTANT TOOL
IN RECORDS MANAGEMENT
Report Title
by
Darlene Wills
Administrative Assistant
Research & Development
Writer
March 15, 1979
Date

FIGURE 8-7. SAMPLE TITLE PAGE

If the report is prepared by an outside consultant, the name and address of the consulting firm is typed on the title page.

```
MANAGEMENT CONSULTANTS, LTD.
 3470 West Adams Boulevard
Sacramento, California 95822
```

The date—month, day, and year—is centered and typed near the bottom of the page by itself.

Letter of Transmittal

8.62 A letter of transmittal, also called a covering letter, accompanies the report for submission to the person or organization who requested or authorized it. The letter mentions the request or authorization and—if the report has no preface—also covers the purpose or scope of the report, the method of study, and a summary of the conclusions or recommendations (see Figure 8-8).

Written in business letter style on company letterhead stationery, it consists of the date of transmittal, inside address, salutation, subject line, body, complimentary closing, and signature line.

ALLIED INSURANCE COMPANY
6650 Wilshire Boulevard
Los Angeles, CA 90036
Area Code (213) 659-2328

July 18, 1979

Mr. Donald L. Busche
Management Consultants, Inc.
1570 East Colorado Boulevard
Pasadena, CA 91106

Dear Mr. Busche:

SUBJECT: Word Processing Center Study

Attached is the report on the Recommendations for the Acquisition and Implementation of a Word Processing Center. The board of directors approved this study at its regular meeting on April 18.

I am particularly pleased with the outcome of this study. According to Don Johnson and the R & D staff, our company can definitely benefit by a word processing installation to eliminate much of the downtime expenses. As mentioned on page 58 of the report, a single factor against such a center would be the attitudes of our present clerical staff. This, however, I believe we can overcome through some well-planned in-service training sessions with personnel and equipment manufacturers.

This report seems to have accomplished all of our objectives--and more! Please do not hesitate to call me if you have any questions or if you need additional information.

Sincerely yours,

Mrs. Janet K. LaCroix
Vice President, Operations

FIGURE 8-8. SAMPLE LETTER OF TRANSMITTAL

8.63 When a preface is included in addition to the transmittal letter, the letter is very brief; it simply describes the recipient's original request, and all detailed information on the report itself is then included in the preface.

Transmittal Memorandum

8.64 When a report is prepared for submission to an individual within the organization, a transmittal memorandum is prepared on interoffice correspondence stationery. It serves the same purpose as the letter of transmittal and contains the same information.

Preface or Foreword

8.65 The preface, or foreword, is the introduction to the report. As noted above, when a preface and letter of transmittal are both included, all explanatory details (purpose of report, method of study, and so on) are contained in the preface; the letter is used only to transmit the report to the recipient. When a letter or

ii

CONTENTS

FIGURE 8-9. SAMPLE CONTENTS PAGE

memorandum of transmittal is *not* included, the preface would also mention the original request or authorization for the report.

Acknowledgments

8.66 The acknowledgments on a separate page give credit to individuals or organizations who assisted in the preparation of the report. The acknowledgments may be a listing of credits, or they may be written in narrative form.

Table of Contents

8.67 A table of contents (headed simply "Contents") lists each major heading in the report with the corresponding page number. The contents usually parallel the Roman numeral and secondary (capital letter) headings in the report outline. While a table of contents is not essential, it should be included when a report is lengthy or is divided into several sections.

TABLES AND CHARTS

FIGURE 8-10. SAMPLE ILLUSTRATION LIST

Illustration List

8.68 When tables, charts, or other illustrations are contained in the report, an illustration list is included either with the table of contents or on a separate page. Each table, chart, or illustration is labeled in sequence by number as *Figure 5* or *Figure 4-2* (i.e., chapter or section 4, second illustration).

The list is typed in the same form as the table of contents. Each illustration is given a title. If illustrations other than charts and tables are included in the report, the list may be headed "Illustrations."

Abstract (Synopsis)

8.69 An abstract, or synopsis, summarizes the report and includes the major facts, results, recommendations, and conclusions. As its name implies, the abstract should cover the substance of the report as concisely as possible.

BODY OF REPORT

8.70 The body of the report, the text itself, includes the introduction, discussion, summary, conclusions, and recommendations. The presentation of information follows the sequence indicated in the report outline.

Introduction

8.71 The introduction provides the reader with background information to help focus attention on the topic. This section includes the following information.

1. **Authorization:** Who authorized the report and when?
2. **Purpose:** What are the objectives or aims?
3. **Scope:** What are the boundaries of the study?
4. **Limitation:** What conditions or problems existed prior to or during the investigation?
5. **Organization of Data:** How is information presented?
6. **History or Background:** What events generated the report?
7. **Method of Investigation:** How was the research conducted? By whom?
8. **Sources of Information:** What authorities were consulted?
9. **Definition of Terms:** How are certain words used in the report?

Discussion

8.72 The discussion is the report itself—the facts, the analyses, and the findings. Written in formal language (third person), the report must be presented in an objective manner. The discussion may contain the following:

1. Strengths and weaknesses of existing situation
2. Details of the methods or functions of existing situation
3. Proposals or recommendations
4. Facts and their substantiating data
5. Narrative or chronology
6. Proposed procedure(s) to improve situation
7. Comparison of procedures and data
8. Alternative methods or routes
9. Advantages and disadvantages of alternatives

Concluding Pages

8.73 The closing parts of the report include the **summary, conclusions,** and **recommendations.** In formal, lengthy reports, all three parts are included for the convenience of the reader in interpreting and summarizing information. Each of these words is typed as a side heading at the left margin to introduce the information in that particular section of the report.

8.74 **Summary.** A summary is a compilation of all the facts and findings contained in the report. It summarizes or brings together the purpose of the report, the main points discussed, and the results of the study or investigation.

8.75 **Conclusions.** The conclusions are statements or inferences based on the writer's interpretation of the facts derived from the study. Conclusions, therefore, should be logical extensions of these facts. Conclusions may be presented in narrative form or listed according to their importance.

8.76 **Recommendations.** Recommendations are suggested methods to be followed or action to be taken as a result of the data presented in the report. Recommendations must be directly related to the original purpose of the study and be fully substantiated by the facts. Alternative methods or actions may also be included.

Quoted Material

8.77 When information is quoted verbatim from another source or when a portion of a direct quotation is cited, the source of the material must be stated.

8.78 **Short quotations** (three or fewer typewritten lines) are typed within the body of the report with quotation marks before and after.

```
The authors note that "Quotations of three or four
typewritten lines are typed within the body of the
report with quotations marks before and after."
```

8.79 A **long quotation** (four or more typewritten lines) is typed as a separate paragraph, single-spaced and indented five spaces from the right and left margins.

```
The authors suggest that longer quotations be typed
in the following manner:

     Quotations of four or more lines should be
     typed in single spacing and indented five
     spaces from the right and left margins.
     Quotation marks should not be used. If the
     first line of the quotation begins a
     paragraph, it is indented five spaces.
     Otherwise the quotation is typed in block
     form.
```

Ellipsis Points

8.80 Ellipsis points are used to indicate the omission of a word, phrase, sentence, or paragraph from a quotation. An ellipsis is made by typing either three or four periods with spaces between them.

8.81 Use **three spaced periods** to indicate omission of part of a sentence.

```
Quotations are easier for a reader to understand
if they include only information that is crucial to
the writer's point.
```

becomes

```
Quotations are easier . . . to understand if they
include only information that is crucial to the
writer's point.
```

8.82 Use **four spaced periods** (a period followed by three spaced periods) to indicate omission of the last part of a sentence, the first part of the next sentence or paragraph, a sentence or more, or a paragraph or more.

End of Sentence:

```
Quotations are easier for a reader to understand
if they include only information that is crucial.
. . . The idea is that ellipses help writers tailor
quoted information to their needs.
```

Beginning of Next Sentence:

```
Quotations are easier for a reader to understand
if they include only information that is crucial to
the writer's point. . . . ellipses help writers
tailor quoted information to their needs.
```

Note that the second sentence does not begin with a capital letter. In this way, the reader knows that the beginning of the sentence has been omitted.

Beginning of Paragraph:

```
Quotations are easier for a reader to understand
if they include information that is crucial to the
writer's point.

     . . . . writers must use ellipses with
restraint.
```

Note that when the beginning of a paragraph is omitted, the ellipsis follows the paragraph indention.

A Sentence or More:

```
Quotations are easier for a reader to understand
if they include only information that is crucial to
the writer's point. . . . Of course, writers must
use ellipses with restraint.
```

Note that the second sentence begins with a capital letter. This indicates that information between the two sentences has been omitted.

A Paragraph or More:

```
Quotations are easier for a reader to understand
if they include only information that is crucial to
the writer's point. . . .

     Of course, writers must use ellipses with
restraint.
```

Note that a new paragraph is begun after the omission of one or more paragraphs.

Lists

8.83 Itemized lists, preceded by Arabic numbers or lowercase letters, present detailed information in a form that is easy to read.

8.84 **Within the paragraph.** Arabic numerals or lowercase letters typed within parentheses are used to introduce lists within a sentence or paragraph of a letter or report. The items are treated as a series and separated by commas.

```
Each of the following items contributes to an
attractive report: (1) arrangement of the headings
to indicate divisions of information, (2) correct
spacing throughout, and (3) correct display of
quoted information.
```

8.85 **Separate lists.** Arabic numerals, followed by a period and two spaces, are used to introduce items when each is listed by itself. No punctuation follows the items unless they are stated as complete sentences.

```
Here is the suggested method for typing a list of
short items (no more than one line each):

1.  Use double spacing in reports.

2.  Use single spacing in letters.

3.  Indent items five spaces.


     1.  Lists of long items may be typed as

separate paragraphs within the body of the report

or letter; they are double-spaced, and the first

line of each item is indented five spaces before

the number is typed.


1.  Long items may also be typed in single
spacing, indented from both right and left margins.

2.  Leave a double space before the list and
between the items in the list.
```

Statistical Data

8.86 Statistical data consist of **tables, graphs,** and **charts.** Such illustrations can save words by presenting complex information in visual form. (See chapter 9 for detailed information on typing tables, graphs, and charts.)

When statistical data are included in the body of a report, use the following guidelines.

1. Arrange information in a logical manner to permit ease in reading.

2. Keep all headings simple and self-explanatory.

3. Type each table, graph, or chart within the text or on a separate page following the related text.

4. Do not describe or explain the contents of the table, graph, or chart; a well-designed graphic presentation should be self-explanatory. All that is needed is a concise summary.

5. Leave sufficient space before and after a graphic presentation that is typed within the text.

6. Cite all sources from which statistical information was obtained in a credit line accompanying each table (see 9.18).

SUPPLEMENTARY PAGES

8.87 Supplementary pages consist of **Notes** or **Bibliography, Appendix,** and **Index.** The decision to include these pages depends on the length and detail of the report. These pages are prepared after the report has been typed and page numbers have been assigned.

Footnotes and Bibliographies

8.88 The sources of all material quoted or paraphrased in the report should be cited in the footnote references and in the bibliography that accompanies the report. See 8.92–8.135 for information on constructing notes and bibliographies. In scientific reports the procedure is somewhat different; see 8.136–8.139.

Appendix

8.89 An appendix consists of additional written or illustrative material that substantiates or expands on a fact or idea presented in the report. These supporting documents, questionnaires or surveys, summary tables, and reference materials are usually more technical or detailed than information in the report. An appendix should be included in the report if it is necessary or desirable for the reader to refer to additional data to interpret the report. Appendix pages may also be referred to as *Exhibits*.

8.90 Materials in the appendix may be combined into one section and labeled *APPENDIX:* or each item can be given a title and labeled individually such as *Appendix 1, 2,* or *3, Appendix A, B,* or *C,* or *Exhibit A, B,* or *C.* When documents are labeled separately, the table of contents should list each item.

APPENDIX 1.	Sample Questionnaire.	87
APPENDIX 2.	Summary Tabulations	89

Index

8.91 An index is an alphabetical list of all topics and subtopics in the report. Each entry in the index is followed by the page number(s) on which the topic is mentioned or discussed. Placed at the end of the report, an index is a valuable aid (particularly in long reports) in helping the reader locate specific information. But it can take a long time to prepare an index, and for most reports, a table of contents is sufficient.

Footnotes[1]

8.92 Footnotes in business reports serve two purposes: (1) they cite the source of a direct or indirect quotation or a specific fact or group of facts; and (2) they provide additional details or elaborate on a point and supply information that might be useful but is not essential to the text of the report itself. The first type is called a **reference or source footnote,** and the second type is called an **explanatory or descriptive footnote.**

Reference footnote:

1. Arthur F. Kinney et al., Symposium (Palo Alto, Calif.: Houghton Mifflin Company, 1969), p. 24.

Explanatory footnote:

2. The circumstances are similar to those in Massey v. FitzSimmons, cited earlier.

NUMBERING FOOTNOTES

8.93 Footnotes are generally numbered consecutively throughout a report. If the report is divided into separate chapters and the overall number of notes is great enough so that consecutive numbering would be awkward, they may be numbered consecutively within each chapter. (A writer may sometimes need to insert a new footnote at the last minute. If notations are numbered consecutively throughout a long report, some hasty renumbering may be necessary, and errors—notes and text references that don't correspond—can result.)

1. The instructions regarding footnotes, bibliographies, and scientific references presented here are based on the University of Chicago Press *Manual of Style,* 12th ed. rev. (Chicago: University of Chicago Press, 1969). Other style books (some of which are listed under Secretarial Handbooks and Textbooks, 15.9) may differ from the *Manual* in certain details of form. The *Manual,* however, does offer the most consistent and common-sense approach to the documentation problems likely to arise in business situations.

TYPING FOOTNOTE NUMBERS

8.94 The Arabic numerals used for footnotes are sometimes typed above the line (superscript) both in the text and within the notation itself at the bottom of the page. However, it is also acceptable to type the numbers above the line *only* at the point of reference in the text: at the end of the last quoted word, sentence, or paragraph or at the end of any factual information that requires a source note. Type the number reference in the text as follows.

1. Use the ratchet release lever on the typewriter and turn the cylinder slightly *toward* you. Type the footnote number and return the ratchet release to its position. Return the cylinder knob to the line of typing.

2. Spacing after the footnote number follows the normal spacing after words or marks of punctuation. For example, since two spaces follow a period, two spaces would be left after the footnote number before the next sentence is begun.

```
. . . same records on paper.6  Microfilming
processes provide reductions . . .
```

8.95 Symbols other than Arabic numerals, such as asterisks and daggers, should not be used for footnotes in business reports.

TYPING FOOTNOTES

8.96 Footnotes (references or explanations) are generally typed at the bottom of the page on which the footnote number appears in the text. While typing the report, observe the number and length of the footnotes that will appear at the bottom of each page. Allow enough space at the bottom of the page for them to be typed. Follow this procedure for typing the footnotes:

1. Allow approximately one-half inch for each footnote at the bottom of the page, using this method:

   a. Place a light pencil mark approximately one inch from the bottom of the page for the bottom margin.

   b. After typing each footnote number within the text, place another pencil mark approximately one-half inch above the first marking(s) to indicate the point where the footnote will be typed.

2. Continue to type the body of the report on the page until a pencil mark is visible. Type a one and one-half inch footnote separating line (using the underscore key) a single space below the last line of the text. Double-space after the line.

3. Indent the first line of each footnote five spaces.

4. Precede each footnote with the reference number typed on the line and followed by a period and two spaces (or typed as a superscript with no space following it).

```
     1.  Marvin Zuckerman, Words Words Words (Bev-
erly Hills, Calif.:  Glencoe Press, 1974), p. 27.
```

5. Type all source and explanatory footnotes in single spacing with double spacing between entries.

6. Type the footnotes within the margin settings used for the report.

8.97 Source and explanatory notes may also be grouped together and typed on a separate page at the end of the report. If this arrangement is used, the word NOTES—not FOOTNOTES—is centered and typed as the heading at the top of the first page of notes. The numbers of the notes are typed on the line, followed by a period and two spaces.

FOOTNOTE ELEMENTS

8.98 The information contained in a footnote varies depending on whether a book, periodical, or public document is being cited; but all footnotes should be as *complete* and as *consistent* as possible. All relevant information that the reader needs to identify each source cited in the text should be included; and all footnotes referring to the same type of source should follow the same pattern. For example, all footnotes for books should follow one pattern, all footnotes for periodicals another pattern, and so on. When a particular work is cited more than once in a report, however, only the first reference must be complete (see Shortened References, 8.123–8.126).

Books

8.99 The first time a book is cited, the notation must include the name(s) of the author(s) and/or editor(s), the full title of the book, the place of publication, the publisher's name, the copyright date, and the page number(s).

```
     1.  Richard Swanson and Charles Marquardt, On
Communication: Listening, Reading, Speaking and
Writing (Beverly Hills, Calif.:  Glencoe Press,
1974), pp. 10-11.
```

8.100 **Author's name.** The author's name, as it appears on the title page of the book, is typed first. The name is typed in normal order—first name, middle name or initial, and surname, followed by a comma.

```
     2.  Arthur M. Okum, The Political Economy of
Prosperity (New York:  W. W. Norton Co., 1970),
p. 256.
```

8.101 If a book has more than one author, the names are listed in the order in which they appear on the title page, even though they may not be in alphabetical order.

3. Farrington Daniels and Robert A. Alberty, Physical Chemistry, 2d ed. (New York: John Wiley & Sons, Inc., 1961), p. 32.

4. Robert M. Carter, Daniel Glaser, and Leslie T. Wilkins, Correctional Institutions (New York: J. B. Lippincott Co., 1972), pp. 104–5.

8.102 If a book has more than three authors, you need list only the name of the author listed first on the title page, followed by the Latin abbreviation **et al.** ("and others"). There is no comma separating the author's name and the abbreviation, and the abbreviation is not underscored. Type a period after the abbreviation. (Note: The abbreviation et al. should not be used in bibliographies.)

5. David Skwire et al., Student's Book of College English (Beverly Hills, Calif.: Glencoe Press, 1975), p. 303.

8.103 **Editors' names.** Three kinds of books include an editor's name on the title page, which means it must be included in a footnote: *anthologies* (writings drawn from various sources), *collected works* (all the works by an important author, usually with comments and introductions by the editor), and *compilations* (information on one subject from different sources, reorganized into a coherent book by the editor).

8.104 When citing *anthologies,* the footnote begins with the author and title of the article, story, or essay quoted in the report and continues with the name of the editor and the title of the book. The book title is underscored; the title of the article is typed within quotation marks.

6. Herbert J. Muller, "Education for the Future," in The Conscious Reader, ed. Caroline Shrodes, Harry Finestone, and Michael Shugrue (New York: Macmillan Publishing Co., Inc., 1974), p. 634.

8.105 When citing *collected works,* note that the author's name usually appears in the title. Thus, if the name of the *author* is mentioned in the report, the footnote begins with the title of the work.

7. The Complete Poems of D. H. Lawrence, ed. Vivian de Sola Pinto and F. Warren Roberts (New York: Viking Press, 1964), p. 32.

If the name of the *editor* is mentioned in the report, the footnote begins with the name(s) of the editor(s).

8. Vivian de Sola Pinto and F. Warren Roberts, eds., The Complete Poems of D.H. Lawrence, . . .

8.106 *Compilations* are cited in the same manner as collected works.

9. Robert E. Spiller et al., eds., Literary History of the United States (New York: Macmillan Publishing Co., Inc., 1974), p. 72.

8.107 **Title.** When a book is cited in a footnote for the first time, the complete title should be supplied, including the subtitle, if any. Book titles are underscored, while chapter or article titles appear within quotation marks.

8.108 **Series title.** If a book is part of a series, the series title and number are written immediately after the book title. Only the title of the book is underscored.

10. Julian H. Steward, ed., Handbook of South American Indians, Smithsonian Institution, Bureau of American Ethnology Bulletin No. 143 (Washington, D.C., 1949), p. 14.

Because the publisher (the Smithsonian) is part of the series title, no publisher's name is included with the place and date of publication.

8.109 **Edition number.** The first edition of a book does not need to be numbered. However, if a book has been published in more than one edition, the edition number will be stated on the copyright page. This number is typed after the book title (or series title) in abbreviated form.

11. Harvey M. Karlen, The Pattern of American Government, 2d ed. (Beverly Hills, Calif.: Glencoe Press, 1975), p. 127.

Note that the abbreviated form for *second* is 2d, instead of 2nd. Note also that no period follows the abbreviated edition number.

If the copyright page includes dates of revisions, this information is included after the edition number.

12. Ernest R. Kamm, Derald D. Hunt, and Jack A. Fleming, Juvenile Law and Procedure in California, 2d ed. rev. (Beverly Hills, Calif.: Glencoe Press, 1971), p. 34.

8.110 **Volume number.** If a work has more than one volume, the footnote for any particular volume usually would cite the total number of volumes in the series, using Arabic numerals. The number of the individual volume is also given in Arabic numerals, even though it may appear on the title page in Roman numerals.

If the volume does not have a specific title, its number is typed after the publication data followed by a colon and the page number for the reference.

```
     13. James A. Gould and H. C. Kiefer, eds.,
The Western Humanities, 2d ed., 2 vols. (New York:
Holt, Rinehart & Winston, Inc., 1971), 2:8.
```

If the volume does have a specific title, the title is typed after the publication data, and the volume number is preceded by the abbreviation `vol.`

```
     14. Ernest A. Baker, A History of the English
Novel, 11 vols. (New York: Barnes & Noble, Inc.,
1960), vol. 7, "The Age of Dickens and Thackeray,"
p. 95.
```

When a work is still in progress (as with the collected works of a particular author, when the volumes may be published one at a time over a long period), the number of volumes may be omitted.

8.111 **Publication data.** This information includes place of publication, publisher's name, and copyright date. It is typed in parentheses following the book title, series title, or volume title.

If the publisher is located in a major city, the city name alone is sufficient.

```
(Chicago: University of Chicago Press, 1976)
```

If the name of the city will not necessarily reveal the publisher's location to the reader, however, the state name should follow in abbreviated form.

```
(Englewood Cliffs, N.J.: Prentice-Hall, Inc., 1977)
```

8.112 The publisher's name is separated from the place of publication by a colon. All publication data should be cited the same way in footnotes and bibliographies. In citing an older book, check to determine the publisher's current name; the name on the copyright page may have changed.

Copyright Page of 1950 Book:

```
Harcourt, Brace & World, 1950
```

Footnote for the Same Book:

```
Harcourt Brace Jovanovich, 1950
```

(The correct wording for the names of all American publishers may be found in *Books in Print* and *Literary Market Place*, both published annually by R. R. Bowker.)

8.113 **Copyright date.** Type the copyright date after the publisher's name, separated by a comma. This information is located on both the title and copyright pages in most books. When more than one copyright date is listed, cite the most recent one.

8.114 **Chapter title.** If a chapter title is to be included for a particular reference, that title is provided after the publication data. "Chapter" is abbreviated "chap.," and the title is typed within quotation marks.

15. Emil Kahn, Elements of Conducting, 2d ed. (New York: Schirmer Books, 1975), chap. 4, "Changes in Tempo and Meter," pp. 63–65.

While a chapter title may be included in a footnote, the title of an article in an anthology *must* be included. The article title precedes the book title and is followed by the page number (see example 6, under 8.104).

8.115 **Page numbers.** Page numbers must be included not only in footnotes that refer to direct quotations but also in notes for a particular fact or group of facts that the report writer has drawn from another author. Page numbers may be omitted, however, when a footnote refers either to an entire book or to a general body of information which has been paraphrased over a few paragraphs in the report. In that case, the footnote should begin "Adapted from" or "Summarized from."

Page numbers are abbreviated **p.** if only one page is cited or **pp.** if several pages are cited. Give specific page numbers whenever possible.

Periodicals

8.116 The major elements of a periodical footnote are the author's name, title of the article (in quotation marks), name of the periodical (underscored), volume number (if any), month and year of publication (or the year, for annuals), and the *inclusive* page numbers of the article—not just the page number from which information was taken.

8.117 **Magazines and journals.** The style of citing magazines and journals depends on how often the periodical is published.

Less often than once a month:

16. E. J. Franco, "Operation Upgrade," Journal of Reading 16 (November 1962), 120–23.

Note the use of the colon to set off the page numbers when the volume number is included in the citation.

Once a month or more often:

17. Fred Schumm, "A Problem-Solving Tool Shed," Industrial Education, March 1975, pp. 66–69.

Note the absence of parentheses around the date when a volume number is not included.

In some magazines, articles are written by teams of writers, and no byline is included with the stories. In that case, the citation is written without an author's name.

18. "New Ideas for Clean Elections," U.S. News and World Report, June 4, 1973, p. 79.

8.118 **Newspapers.** An author's name is not required for articles or editorials that appear without a byline. The name of the newspaper, as well as the city of publication, is underscored. Such newspapers as the *Wall Street Journal* and the *Christian Science Monitor,* however, do not need a city name for identification.

19. Bill Boyarsky, "Way Cleared for Voting Act Renewal," Los Angeles Times, July 17, 1975, p. 1.

20. "High-Energy Studies Indicate the Existence of New Particle," New York Times, February 3, 1975, p. 48.

Public Documents

8.119 The information included in footnotes for public documents varies considerably depending on the kind of document cited. Notes for some basic documents are illustrated here.

8.120 **Legal cases.** The citation for a legal case refers to the official report of that case by volume number, abbreviation of volume title, page number, district number (where applicable), and date. For example, the official records of the Supreme Court cases are published in a series of volumes called the *Supreme Court Reporter* (abbreviated "U.S."); and federal courts of appeal and district court cases are published in the *Federal Reporter Series* (abbreviated "F.2d" or "F.Supp.," for second series and federal supplement).

21. Covington v. Harris, 419 F2d 617 (D.C. Cir. 1969).

8.121 **Government publications.** Most government publications do not include an author's name, so the following information would be sufficient to locate an original document: name of the government agency, title of the publication (underscored), the publication, bulletin, or volume number (if any), place and date of publication (in parentheses), and the page reference.

22. U.S. Department of State, The Suez Canal Problem: July 26–Sept. 22, 1956, Documentary Publication no. 6392 (Washington, D.C., 1956), p. 18.

23. U.S. Department of Labor, Labor Laws That Have Been Declared Unconstitutional, by David Lindley Clark, Bureau of Labor Statistics Bulletin no. 321 (Washington, D.C., 1922), p. 14.

Note that example 23 above includes the name of an author. In such a case, an acceptable alternative form would list the author's name first, with the department name written as the publisher.

24. David Lindley Clark, Labor Laws That Have Been Declared Unconstitutional, U.S. Department of Labor, Bureau of Labor Statistics Bulletin no. 321 (Washington, D.C., 1922), p. 14.

8.122 **U.S. Constitution.** When citing the Constitution, identify the material quoted or referred to by article and section or other division. Do not underscore "Constitution," and do not spell out "United States."

25. U.S. Constitution, Article II, sec. 4.

26. U.S. Constitution, Amendment XVI, sec. 3.

SHORTENED REFERENCES

8.123 After a book or article has been cited in full the first time in a footnote, subsequent references may be shortened somewhat by the use of certain Latin abbreviations or abbreviated titles.

8.124 **Ibid.** (ibidem) is used to cite consecutive references to the same work, whether it is the same page or a different page. If the page number is different from that originally stated, the new page number is written in the subsequent reference.

27. Alvin Toffler, Future Shock (New York: Bantam Books, 1970), pp. 169–172.

28. Ibid. [exact work, including page number]

29. Ibid., p. 175. [exact work but different page]

8.125 **Op. cit.** (opere citato) is used to cite nonconsecutive references to a work previously listed, whether it is the same page or a different page. If the page number is different from that originally cited, the new page number is written in the subsequent reference. Type the surname of the author(s) to identify that previous work and the page number.

30. William E. Strunk and E. B. White, The Elements of Style (New York: Macmillan Publishing Co., Inc., 1972), pp. 59–75.

31. Fred Kline, "Baltimore: The Hidden City," National Geographic, February 1975, pp. 188–215.

32. Strunk and White, op. cit., p. 77. [Refers to footnote 30 above, but on a different page.]

8.126 **Loc. cit.** (loco citato) is used when a subsequent but nonconsecutive reference is made to the same volume or page as that previously cited. Type the surname of the author(s) to identify that previous work.

33. James K. Bell and Adrian A. Cohn, Handbook of Grammar, Style, and Usage (Beverly Hills, Calif.: Glencoe Press, 1972), p. 84.

34. Toffler, loc. cit. [Refers to footnote 27 above—the same work and the same page.]

Bibliographies

8.127 For business report purposes, a *bibliography* is a list of all sources cited in the report and all other works consulted by the writer in preparing the report. The bibliography is typed on a separate page (or pages) and is placed at the end of the report.

8.128 An **annotated bibliography** includes a brief comment for each book and article in the bibliography, explaining why it was useful in preparing the report and why it might be of interest to readers. (For an example, see 8.130.)

8.129 **Lengthy bibliography.** A very lengthy bibliography may be divided into sections, as follows:

By type of work: books
periodicals
government publications
unpublished works

By an author's works: subjects (all the works on a given subject grouped together)
dates (all the works published in a given year or period grouped together)

By importance: primary sources
secondary sources

Leave a triple space before and after the division heading, which is centered on the page:

```
                    BOOKS


Spence, William P.  Architecture: Design,
     Engineering, Drawing.  2d ed.  Bloomington,
     Ill.:  McKnight & McKnight Publishing Co.,
     1972.
```

TYPING A BIBLIOGRAPHY

8.130 The heading BIBLIOGRAPHY (the singular form of the word, although there are multiple entries and/or several pages) or ANNOTATED BIBLIOGRAPHY (if appropriate) is centered and typed on a separate page to be added to the end of the report. Follow these guidelines:

1. Use the same margin setting that was used for the report.

2. Type the first line of each entry beginning at the left margin. Succeeding lines are typed beginning at a five-space indentation.

```
Bell, James K., and Adrian A. Cohn.  Handbook
     of Grammar, Style, and Usage.  Beverly
     Hills, Calif.:  Glencoe Press, 1972.
```

3. Type each entry in single spacing; double-space between entries.

4. For an annotated bibliography, type the annotation on a new line a double space below the bibliographic entry. Each line of the annotation begins at the indention.

> Bell, James K., and Adrian A. Cohn. Handbook of Grammar, Style, and Usage. Beverly Hills, Calif.: Glencoe Press, 1972.
>
> Presents standard guidelines for grammar, word usage, punctuation, and writing style in alphabetical order so a reader can use it like a dictionary.

Note that this annotation is not written in sentence form. Consistency should be maintained, however, in the wording of each annotation so all annotations are written in the same form—either complete sentences or phrases.

ELEMENTS OF A BIBLIOGRAPHIC ENTRY

8.131 Bibliographic entries contain the same information as that in footnotes but are arranged somewhat differently. Entries are listed in alphabetic sequence by authors' surnames, so that each name is inverted—surname, first name, and middle name or initial.

The elements of each entry include the name(s) of the author(s) or editor(s), title, edition number (if any), and publication data. Note that the parts of an entry are separated by periods rather than commas or parentheses.

> Johnson, H. Webster. How to Use the Business Library. Cincinnati: South-Western Publishing Company, 1972.

Author's name.

8.132 The author's name is inverted so the surname appears first. Separate the surname from the rest of the name with a comma.

Author's and editor's names

8.133 When a work has several authors or editors, only the first author's name is inverted, but all names that appear on the title page or byline must be listed. The abbreviation et al. should not be used in bibliographies, even if a work has more than three authors or editors.

> Maedke, Wilmer O., Mary F. Robek, and Gerald F. Brown. Information and Records Management. Beverly Hills, Calif.: Glencoe Press, 1974.
>
> Maxwell, Gerald W., and William L. Winnett, eds. Relevance in the Education of Today's Business Student. Washington, D.C.: National Business Education Association, 1972.

If more than one work by the same author is listed, do not repeat the name in succeeding entries. Type eight hyphens at the beginning of the line, followed by a period and two spaces before the entry. A series of eight underscores may be typed instead of the hyphens.

Solzhenitsyn, Aleksandr I. The Gulag Archipelago 1918-1956: An Experiment in Literary Investigation. Translated by Thomas P. Whitney. New York: Harper & Row, 1974.

________. The Cancer Ward. Translated by Rebecca Frank. New York: Dial Press, 1968.

Titles

8.134 Titles of books and magazines are underscored, as in footnotes.

Strunk, William, Jr., and E. B. White. The Elements of Style. New York: Macmillan, 1972.

Chapters or articles from books and magazines are typed within quotation marks before the name of the book or magazine.

Strunk, William, Jr., and E. B. White. "A Few Matters of Form." The Elements of Style. New York: Macmillan, 1972.

When a work does not have an author, or the author is unknown, the work is listed in alphabetic order by the first word in the title, except for the words "A," "An," and "The."

Volume numbers

8.135 Volume numbers are included for periodicals that are published less than once a month. For books published in more than one volume, the total number in the series is cited in the bibliography, even though only one volume was referred to in preparing the report. (The specific number and title of that volume is included in the footnote reference, but the work *as a whole* is cited in the bibliography.)

Scientific References and Bibliographies

8.136 When a report deals with a scientific or technical subject, the references are cited in abbreviated form within the text rather than as footnotes. The bibliography appearing at the end of the report contains the full citation for each work mentioned in the text.

ELEMENTS OF A CITATION

8.137 The citation includes two or three elements written in parentheses: the author's last name, the date of the work being cited, and the page number (if reference is to a direct quotation). An alternative method involves numbering each bibliographic reference beforehand and inserting the reference number in the text wherever it is cited. This method makes it difficult for the reader to identify the source, however, and increases the chance of errors in citations.

TYPING CITATIONS
8.138

Type the author's name, the date of the work, and the page number (if any) in parentheses, and place the citation at the end of the sentence to which it refers, before the period.

```
    Rutherford's atomic model sharply undermined
a traditional premise of scientific investigation:
the assumption that scientists should accept only
the evidence of their own eyes (Hameka 1967).
```

If a citation refers to part of a sentence, place the citation at a logical break in the sentence, ideally before a comma or other mark of punctuation.

```
    The rate of erosion is usually highest "in
semiarid and arid regions where vegetation is
sparse or absent" (Kolendow 1974, p. 352),
because in humid areas the moisture stimulates
growth of sufficient vegetation to retard erosion.
```

If the author's name is already mentioned in the sentence, only the date and page number (if necessary) are typed in the citation.

```
This conclusion is based on the success of the
process modules for investigating environmental
science that were devised by Litherland and
Hungerford (1975).
```

SCIENTIFIC BIBLIOGRAPHIES
8.139

Entries for the references cited in scientific reports contain the same elements as other bibliographies (see 8.127–8.135), but the elements are arranged differently. The following illustrate the bibliographic entries for the works mentioned above.

Type the date following the author's name. Capitalize only the first letter of the title of the work.

```
Hameka, Hendrik F.  1967.  Introduction to quantum
     theory.  New York:  Harper & Row.
```

When reference is to a journal article, the title of the article is typed with only the first letter capitalized. The journal title is underscored, with the first letter of important words capitalized. Volume number follows journal title with no punctuation between; volume and page numbers are separated by a colon.

```
Litherland, Ralph A., and Harold R. Hungerford.
     1975.  Process modules for investigating
     environmental science.  The Science
     Teacher 42:40–47.
```

Nine

Statistical Data

Introduction

9.1 Tables, charts, and graphs provide the most effective and compact way to illustrate statistical relationships and comparisons. The data may be presented within the body of a letter, memorandum, or report, or placed on a separate page and attached to the communication.

Tables

9.2 A table presents figures and/or words in columnar form. Thus, it is useful for presenting comparisons involving numbers, dates, or amounts.

PLACEMENT OF TABLES

9.3 Short tables generally are typed within the text of the document —letter, memorandum, or report—to which they refer. Longer tables are typed on separate pages and inserted close to the related discussion. In either case, tables should be constructed so they are self-explanatory and can be understood without reading the related discussion.

Within the Text (Figure 9-1)

9.4 1. Type the table within the margin settings for the letter, memorandum, or report.

2. Precede the table with a double or triple space; follow it with a double space before continuing the text.

3. Single-space the information within the table unless it includes long columns of figures, which should be double-spaced.

4. Type the entire table on one page.

5. Introduce the table with a brief statement preceding it in the text; any discussion or explanation should be placed after the table.

Outside the Text (Figure 9-2)

9.5 1. Use plain bond paper of the same quality as that used for other pages of the letter, memorandum, or report.

2. Change the type style, if necessary, to accommodate the information in the table (e.g., pica type for a table with many figures) or the size of the table (e.g., elite type for a long table with few or no figures).

3. Type the table so it is attractively displayed both horizontally and vertically (see 9.19–9.26 for centering methods). If the table is part of a bound report, allow an extra half inch for the binding.

4. Use either single or double spacing depending on the length and detail of the table.

5. Rule or box the table if it does not occupy the full page.

Lark Corporation

85-76 Moreno Avenue
Encino, California 91316

August 15, 1979

Mr. and Mrs. Gerald Jann
913 McKenzie Avenue
Salem, Oregon 97201

Dear Mr. and Mrs. Jann:

SUBJECT: Typing a Table Within the Letter

Below is an illustration of a table typed within the body of a letter. This letter is typed in the modified block style with mixed punctuation, and it follows the guidelines for typing business correspondence.

Only a short table should be typed within the body of business correspondence; lengthy tables should be typed on separate pages. Lengthy tables should be identified by number and/or title and should be placed close to its discussion or explanation in the letter, memorandum, or report.

The table must be typed within the margin settings of the letter and should be preceded and followed by either a double or triple space. The following illustrates the form and spacing suggested for typing short tables:

TERM INSURANCE PREMIUM FOR FIVE-YEAR PERIODS

(Face Value at $25,000)

Age	Annual Premium
25	$104
30	106
35	119
40	155

Sincerely yours,

Reynaldo B. Cruces
Underwriter

FIGURE 9-1. TABLE WITHIN BUSINESS LETTER

6. Identify each table by number and/or title so that a specific reference can be made in the text.

7. Place the table close to its related discussion, with any explanation or discussion following the table.

ELEMENTS OF A TABLE (Figure 9-2)

Main Heading

9.6 The main heading, the title of the entire table, is centered and typed in solid capital letters. It may consist of one, two, or possibly three lines. Double space two- or three-line headings. The title should be specific in identifying the information presented. A triple space follows the main heading except when a secondary heading is used.

Secondary Heading

9.7 A secondary heading further identifies the contents of the table. This heading is typed a double space below the main heading. Only the first letter of important words is capitalized. The secondary heading may be enclosed in parentheses. Triple-space after the entire heading before beginning the table.

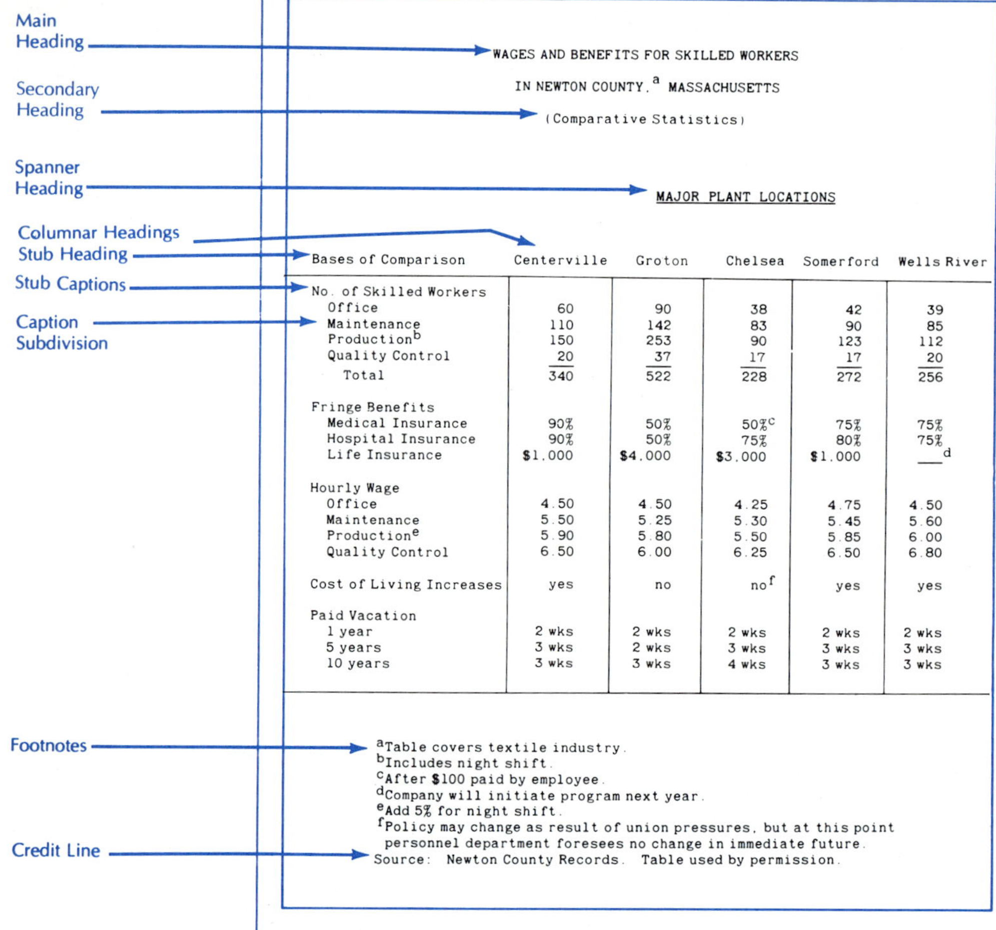

WAGES AND BENEFITS FOR SKILLED WORKERS

IN NEWTON COUNTY,[a] MASSACHUSETTS

(Comparative Statistics)

	MAJOR PLANT LOCATIONS				
Bases of Comparison	Centerville	Groton	Chelsea	Somerford	Wells River
No. of Skilled Workers					
Office	60	90	38	42	39
Maintenance	110	142	83	90	85
Production[b]	150	253	90	123	112
Quality Control	20	37	17	17	20
Total	340	522	228	272	256
Fringe Benefits					
Medical Insurance	90%	50%	50%[c]	75%	75%
Hospital Insurance	90%	50%	75%	80%	75%
Life Insurance	$1,000	$4,000	$3,000	$1,000	___[d]
Hourly Wage					
Office	4.50	4.50	4.25	4.75	4.50
Maintenance	5.50	5.25	5.30	5.45	5.60
Production[e]	5.90	5.80	5.50	5.85	6.00
Quality Control	6.50	6.00	6.25	6.50	6.80
Cost of Living Increases	yes	no	no[f]	yes	yes
Paid Vacation					
1 year	2 wks	2 wks	2 wks	2 wks	2 wks
5 years	3 wks	2 wks	3 wks	3 wks	3 wks
10 years	3 wks	3 wks	4 wks	3 wks	3 wks

[a]Table covers textile industry.
[b]Includes night shift.
[c]After $100 paid by employee.
[d]Company will initiate program next year.
[e]Add 5% for night shift.
[f]Policy may change as result of union pressures, but at this point personnel department foresees no change in immediate future.
Source: Newton County Records. Table used by permission.

FIGURE 9-2. TABLE ON SEPARATE PAGE

Spanner Heading

9.8 A spanner heading "spans" or extends over two or more columns of information to group different categories or classifications of data. It is centered and typed a single or double space above the columnar headings to which it refers. Spanner headings are helpful in lengthy or detailed tables (see "Major Plant Locations," Figure 9-2).

Columnar Heading

9.9 Columnar headings are titles or captions centered and typed above each column of information. The number of columns and the length of the entries within each column determine the length of the columnar headings. Tables with few columns across the page may have longer headings; tables with many columns would need either short headings or headings centered and typed in two or three lines. Columnar headings are typed a single or double space below the spanner heading and a double space above the first columnar entries.

Stub Heading

9.10 A stub heading is the heading centered and typed above the captions (stubs) in the lefthand column of the table. This heading identifies the categories of information within that column.

Stubs

9.11 The captions in the lefthand column of the table are called stubs. Each stub consists of words that relate to or describe the data in the columns across the page opposite it. The stubs are typed beginning at the left margin.

Stub Caption or Line Caption

9.12 When the information within each stub is divided into categories, these stub captions or line captions are typed below the stub. The stub is typed at the left margin and may be underscored; the stub captions are typed below the stub in single spacing and indented two or three spaces. Depending on the length and detail of the table, a single or double space may precede the next stub.

Caption Subdivision

9.13 In addition to the stub caption, a second subdivision below the stub may be useful. This subdivision, typed below the stub caption, is indented two or three spaces from the beginning of the stub caption.

Footnotes

9.14 Footnotes are used to explain or expand on the data in the table **(explanatory footnote)** or to cite the source of a specific piece of data **(source footnote)**. The source of the table as a whole is referred to as the **credit line** (see 9.18).

9.15 Footnote references are typed within the table in consecutive sequence. The words or figures to which the footnotes apply are indicated by lowercase letters, rather than the Arabic numerals used in the text of a report; otherwise, the numerals would not stand out within columns of figures. The lowercase letters are typed as superscripts—to the right of the words or figures in question.

```
Production^b      50%^c
```

To place the footnote reference within the table, move from left to right and top to bottom of the table (see location of superscripts a–f in Figure 9-2).

9.16 Type a footnote separating line of 15 to 18 underscores a single space below the data. Double-space after the footnote separating line before typing the notes. If the table is boxed or ruled, the separating line is not necessary.

9.17 The footnotes are typed single-spaced, with a double space between them. Begin each note at the left margin by typing its identifying lowercase letter as a superscript; the note itself is typed immediately after the superscript. Succeeding lines of each footnote may begin either at the left margin or even with the first word in the first line (see note f, Figure 9-2).

Credit Line

9.18 The source from which the table was obtained is cited at the end of the table below the last footnote, if any. It is usually preceded by the word "Source," followed by a colon (see Figure 9-2); but if the table has no footnotes, this identification is not necessary.

CENTERING TABLE COLUMNS

9.19 Tables must be centered on the page both vertically and horizontally, to ensure even margins at top, bottom, and sides and even spaces between the columns. Table 9-1, Standard Paper Dimensions, is a useful aid in centering tables.

Width of Paper	8½ Inches	11 Inches	13 Inches
Elite Type:			
Spaces per inch	12	12	12
Spaces on page	102	132	156
Center point	51	66	78
Vertical lines (Paper on side)	51	66	78
Pica Type			
Spaces per inch	10	10	10
Spaces on page	85	110	130
Center point	42	55	65
Vertical lines (Paper on side)	51	66	78

TABLE 9-1. STANDARD PAPER DIMENSIONS

Horizontal Centering

9.20 Effective methods of centering horizontally include the backspace-from-center method, the mathematical method, and the eye judgment method.

9.21 **Backspace-from-center method.** As its name implies, this tabulation method (used to type tables that are separate from the related text) involves backspacing from the center point of the paper to determine the left margin setting. There are three major tasks: determining the left margin setting; setting tabulator stops for the columns; and centering columnar headings. In each case, you must work with the longest item in each column. The procedure is as follows:

1. Clear all tab stops; move margin stops to the ends.
2. To find left margin for table:

   a. Find the *longest item* in each column of the table.

   b. Determine how many spaces are to be left between columns. (It should be an even number, such as 4, 6, 8, 10, or 12, depending on the number and lengths of the columns.)

c. From the center of the paper, backspace once for every two letters *in the longest item* in each column. Begin with the longest item in column 1, then to the longest item in column 2, etc. As you go from one column to the next, if there is an extra letter in one column, carry it over into the longest item in the next column. Continue backspacing once for every two letters in the longest item in each column across the page.

d. Backspace once for every two spaces to be left between columns. (For instance, if you are to leave 10 spaces between columns, backspace 5 for the space between the first and second columns, 5 for the space between the second and third columns, etc.)

e. After you have backspaced for every two letters in the longest item of each column and backspaced once for every two spaces to be left between columns, where you stop is the left margin. Set your left margin here.

3. To find tab stops before typing the table:

a. From the left margin, space *forward once* for *every* letter in the *longest item* in the first column. Space *forward* once for each space to be left between columns 1 and 2. Set your first tab stop here.

b. From the beginning of column 2, space forward once for each letter in the longest item of the second column, plus once for each space to be left between columns 2 and 3. Set a second tab stop here.

c. Continue spacing forward in this manner until tab stops have been set for all columns to be typed across the page.

Note: You must space forward to set your tab stops because each letter to be typed must occupy one space across the page; each space between the columns must also be accounted for. Thus you are allowing for each letter and each space.

4. To type columnar headings:

a. Once the tab stops have been set across the page, columnar headings can be centered and typed before typing the table.

b. Columnar headings must be centered above each column of information. In some cases, column headings may be the longest item in the columns so that the information within the column will be centered below the heading.

c. You must find the exact center of each column before the column heading can be typed. Find the longest item in each column. Space forward *once* for *every two letters* in the longest item in the first column (if there is an extra letter, disregard it). This is the center of the column.

d. To center the heading from the center of the column: backspace once for every two letters in the heading.

e. Begin typing the heading at this point. The heading should be centered above the longest item in the column. (When the heading is the longest item within the column, find the center point of the column based on the heading; find the longest item below the heading and backspace-center it. This will now be the new tab stop for this column, and other items within this column will not seem centered. In other words, the second longest item in the column *will* be centered below the columnar heading.)

f. Continue to find the center of each column. Tab over to the next column, spacing forward once for every two letters in the longest item within the column. Then backspace-center the heading and type.

9.22 **Mathematical method.** This method of horizontal centering is used when information must be typed to accommodate specific dimensions of the page. Like the preceding method, it is used when the table is typed on a separate page. The procedure is as follows:

1. Use the boxes illustrated below and count the letters and spaces of the longest entry in each column of data across the page.

Nevada	230	500	80	2,050
California	185	75	45	965
New Jersey	1,025	135	115	1,440
Utah	290	210	100	850
10	5	3	3	5

2. Add all of these figures to determine the total number of spaces to be used for the table.

10 5 3 3 5 = 26

3. Determine the number of spaces remaining and specify the number of spaces to leave between columns. Leave a minimum of four spaces and a maximum of ten spaces between columns for easier reading.

4. Add the remaining spaces to the right and left margins.

5. Insert the paper so the left edge is even with the zero or its equivalent on the paper scale.

6. Clear all tabulator stops. Position the carriage or the carrier to correspond with the center point of the page (42 for pica and 50 or 51 for elite on 8½-inch wide paper; 55 for pica and 65 for elite on 11-inch wide paper.)

7. Set the left margin as indicated by the rough sketch in item 2 above. The right margin does not need to be set.

8. Set tabulator stops before beginning to type the data.

a. From the left margin, space *forward* once for *every* letter in the longest entry in the first column plus once for *every* space between the first and second columns. Set the first tab stop here.

b. From the beginning of column 2, space forward once for each letter in the longest entry of the second column, plus once for each space between the second and third columns. Set a second tab stop here.

c. Continue spacing forward in this manner until tabulator stops have been set for all columns in the table.

9. Type columnar headings, following the procedure outlined in item 4 under the backspace-from-center method (9.21).

9.23 **Judgment method.** A two-, three-, or four-column table included within the text of a letter, memorandum, or report may be centered by using eye judgment rather than a more precise and involved method. The table must be typed within the margins set for the correspondence.

9.24 If the table is to be indented from the right and left margins, follow these steps. (This style cannot be used if the letter is typed in the full block style.)

1. Decide on the number of spaces for the indention from both margins.

2. Space forward from the left margin and reset the margin; backspace from the right margin and reset the margin.

3. Begin the first column at the indention; type the last column so it ends even with or near the right margin.

4. Using eye judgment, center and type the middle column or columns so the number of spaces between the columns is approximately the same.

9.25 If the table is not to be indented, follow these steps:

1. Begin the first column at the left margin; type the last column so it ends even with or near the right margin.

2. Using eye judgment, center and type the middle column or columns so the number of spaces between the columns is approximately the same.

To type columnar headings, follow the procedure outlined in item 4 under the backspace-from-center method (9.21).

Vertical Centering

9.26 Tables are usually centered vertically so that top and bottom margins are even, but they may also be typed a little higher on the page than vertical center for a more pleasing appearance. Follow these steps to plan the vertical centering of a table.

1. Determine the vertical spacing for the different parts of the table: main heading, spanner heading, columnar headings, columnar entries.

2. Count the total number of lines the table will take; include the blank lines between the typewritten ones. (A double space equals one blank line; a triple space equals two blank lines.)

3. Subtract this figure from the total number of lines on the page vertically (8½-inch length equals 51 lines; 11-inch length equals 66 lines).

4. Divide this figure by two to arrive at the number of lines to leave for the top and bottom margins. (If there is an odd number, round it to the next lower number.)

5. Type the table a little higher than vertical center, if desired, beginning two or three lines higher than the figure obtained in step 4.

TYPING FIGURES IN COLUMNS

Whole Numbers

9.27 Type whole numbers so they are aligned at the right. Use a comma to separate every three digits from the right.

```
  905
2,378
   25
```

Decimal Figures

9.28 Type numbers with decimal points so the decimal points are aligned.

```
11.5
  .9
 2.155
```

Mathematical Symbols

9.29 Type mathematical symbols so they are aligned in a column in front of the figures. Thus, the figures should be aligned at the right.

```
+ 59
+100
-  7
```

Percent Figures

9.30 Type the percent symbols so they are aligned in a column after the figures. When the entire column consists of percents, type the percent symbol only after the first entry and after subtotals and totals within the column.

```
100%       12.500%
 12       137.875
 96         1.5
 14          .5
  2       152.375%
224%
```

Dollar Signs

9.31 Type dollar signs so they are aligned in a column in front of the amounts. When the entire column consists of dollar amounts, type the dollar sign before the first entry only and before subtotals and the total within the column.

```
$1,535.07      $ 5,000.00
   200.00          150.50
 3,216.45           35.75
     2.50        8,750.25
$4,954.02           14.85
    24.95      $13,951.35
   100.00
$5,078.97
```

9.32 Type the dollar sign before both amounts in the first entry only when a range of amounts is shown.

```
$1,500-$2,500      $   125.00-$   550.00
 7,000- 8,500           25.75-     28.50
   400-   750        1,100.00- 1,300.00
```

Align the dollar sign with the longest dollar amount.

Fractions

9.33 Type fractions consistently by using the ¼ and ½ keys on the typewriter or by using the number keys for all fractions. Align the fractions in a column after the figures. When a whole number precedes the fraction, a hyphen may be typed to separate the whole number from the fraction.

```
10-1/2      13-1/4      5-3/4
```

Different Figures

9.34 Type various kinds of figures either aligned at the *left* or centered above one another.

```
$190.00           $190.00
10 pounds        10 pounds
#1225-A           #1225-A
39-1/2%           39-1/2%
$3,500.86        $3,500.86
```

TYPING RULED OR BOXED TABLES

9.35 **Ruled tables** consist of horizontal lines, typed across the table to separate various headings, and vertical lines, which separate the columns of data. These ruled lines aid the reader in following information from column to column and down the page.

PERCENT OF EMPLOYEE TURNOVER

AT PROSPECTS CORPORATION*

(Period from December, 1980, to June, 1981)

Branch/Office	December	January	February	March	April	May	June
Arizona							
Flagstaff	---	---	2.0%	---	---	---	---
Phoenix	.4	1.0	---	---	2.0%	.4%	.5%
Tucson	---	.8	---	---	---	1.2	---
California							
Los Angeles	.5	.9	1.0	3.5	---	1.0	2.0
San Francisco	.4	.5	1.0	2.0	**	---	3.5
San Raphael	---	---	---	---	1.5	---	**
Nevada							
Las Vegas	1.0	.9	---	---	---	1.0	2.0
Reno	---	---	**	.5	---	---	---

*Survey based on 350 employees during the six-month period.

**Data not available.

FIGURE 9-3. BOXED TABLE

9.36 **Boxed tables** are ruled horizontally at the top, below the columnar headings, and at the end of the table. This table is ruled vertically between the columns in addition to being ruled at the sides (see Figure 9-3). Thus, the entire table is enclosed.

Horizontal Rules

9.37 **Top of the table.** A double horizontal line is typed at the top of the table below the main or secondary heading. Triple-space after the heading and type an underscore the width of the table. Return the carriage or carrier. Engage the ratchet release lever and roll the cylinder slightly away from you. Type the second underscore below the first one, being sure to end the line at the same point as the first line. Return the ratchet release lever to its position to continue the table.

MAIN HEADING

Secondary Heading

9.38 **Below columnar headings.** Separate the columnar headings by a single horizontal underscore. Begin this line at the left margin a single space below the columnar headings. This line should end at the same point as the double horizontal lines above.

Branch/Office December January February March April

9.39 **End of table.** Leave a single space after the last item in the table and type a single horizontal line across the width of the table.

This line should end at the same point as the other horizontal lines.

Oregon	13.0	13.5	14.1	15.8
South Dakota	12.5	13.2	10.0	14.6

Vertical Rules

9.40 Vertical lines are used to separate the data within the columns, especially if the columns are close together.

9.41 **Typewritten lines.** When all information has been typed in the table, remove the page from the typewriter and insert it on its side. The paper must be inserted straight so that the lines are straight and the columns appear evenly spaced.

Use the underscore key to type the lines between the columns. Type each line in the middle of the spaces between columns. The line should not extend beyond the double horizontal lines at the top of the table nor the single line at the bottom of the table.

9.42 **Hand-drawn lines.** Remove the page from the typewriter when all information has been typed in the table. Use a fine-point black-ink pen and a ruler or other straightedge to draw the vertical lines. Draw each line in the middle of the space between columns. The line should not extend beyond the double horizontal lines at the top of the table nor the single line at the bottom of the table.

NUMBERING TABLES

9.43 Tables typed on separate pages should be placed within the letter, memorandum, or report immediately after the related discussion or explanation. Each table within the communication should be given a number and title so it can be referred to easily within the text.

The tables are numbered consecutively within the communication, preferably in Arabic numerals. The number is typed a double space above the title of the table.

TABLE 4

PERCENT OF LEGAL SECRETARIES IN THE DALLAS AREA

PURSUING PARALEGAL OR LEGAL ASSISTANT JOBS

NUMBERING PAGES

9.44 Each table within the letter, memorandum, or report is assigned a page number. An 8½-inch wide page with a table is numbered in the upper right corner at the right margin, except for topbound report pages, which are numbered at the bottom of the page centered.

When a table is typed on an 11-inch wide page, the page is numbered like the other pages in the report, usually in the upper right corner. The top of the table becomes the left-hand side of the page.

Charts and Graphs

9.45 A chart is another means of conveying statistical data in a visual presentation. Three common chart styles are the **pie chart, bar chart,** and **line chart** or **graph.** While charts do not present data in as detailed a form as tables, they are excellent in providing concise comparisons and relationships.

Charts are prepared on separate pages and incorporated into the report immediately after the related discussion. Charts are numbered consecutively throughout the report or within each chapter or section. Charts are referred to as figures.

PIE CHARTS

9.46 A pie chart is a circle that is divided into sections to represent various data (see Figure 9-4). The entire circle represents 100 percent, or the *whole* of something. Therefore, each figure represents a percentage, and the pie is divided into segments proportionate to the percentage figures.

Use a protractor to draw the circle and to determine the size of the sections representing the pieces of information. Regardless of the size of circle drawn, the distance around the circle (circumference) represents 360 degrees. Thus the 360 degrees must be divided proportionately for each section.

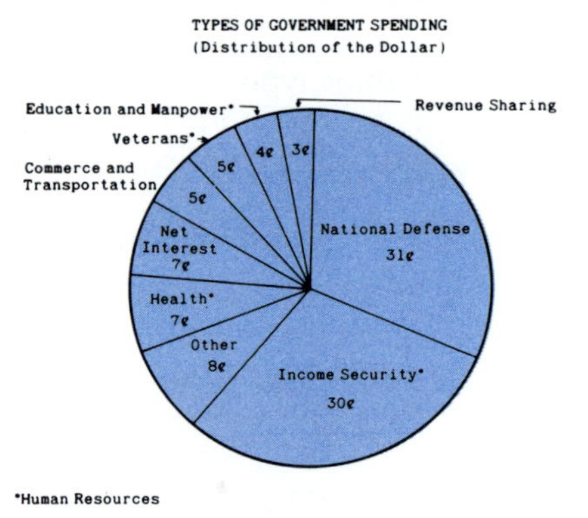

FIGURE 9-4. TYPICAL PIE CHART

From Internal Revenue Service, *Understanding Taxes,* 1975.

Constructing a Pie Chart

9.47 1. Convert each figure to be represented into a percentage.

2. Begin at the top of the circle (12 o'clock position), going clockwise, and mark off the appropriate sections of the pie, starting with the largest figure and ending with the smallest figure.

3. Label each section of the pie, using as few words as possible. Type the caption within its section. If there is not enough space within the section, type the caption outside the circle and use an arrow or line to indicate its relationship.

4. Number each chart consecutively (after all charts have been completed and placed in sequence). The charts may be numbered consecutively throughout the report as Figure 1, Figure 2, Figure 3, etc.; or the charts may be numbered consecutively within each chapter or section, as Figure 1-1, Figure 1-2, etc. (referring to charts 1 and 2 in chapter 1).

Typing Information in Pie Charts

9.48

1. Type the main heading in solid capital letters a triple space above the top of the pie chart. The heading is centered horizontally across the page. If a secondary heading is used, begin the main heading three lines higher on the page.

2. Type a secondary heading, if used, a double space below the main heading. It is centered horizontally across the page, and only the first letter of each important word is capitalized.

3. All captions within the pie chart sections are typed in the same direction rather than being slanted. Each caption should be contained within its section; concise headings should be used. Information typed outside the pie chart must also be typed in the same direction.

4. Footnote references and explanations are not commonly included on pie charts because they would be incorporated into the text of the report. However, if the source is to be cited or a brief explanation is to be given, type this information below the chart preceding the number and title of the chart.

5. Type the page number for each chart in the same manner as the other pages of the report.

BAR CHARTS

9.49

Horizontal and vertical bar charts are used to compare magnitudes or quantities of similar items or of time. Data on bar charts may be represented by horizontal or vertical bars. On both types of bar charts, a vertical axis and a horizontal axis are drawn perpendicular to one another to relate the constant data and the variable data being compared.

Horizontal Bar Chart

9.50

The horizontal bar chart (Figure 9-5) is read from left to right, with the greater magnitudes or quantities to the right. The horizontal axis shows the sequence of amounts, percentages, dates, or time (constant information); the variable information being compared is listed down the vertical axis.

9.51 Use a ruler or other straightedge to draw the horizontal and vertical axes. Determine the degrees or magnitudes for the constant information on the horizontal axis. The degrees on this scale should be in uniform segments. The point at which the two axes meet represents the lowest degree on the horizontal scale.

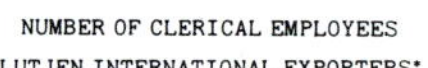

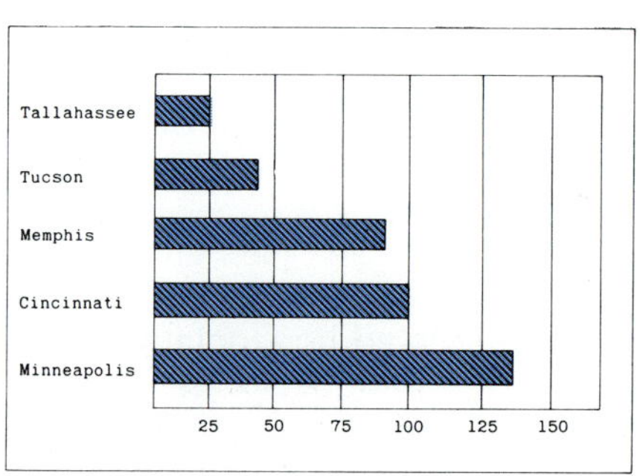

*Data as of December 31, 1978

Constructing Horizontal Bar Charts

FIGURE 9-5. TYPICAL HORIZONTAL BAR CHART

9.52 1. Determine the kind of constant information that is to be represented on the horizontal axis: dollars, percentages, years, amounts, or numbers. Decide on the distribution of numbers across the scale. The range of numbers should be confined to the extent of the smallest and largest items being compared.

2. Determine the variable information to be listed down the left side of the chart. These captions may be listed in these ways:

   a. Largest quantity or number to smallest (descending order)

   b. Smallest quantity or number to largest (ascending order)

   c. Earliest year to latest year (chronological order)

3. Draw each bar to correspond with the appropriate quantity or number for each caption. Each bar is approximately one-quarter inch wide, depending on the number of captions included. The space between the bars should equal the width of the bars.

4. Number each chart consecutively (after all charts have been completed and placed in sequence). The charts may be numbered consecutively throughout the report as Figure 1, Figure 2, Figure 3, etc.; or the charts may be numbered consecutively within each chapter or section, as Figure 1-1, Figure 1-2, etc. (referring to charts 1 and 2 in chapter 1).

5. Determine the number of spaces to be left between the numbers across the horizontal scale. Use eye judgment to place these numbers evenly across the scale. Type the numbers at uniform intervals, from the lowest number or earliest date to the highest number or latest date.

```
______________________________________________________
  1960       1965       1970       1975       1980
```

6. Draw a vertical line if desired, to separate each segment of numbers across the horizontal scale into columns.

7. Type the total of each bar, if desired, at the end of the bar to assist the reader in interpreting the data.

8. Use the underscore key on the typewriter to enclose the bars of the chart so this information will stand out from the captions and numbers. Leave an even amount of space above and below the bars to prevent crowding or confusion with extra lines.

9. Type the page number for each chart in the same manner as other pages in the report.

Typing Information in Horizontal Bar Charts (Figure 9-5)

9.53 1. Arrange the bar chart so it is approximately centered horizontally and vertically on the page.

2. Type the main heading in solid capital letters above the chart and centered horizontally across the page. A two- or three-line heading is double-spaced. Triple-space after the main heading except when a secondary heading is used. (Headings may be typed below the chart instead of above it. In this case, the heading would be preceded by the chart number within the report.)

```
        SALES VOLUME FOR FOTOLINE PRODUCTS

                  February 1979

 ______________________________________________
   Figure 13. Sales Volume, February 1979
```

3. Type the secondary heading, if used, a double space below the main heading. It is centered horizontally across the page, and only the first letter of each important word is capitalized. Triple-space after this heading.

4. Type the captions on the left side of the chart so that they all either begin or end at the same point. Type the captions either according to their ascending or descending order of quantities or numbers, or in chronological order. Triple-space between each caption.

```
Robert Morrisey        |        Robert Morrisey |
                       |                        |
Kenneth C. Chambers    |    Kenneth C. Chambers |
                       |                        |
Judith A. Molina       |       Judith A. Molina |
```

5. Type any footnotes outside the boxed chart, below the bottom line. Type them beginning at the left margin set for the captions and a double space below the line. (See Figure 9-5.)

6. Type the source of the chart a double space below the footnote references or explanations.

Vertical or Columnar Bar Charts

9.54 Bar charts may also be presented in vertical or columnar form. These charts contain the same elements as the horizontal bar charts, but they are reversed: the constant data is represented along the vertical axis, the variable data being compared is represented on the horizontal axis; and the bars or columns are drawn to represent the quantities or magnitudes (see Figure 9-6). The bars are drawn as vertical columns along the horizontal scale; the height of each column or bar corresponds to the numbers along the vertical axis.

9.55 The **vertical axis** contains dollar amounts, percentages, or numbers rather than people, places, or things; and the **horizontal axis** contains dates (months, years, and so on).

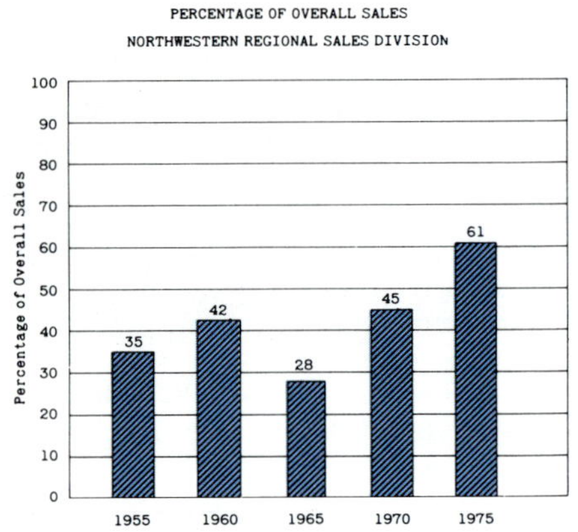

FIGURE 9-6. TYPICAL VERTICAL BAR CHART

Constructing Vertical Bar Charts

9.56 1. Determine the kind of constant information that is to be represented along the vertical axis—dollars, percentages, or other amounts. This information is listed in ascending order, beginning with zero at the perpendicular point of the two axes. Each item is called a **caption.**

2. Decide on the distribution of numbers on the vertical axis. The range of numbers should be confined to the extent of the smallest and largest items being compared on the horizontal axis. The numbers should be in equal units and large enough so information can be easily read and data accurately presented (see Figure 9-6).

3. Identify the numbers along the vertical axis as dollars, percentages, or other amounts. This information may be typed above or alongside the column of numbers (see Figure 9-6).

```
Dollars          PERCENTAGE OF TURNOVER
(000's)
                      100
  125
                       75
  100
                       50
   75
                       25

                        0
```

When large dollar amounts or numbers are to be presented, delete the extra zeros for even amounts of thousands and millions and indicate this in the columnar or secondary headings as follows.

```
                    SALES VOLUME FOR FOTOLINE PRODUCTS

                              February 1979
```

Secondary Head: *(in thousands of dollars)*

4. Determine the variable information to be listed across the horizontal axis. Dates are usually listed in chronological order from the earliest month or year to the latest.

5. Draw each columnar bar to correspond with the appropriate amount, percentage, or other number on the vertical axis. Each bar is approximately one-quarter inch wide, depending on the number of items included. The space between the bars should equal the width of the bars.

6. Number each chart consecutively after all charts have been completed and placed in sequence within the report. All charts are labeled Figure 1, Figure 2, Figure 3, etc.; or the charts may be numbered consecutively within each chapter or section, as Figure 1-1, Figure 1-2, etc. (referring to charts 1 and 2 within chapter 1).

Typing Information in Vertical Bar Charts (Figure 9-6)

9.57 1. Arrange the bar chart so it is centered horizontally and vertically on the page.

2. Type the main heading in solid capital letters above the chart, centered horizontally across the page. A two- or three-line heading is double-spaced. Triple-space after the main heading, except when a secondary heading is used. (Headings may be typed below the chart instead of above it. In this case, the number of the chart precedes the heading.)

3. Type the secondary heading, if used, a double space below the main heading. Center it horizontally across the

page, and capitalize only the first letter of each important word. Triple-space after this heading.

4. Type the captions (amounts or percentages) along the vertical axis so that all numbers are aligned at the right. Type the numbers in ascending sequence, beginning with zero at the perpendicular point of the two axes. Triple-space between each number.

5. Use the underscore key to draw horizontal lines from the numbers along the vertical axis to the right of the chart, for ease in reading the columnar information.

6. Determine the captions to be typed along the horizontal axis and the number of spaces to be left between them. Use eye judgment to place these numbers proportionately across the scale, beginning with the earliest date to the latest.

```
____________________________________________________
   1960      1965      1970      1975      1980
```

7. Use the underscore key to enclose the bars of the chart so this information will stand out from the captions and other numbers. Leave an even amount of space to the right of the last bar and to the left of the first bar.

8. Type footnote references or explanations outside the boxed chart below the typewritten line. Type these references beginning at the left margin set for the captions and a double space below the line.

9. Type the source a double space below the footnote references or explanations.

LINE CHARTS OR GRAPHS

9.58 A line chart or graph is used to illustrate continuous changes or movement of data over a particular period of time—daily, weekly, monthly, annually, and so on. The interrelationships are indicated by plotting dots placed across the chart or graph and connected by lines. Charts may be prepared on the typewriter, or specially ruled grid paper may be used for more accurate representations.

9.59 The horizontal axis represents the variable—time—and the vertical axis represents the constant amounts, percentages, or other numbers. Up to four series of lines may be shown on one line chart or graph to provide comparisons of other related items (see Figure 9-7). Colored lines, colored dots, dashes, or other devices should be used to distinguish each series of lines.

Constructing Line Charts or Graphs

9.60 1. Begin the vertical axis at zero, regardless of the highest point to be plotted on this axis, to ensure a more accurate reading of the points along this line. If there is a wide gap between zero and the first number plotted, the break may be indicated by a zigzag or wavy line.

2. The divisions and spaces on both the vertical and horizontal axes must be equally proportioned on the grid to

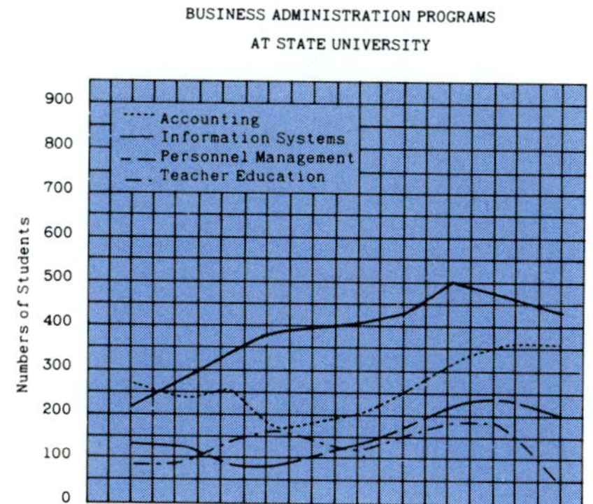

FIGURE 9-7. TYPICAL LINE CHART

give an accurate picture of any movement across the chart. Widening spaces or lines will create a distorted picture and a misinterpretation of the facts.

3. Determine the kind of constant information that is to be represented along the vertical axis: dollars, percentages, or other amounts. List these numbers in ascending order beginning with zero at the perpendicular point of the two axes. Each number is called a **caption.**

4. Identify the numbers along the vertical axis as dollars, percentages, or other amounts. This information should be spaced in the same proportion as the numbers along the horizontal axis. Place the identifying information above the column of numbers or type it sideways on the page.

When large dollar amounts or numbers are to be presented, delete the extra zeros for even amounts of thousands and millions and indicate this in the secondary heading or columnar heading as follows:

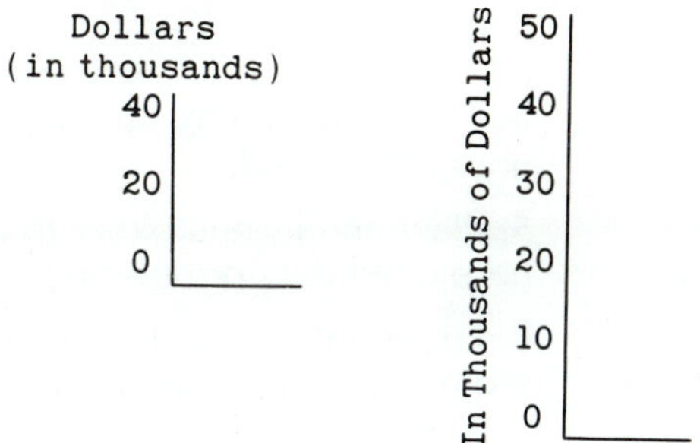

PRODUCTION COSTS FOR WORD PROCESSING

(In Thousands of Dollars)

5. Decide on the distribution of time across the horizontal axis. These **time captions** are listed from the earliest time to

the latest. Provide a proportionate amount of space for each date on the horizontal axis as well as for the numbers along the vertical axis.

When the months of the year are to be plotted on this axis, use the first letter of each month instead of spelling out each month:

```
|_____________________________________________
   J  F  M  A  M  J  J  A  S  O  N  D
```

6. Plot the appropriate data on the chart following the numbers and dates on both axes. Place a dot at each point. Beginning at the vertical axis, connect these lines to form a continuous line across the chart. For subsequent lines plotted on the same chart, use different color lines or dots or dashes to represent additional series.

7. Identify each line by title or by a legend placed at the top or bottom of the chart when more than one line is plotted on the chart. The legend explains which symbols and/or colors represent which information on the chart.

```
----      Michigan
._._._    Nebraska
......    New Jersey
```

Typing Information in Line Charts

9.61

1. Center the chart horizontally and vertically on the page.

2. Type the main heading in solid capital letters above the chart, centered horizontally across the page. Headings may also be typed below the chart. If a secondary heading is used, it is typed a double space below the main heading.

3. Type the captions along the vertical axis so that all numbers are aligned at the right. Type the numbers in ascending sequence, beginning with the zero at the perpendicular point of the axes. Triple-space between each caption, or be guided by the specially ruled grid paper for spacing.

4. If the entire chart is to be typewritten, use the underscore key to draw both horizontal and vertical lines for the grid, leaving proportionate spacing for the data. If grid paper is used for plotting and is to be affixed to the page, be sure the typewritten information is carefully aligned with the lines on the grid.

5. Place the legend either in a corner of the chart that has no plotted data or outside the grid lines.

6. Enclose the grid of the chart in a box using the underscore key or a pen and straightedge. Do not enclose the numbers along the two axes within the box.

7. Type footnote references or explanations outside the boxed chart. Type these references beginning at the left margin for the captions.

8. Type the source a double space below the last footnote reference or explanation.

Ten

Business Mathematics

Calculating Discounts

10.1 A discount is a percentage figure by which a dollar amount is reduced from the original price.

Example: \$44.95 less 3% discount = \$43.60

To calculate the discount:

1. Convert the percentage rate of discount to its decimal equivalent.

```
3% = .03
```

2. Multiply the gross amount by the discount. Insert the decimal point in the appropriate position.

```
$44.95
 x .03
 13485 = 1.3485
```

3. Round the answer to the nearest cent.

```
1.3485 = $1.35 discount
```

CASH DISCOUNTS

10.2 A cash discount is an amount deducted from an invoice amount to encourage customers to make payment promptly upon receipt of the invoice. The following terms are commonly used to describe various methods of cash discounting:

2/10, n/30 2 percent discount if invoice paid within 10 days of invoice date; otherwise, net amount must be paid within 30 days

2/10 EOM 2 percent discount if invoice paid within 10 days after the end of the month

2/10 ROG 2 percent discount if invoice paid within 10 days of receipt of goods

To calculate discounts:

1. Determine in all instances whether payment was made within the discount period allowed.

2. Convert the percent of the discount to its decimal equivalent.

3. Multiply the invoice amount by the rate of discount to obtain the amount of the discount.

4. Subtract the amount of the discount from the invoice amount to determine the net amount.

CHAIN DISCOUNTS

10.3 A chain discount is a series of two or more discounts allowed in a sales transaction. (*Note:* Never add up chain discounts and multiply by their total!)

EXAMPLE: $175.50 less 10%–5%

To calculate the discount:

1. Convert the percentages to their decimal equivalents.
2. Determine the complement of each discount rate.

(A complement of any number is the difference between it and the next higher power of 10.)

```
 100%    1.00          100%    1.00
- 10%     .10         -  5%     .05
  90%     .90           95%     .95
```

3. Multiply the gross amount by the complement of the first discount. Insert the decimal point at the appropriate place.

```
$175.50
x   .90
 157.9500 = $157.95
```

4. The new net amount becomes the gross amount, to be multiplied by the second discount.

5. Multiply the new gross amount by the complement of the second discount.

```
$157.95
x   .95
 150.0525 = $150.05 = net amount
```

6. The amount of the discount is determined by subtracting the net amount from the original gross amount.

```
 $175.50
 -150.05
  $25.45
```

10.4 DISCOUNT AND NET AMOUNTS

The discount-and-net amounts method of computation provides both the amount of the discount and the net amount (the gross amount less the discount).

EXAMPLE: $285 less 12% discount = $250.80

To use this method:

1. Determine the amount of the discount as explained in 10.1 and 10.2.

```
   $285   gross amount
  x .12   rate of discount
 $34.20=  amount of discount
```

2. Subtract the amount of the discount from the gross amount.

```
$285.00
- 34.20
$250.80 = net amount
```

NET AMOUNTS

10.5 The net amount is the gross amount less the amount of the discount.

EXAMPLE: $150 less 15% discount = $127.50

1. Convert the rate of discount to its decimal equivalent.

```
15% = .15
```

2. Subtract the discount rate from 100%. The gross amount is equal to 100%, and the discount is a reduction from 100%. (The difference is known as the complement.)

```
 100%      1.00
 -15%      -.15
 ----      ----
  85%       .85
```

3. Multiply the gross amount by the complement. Insert the decimal point in the appropriate position.

```
    $150
    x.85
--------
  127.50 = $127.50 = net amount
```

Computing Interest

10.6 Interest is the amount of money charged for borrowing money. Interest is calculated on the basis of one year—either 360 or 365 days.

INTEREST DIVISOR METHOD

10.7 Interest divisor tables, available from financial institutions, eliminate the need to multiply by the percentage rate when computing the amount of interest charged on loans. The illustrations below show the percentage rate on the vertical axis and the fractions of percentages on the horizontal axis.

When an interest divisor table is used, the formula for computing interest is:

$$\frac{\textbf{Principal} \times \textbf{Time}}{\textbf{Interest Divisor}} = \textbf{Interest}$$

EXAMPLES:	*Principal*	*Rate*	*Time (360-day basis)*
	$ 260	7 1/4%	287 days

To calculate the amount of interest:

1. Multiply the principal amount by the time—in days.

```
 $260
x 287 days
-----
74620
```

2. Refer to the interest divisor table for the appropriate percentage rate and obtain the amount.

```
7 1/4% = $4,965.52
```

%		1/4	1/2	3/4
0		144000.00	72000.00	48000.00
1	36000.00	28800.00	24000.00	20571.43
2	18000.00	16000.00	14400.00	13090.91
3	12000.00	11076.92	10285.71	9600.00
4	9000.00	8470.59	8000.00	7578.95
5	7200.00	6857.14	6545.45	6260.87
6	6000.00	5760.00	5538.46	5333.33
7	5142.86	4965.52	4800.00	4645.16
8	4500.00	4363.64	4235.29	4114.29
9	4000.00	3891.89	3789.47	3692.31
10	3600.00	3512.20	3428.57	3348.84

TABLE 10-1. INTEREST DIVISORS–360 DAY BASIS

%		1/4	1/2	3/4
0		146000.00	73000.00	48666.67
1	36500.00	29200.00	24333.33	20857.14
2	18250.00	16222.22	14600.00	13272.73
3	12166.67	11230.77	10428.57	9773.33
4	9125.00	8588.24	8111.11	7684.21
5	7300.00	6952.38	6636.36	6347.83
6	6083.33	5840.00	5615.38	5407.41
7	5214.29	5034.48	4866.67	4709.68
8	4562.50	4424.24	4294.12	4171.43
9	4055.56	3945.95	3842.11	3743.59
10	3650.00	3560.98	3476.19	3395.35

TABLE 10-2. INTEREST DIVISORS–365 DAY BASIS

3. Divide this amount into the number obtained when the principal was multiplied by time.

```
            15.027
4965.52 )74620.00000
```

4. Convert the decimal quotient into a dollar amount, rounding to the nearest cent.

```
15.027 = $15.027 = $15.03 = amount of interest
```

SIMPLE INTEREST 10.8

Simple interest is calculated by using the following formula:

$$\frac{\text{Principal} \times \text{Rate} \times \text{Time}}{\text{360 or 365 Days}} = \text{Interest}$$

EXAMPLE: Principal = $7,450

Rate = 9 1/4%

Time (360-day basis) = 2 years

To calculate the amount of interest:

1. Convert the percentage rate into its decimal equivalent.

   `9 1/4% = .0925`

2. Convert the time in years to days.

   `2 years = 720 days`

3. Multiply the principal amount by the rate.

   `$7450 x .0925 = 689.1250`

4. Multiply the result by time.

   `689.1250 x 720 = 496170.0000`

5. Divide this result by 360 days.

```
        1378.25 =amount of interest
360 )496170.0000
```

Computing Percentages

10.9 Determining the relationship that one number has to another in order to express that relationship as a percentage figure is the purpose of computing percentages. A percentage is a fraction of a total amount expressed in hundredths (see Table 10-3).

AMOUNT AND PERCENT OF DECREASE/INCREASE

10.10 Computing the percentage of decrease or increase provides a comparison of figures on which management decisions may be based. Such comparisons may be expressed in dollar amounts as well as percentage figures.

1/3	=	.33333	1/6	=	.16667	1/12	=	.08333
2/3	=	.66667	2/6	=	.33333	2/12	=	.16667
1/4	=	.25	3/6	=	.50	3/12	=	.25
2/4	=	.50	4/6	=	.66667	4/12	=	.33333
3/4	=	.75	5/6	=	.83333	5/12	=	.41665
1/5	=	.20	1/8	=	.125	6/12	=	.50
2/5	=	.40	2/8	=	.25	7/12	=	.58333
3/5	=	.60	3/8	=	.375	8/12	=	.66667
4/5	=	.80	4/8	=	.50	9/12	=	.75
			5/8	=	.625	10/12	=	.83333
			6/8	=	.75	11/12	=	.91666
			7/8	=	.875			

TABLE 10-3. DECIMAL EQUIVALENTS OF COMMON FRACTIONS

The decimal equivalent of a common fraction is calculated by dividing the denominator (bottom number of the fraction) into the numerator (top number of the fraction) and carrying the quotient to at least five decimal places to the right to round out the fourth decimal.

To calculate percent and amount of increase or decrease:

1. Obtain the amounts of the figures to be compared, such as the previous year's sales and the current year's sales, the previous year's expenses and the current year's expenses, etc.

Department	Sales: Previous Year	Sales: Current Year	Amt. of Increase/ Decrease	% of Increase/ Decrease
A	$10,205	$12,368	$2,163	21.20%
B	3,562	2,117	(1,445)	(40.57)

2. Determine the amount of increase or decrease between the previous year and the current year, using the figure for the previous year as the base for the comparison.

```
(A)  $12,368 = current        (B)  $3,562 = previous
     -10,205 = previous            -2,117 = current
     $ 2,163 = difference          $1,445 = difference
```

3. Divide the difference by the previous year's or month's figure to determine the percent of increase or decrease.

```
                .211954                      .40567
(A) 10,205 )2163.000000      (B) 3562 )1445.00000
```

4. Convert the quotient to a percentage figure by moving the decimal point two places to the right.

```
(A) .211954 = 21.20%          (B) .40567 = 40.57%
              increase                     decrease
```

5. Indicate a percentage decrease by enclosing the figure in parentheses.

```
(A) 21.20% increase           (B) (40.57%)
```

BASE AMOUNTS 10.11

In determining the base amount, the percentage amount and the percentage rate are known.

EXAMPLE: $560 is 12½% of what amount?

To calculate the base amount:

1. The percentage rate is the **divisor** and the amount is the **dividend.**

2. Convert the percentage rate into its decimal equivalent.

$12\frac{1}{2}\% = .125$

3. Divide the amount by the percentage rate.

```
        4.480   = $4,480
.125 )560.000
```

4. To check the calculation, multiply the percentage rate by the quotient, rounding off to the next higher number where necessary.

$4480 x 12.5 = $560

$560 is 12½% of $4,480

RATE PERCENTAGES

10.12 In calculating rate percentages, the dollar amounts are known.

EXAMPLE: $3,000 is what % of $4,500?

To calculate the rate percentage:

1. Determine the base number to which the other number is being compared. The base number follows the word **of.**

2. Convert the numbers into a fraction. The base number becomes the denominator.

```
3000 numerator
4500 denominator
```

3. Divide the numerator by the denominator, carrying the quotient to at least four decimal places.

```
           .66666
4500 )3000.00000
```

4. Convert the quotient into a percentage by moving the decimal point two places to the right, rounding off where necessary.

```
.66666 = 66.67%
```

5. To check the calculation, multiply the base amount by the quotient, rounding off to the next higher number where necessary.

```
$4,500 x .66666 = 2999.70000 = $3,000
```

Estimating Answers in Multiplication

10.13 Often, an estimate will provide the necessary information when an approximation is sufficient to obtain an estimated answer to a problem, increase one factor and decrease the other to the nearest number that is easy to work with.

Problem: 578 x 321 **Estimate:** 600 x 300

```
   578                  600
 x 321                x 300
   578               180000 = estimated product
  1156
 1734
185538 = product
```

When a multiplication problem involves decimal points, the decimal fraction should be dropped. One of the remaining factors is increased, the other is decreased. (If the estimate must include the decimal, round it off as a fraction by referring to Table 10-3.)

Problem: 436.25 x 28.75 **Estimate:** 400 x 30

```
    436.25
  x  28.75
    218125
   305375
  349000
  87250
12,542.1875 = product
```

```
   400
 x  30
12,000 = estimated product
```

Proration

10.14 Prorating means proportionately distributing an amount among several individual amounts.

EXAMPLE:

Department	Gross Revenue	% of Revenue
A	$15,650	27.82%
B	10,073	17.90
C	12,245	21.77
D	9,830	17.47
E	8,462	15.04
	$56,260	100.00%

To prorate the revenue:

1. Determine the total amount of sales, revenue, expenses, etc., involved. It is this total—100 percent of the revenue—that will be prorated among the other departments, sections, divisions, branches, etc.

2. Divide this total into the individual revenue figures indicated on the chart above.

```
          .27817
56260 )15650.00000
```

3. Convert the quotient to a percentage figure by moving the decimal point two places to the right.

.27817 = 27.82%

4. Continue in the same manner until all percentages have been calculated. When all percentages are determined, they will total 100 percent or slightly more or less, depending on rounding.

Eleven

Units of Measure

Standard Measures

APOTHECARIES' FLUID MEASURE 11.1

		Metric Equivalent
	1 minim or drop (min. or M)	= 0.0616 ml
60 min.	= 1 fluid dram (fl. dr.)	= 3.6966 ml
8 fl. dr.	= 1 fluid ounce (fl. oz.)	= 0.0295 *l*

CIRCULAR AND ANGULAR MEASURE 11.2

	1 second (″)
60 sec.	= 1 minute (′)
60 min.	= 1 degree (°)
90 deg.	= 1 quandrant or 1 right angle
360 deg.	= 1 circumference = 1 circle

COUNTING MEASURE 11.3

	1 dozen	= 12 units
12 doz.	= 1 gross	= 144 units
12 gr.	= 1 great gross	= 1,728 units

CUBIC AND CAPACITY MEASURE 11.4

This measures length, width, and depth.

		Metric Equivalent
	1 cubic inch (cu. in.)	
1,728 cu. in.	= 1 cubic foot (cu. ft.)	= 0.0283 m^3
27 cu. ft.	= cubic yard (cu. yd.)	= 0.7646 m^3

DRY CAPACITY MEASURE 11.5

			Metric Equivalent
	1 pint (pt.)	= 33.6 cu. in.	= 0.5506 *l*
2 pt.	= 1 quart (qt.)	= 67.2 cu. in.	= 1.1012 *l*
8 qt.	= 1 peck (pk.)	= 537.61 cu. in.	= 8.8096 *l*
4 pk.	= 1 bushel (bu.)	= 2,150.42 cu. in.	= 35.2383 *l*
	1 barrel (bbl.)	= 7,056 cu. in.	= 115.62 *l*

LINEAR MEASURE 11.6

This measures length and distance on a straight line from one point to another.

		Metric Equivalent
	1 inch (in.)	= 2.54 cm
12 in.	= 1 foot (ft.)	= 30.48 cm
3 ft.	= 1 yard (yd.)	= 0.9144 m
5½ yd.	= 1 rod (rd.)	= 5.0292 m
40 rd. or ⅛ mi.	= 1 furlong (fur.)	= 201.168 m
320 rd.	= 1 mile (mi.)	= 1.609 km
3 mi.	= 1 league	= 4.828 km

LIQUID CAPACITY

11.7

			Metric Equivalent
	1 fluid ounce (fl. oz.)	= 1.804 cu. in.	= 29.57 ml
16 fl. oz.	= 1 pint (pt.)	= 28.875 cu. in.	= 0.4732 *l*
2 pt.	= 1 quart (qt.)	= 57.75 cu. in.	= 0.9463 *l*
4 qt.	= 1 gallon (gal.)	= 231 cu. in.	= 3.7853 *l*
31.5 gal.	= 1 barrel liquid (bbl.)		= 119.24 *l*

MEASURE OF TIME

11.8

60 seconds (sec.)	= 1 minute (min.)
60 minutes	= 1 hour (hr.)
24 hours	= 1 day (d.)
7 days	= 1 week (wk.)
365 days	= 1 common year (yr.)
366 days	= 1 leap year
10 years	= 1 decade
100 years	= 1 century
1,000 years	= 1 millenium

PAPER MEASURE

11.9

24–25 sheets	= 1 quire (qr.)
500 sheets	= 1 ream (rm.)
2 rm.	= 1 bundle (bdl.)
5 bdl.	= 1 bale

SQUARE MEASURE

11.10

This measures both length and width and expresses the area of a surface.

		Metric Equivalent
	1 square inch. (sq. in.)	= 6.4516 cm^2
144 sq. in.	= 1 square foot (sq. ft.)	= 0.0929 m^2
9 sq. ft.	= 1 square yard (sq. yd.)	= 0.8361 m^2
30¼ sq. yd.	= 1 square rod (sq. rd.)	= 25.293 m^2
160 sq. rd.	= 1 acre (A.)	= 0.4047 ha
640 A.	= 1 square mile (sq. mi.)	= 258.9998 ha or 2.5899 km^2

Standard Weights

APOTHECARIES' WEIGHT

11.11

This measures drugs and medicines.

		Metric Equivalent
	1 grain (gr.)	= 0.0648 g
20 gr.	= 1 scruple (s. ap.)	= 1.296 g
3 s. ap.	= 1 dram (dr. ap.)	= 3.888 g
8 dr. ap.	= 1 ounce (oz. ap.)	= 31.1035 g
12 oz. ap.	= 1 pound (lb. ap.)	= 373.24 g

AVOIRDUPOIS WEIGHT

11.12 This measures ordinary materials.

		Metric Equivalent
	1 grain (gr.)	= 0.0648 g
27.343,75 gr.	= 1 dram (dr.)	= 1.7718 g
16 dr.	= 1 ounce (oz.)	= 28.3495 g
16 oz.	= 1 pound (lb.)	= 453.5924 g or 0.4536 kg
100 lb.	= 1 hundredweight (cwt.)	= 45.3592 kg
2,000 lb.	= 2 short ton (s.t.)	= 907.18 kg

TROY WEIGHT

11.13 This measures precious metals and gems.

		Metric Equivalent
	1 grain (gr.)	= 0.0648 g
3.086 gr.	= 1 carat (c.)	= 0.2 g
24 gr.	= 1 pennyweight (dwt.)	= 1.55 g
20 dwt.	= 1 ounce (oz. t.)	= 31.1035 g
12 oz.	= 1 pound (lb. t.)	= 373.24 g

The Metric System

11.14 The metric system is a decimal system of measurement that is accepted and used by 90 percent of the world's population. Metric system units are based on a scale of ten within each of the following seven basic units:

Unit	*Symbol*	*Quantity*
meter	m	length or distance
liter	*l*	capacity
kilogram	kg	mass weight
degrees Celsius	°C	temperature
second	s	time
ampere	A	electric current
mole	mol	matter or amount of substance

METRIC PREFIXES AND MEANINGS

11.15

Prefix	*Symbol*	*Decimal Meaning*
pico-	p	0.000000000001
nano-	n	0.0000000001
micro-	μ	0.0000001
milli-	m	0.001
centi-	c	0.01
deci-	d	0.1
deka-	ka	10
hecto-	h	100
kilo-	k	1,000
myria-	my	10,000
mega-	M	1,000,000
giga-	G	1,000,000,000
tera-	T	1,000,000,000,000

Metric Measures

MEASURES OF AREA (*surface*)

11.16

1 square kilometer (km^2)	1 000 000	square meters
1 square hectometer (hm^2) or 1 hectare	10 000	square meters
1 square dekameter (dkm^2)	100	square meters
1 square meter (m^2)	10	dekameters
1 square decimeter (dm^2)	0.01	square meter
1 square centimeter (cm^2)	0.0001	square meter
1 square millimeter (mm^2)	0.000001	square meter

MEASURES OF CAPACITY

11.17

1 hectoliter (hl)	100	liters
1 dekaliter (dkl)	10	liters
1 liter (*l*)	1	liter
1 deciliter (dl)	0.1	liter
1 centiliter (cl)	0.01	liter
1 milliliter (ml)	0.001	liter

MEASURES OF LENGTH

11.18

1 kilometer (km)	1 000	meters
1 hectometer (hm)	100	meters
1 dekameter (dkm)	10	meters
1 meter (m)	1	meter
1 decimeter (dm)	0.1	meter
1 centimeter (cm)	0.01	meter
1 millimeter (mm)	0.001	meter

MEASURES OF VOLUME

11.19

1 cubic kilometer (km^3)	10^9	cubic meters
1 cubic hectometer (hm^3)	10^6	cubic meters
1 cubic dekameter (dkm^3)	10^3	cubic meters
1 cubic decimeter (dm^3)	10^{-3}	cubic meter
1 cubic centimeter (dm^3)	10^{-6}	cubic meter
1 cubic meter (m^3)	1	cubic meter

MEASURES OF WEIGHT

11.20

1 kilogram (kg)	1 000	grams
1 hectogram (hg)	100	grams
1 dekagram (dkg)	10	grams
1 gram (g)	1	gram
1 decigram (dg)	0.1	gram
1 centigram (cg)	0.01	gram
1 milligram (mg)	0.001	gram

MEASURES OF TEMPERATURE

11.21

0°Celsius	freezing point of water (32°F)
10°C	warm winter day (50°F)
20°C	mild spring day (60°F)
30°C	warm—almost hot day (86°F)
37°C	normal body temperature (98.6°F)
40°C	heat wave conditions (104°F)
100°C	boiling point of water (212°F)

Conversions from Customary System to Metric System

LENGTH/DISTANCE

11.22

From	To	Multiply by
inches (in.)	millimeters (mm)	25.4
inches (in.)	centimeters (cm)	2.5
feet (ft.)	meters (m)	0.3048
yards (yd.)	meters (m)	0.9144
miles (mi.)	kilometers (km)	1.609

AREA

11.23

From	To	Multiply by
square inches (sq. in.)	square centimeters (cm^2)	6.452
square feet (sq. ft.)	square meters (m^2)	0.0929
square yards (sq. yd.)	square meters (m^2)	0.836
acres (A.)	hectares (h)	0.4047
square miles (sq. mi.)	square kilometers (km^2)	2.590
square miles (sq. mi.)	hectares (h)	259.0

CAPACITY

11.24

From	To	Multiply by
fluid ounces (fl. oz.)	cubic centimeters (cm^3)	29.57
liquid pints (pt.)	liters (*l*)	0.4732
liquid quarts (qt.)	liters (*l*)	0.9463
gallons (gal.)	liters (*l*)	3.785
bushels (bu.)	hectoliters (hl)	0.352
bushels (bu.)	liters (*l*)	35.24
dry quart (qt.)	liters (*l*)	1.101

VOLUME

11.25

From	To	Multiply by
cubic inches (cu. in.)	cubic centimeters (cm^3)	16.387
cubic feet (cu. ft.)	cubic meters (m^3)	0.0283
cubic yards (cu. yd.)	cubic meters (m^3)	0.7646

WEIGHT

11.26

From	To	Multiply by
grains (gr.)	grams (g)	0.0648
avoirdupois ounces	grams (g)	28.35
avoirdupois pounds	kilograms (kg)	0.4536
short ton (2,000 lbs.)	metric ton	0.9072
long ton (2,240 lbs.)	metric ton	1.016

TEMPERATURE

11.27

To convert degrees Fahrenheit to degrees Celsius:

°Celsius = 5/9 (°F − 32) — for exact conversion

°Celsius = ½ °F − 15 — for approximate conversion

Twelve
Filing Systems

Introduction

12.1 There are five commonly used business filing systems: **alphabetic, numeric, subject, geographic,** and **chronologic.**

Filing procedures vary according to the functions of each office: the ways records are used determines the choice of filing system. All systems, however, share certain specific procedures, some of which occur simultaneously:

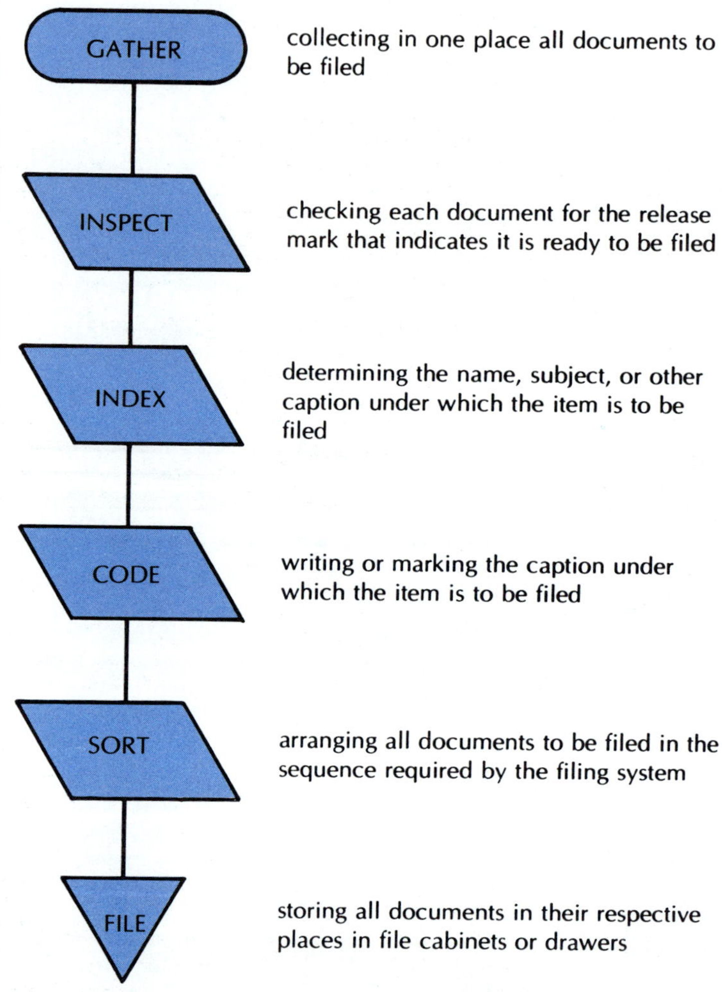

GATHER
collecting in one place all documents to be filed
INSPECT
checking each document for the release mark that indicates it is ready to be filed
INDEX
determining the name, subject, or other caption under which the item is to be filed
CODE
writing or marking the caption under which the item is to be filed
SORT
arranging all documents to be filed in the sequence required by the filing system
FILE
storing all documents in their respective places in file cabinets or drawers

FIGURE 12-1. FLOW CHART: FILING PROCEDURES

The list below offers general hints that apply to all filing tasks.

1. Follow the prescribed sequence of tasks for each type of filing system to save time and effort during filing.

2. Use spare moments during the day to file or at least sort papers prior to filing.

3. Do not allow papers to accumulate from day to day; papers that are not filed are likely to become lost or misfiled.

4. Do not allow files to be kept in desk drawers. For safety and more efficient office procedures, keep all files in their appropriate places.

5. When a file is removed from the files, an out-card system should be used to indicate who has the file and when it was borrowed.

Alphabetic System

12.2 The alphabetic filing system, based on the letters of the alphabet, is a direct method of filing and retrieving. When the file caption is known, the file may be located by simply checking the files under the letter(s) in question. The rules for alphabetic filing are presented in four segments: names of **individuals, businesses, institutions,** and **government agencies.**

NAMES OF INDIVIDUALS

12.3 Names of individuals are arranged with the last name first, then the first name or initial, then any middle name or initial. When names are transposed, a comma separates the last name or surname from the rest of the name.

Gomes, Joseph C.
Lau, J. Dennis

12.4 Each part of an individual's name is an indexing unit; the more words in the name, the more indexing units there will be. Indexing units are compared letter by letter until a difference is found, to determine where the file will be placed. An individual's last name is the first indexing unit; his or her first name is the second indexing unit; and his or her middle name or initial, if any, is the third indexing unit.

Abbreviated Given Names

12.5 Abbreviated given names are indexed as though they were spelled out in full.

Chas. D. Thomas	Thomas, **Charles** D.
Wm. C. Thompson	Thompson, **William** C.

Foreign or Unusual Names

12.6 Use the last part of an unusual or foreign name as the surname if the name is not distinctly separated.

Bing Yee	**Yee,** Bing
Xavier Douglas	**Douglas,** Xavier

Hyphenated Surnames

12.7 A surname containing a hyphen is indexed as one word; in other words, the hyphen is disregarded and the name is **visualized as one word.**

Sylvia Lopez-Tiana	**Lopeztiana,** Sylvia
Louis C. Lopes-Blanco	**Lopesblanco,** Louis C.

Identifying Elements

12.8 When all indexing units of individuals' names are identical, use the **cities, states, street names,** and then **house numbers** as identifying elements to determine the correct filing sequence.

Kane, Daniel (Pasadena, Texas)
Kane, Daniel (Boston)
Kane, Daniel (Pasadena, California)

Correct Order: Kane, Daniel (**Boston**)
Kane, Daniel (Pasadena, **California**)
Kane, Daniel (Pasadena, **Texas**)

Initials

12.9 An initial is an indexing unit and is placed before a word starting with the same letter.

Johnson	James	**H.**
Johnson	James	**Henry**
Johnson	**S.**	**R.**

Married Women

12.10 Names of married women are indexed and coded under the legal names—first name; middle name, middle initial, or maiden name; and husband's surname. If her legal name cannot be determined, index under the husband's name.

Mary Alice Xanders (Mrs. Randolph L.) =
Xanders, Mary Alice (Mrs.)

Nicknames

12.11 A nickname is changed to the person's given name if the given name can be determined. (Note: The legal name of some persons may be a known nickname.)

Bob C. Underwood Underwood, **Robert** C.

Personal Titles

12.12 A title before or after an individual's complete name is treated as an identifying element; the title is not considered an indexing unit.

Dr. James D. Wise Wise, James D. (**Doctor**)

A title preceding an individual's given name or surname alone is indexed as a separate unit as written.

Prince William **Prince** William

Professional Degrees

12.13 A professional degree following an individual's name is treated as an identifying element; it is not considered an indexing unit.

Louis Wortz, M.D.	Wortz, Louis (**M.D.**)

Seniority Titles

12.14 Seniority titles such as Jr., Sr., II, 2d, and III are considered identifying elements only.

Norman Vanderveen, Jr.	Vanderveen, Norman (**Jr.**)

Similar Names

12.15 In similar but not identical names, the one with the fewest letters is filed first. (Principle: Nothing comes before something.)

Haskin, Samuel
Haskin**s**, David

Surname Prefixes

12.16 A surname containing a prefix is indexed as though it were written as one word. Surname prefixes include A', D', de, De la, Des, Di, Du, Fitz, La, Le, M', Mac, Mc, O', Van, Van der, Von and Von der.

Sandra O'Hara	**Ohara,** Sandra
Jerry MacKenzie	**Mackenzie,** Jerry

NAMES OF BUSINESSES

12.17 Company names are generally indexed in the order in which the words are written. Each significant word in the name is indexed as a separate unit.

Abbreviations

12.18 Determine what the abbreviation represents. Then index the abbreviation as though it were spelled out, with each word being a separate unit.

Harper Mfg. Co.	Harper **Manufacturing Company**
Mielke Electrical Corp.	Mielke Electrical **Corporation**

Article "The"

12.19 The article "the" is not an indexing unit. However, to indicate the correct full name of the company, "the" must be written in parentheses. If "the" appears as the first word in the name, it is written in parentheses and placed at the end of the name. If "the" appears in the middle of a name, it is placed in parentheses in its proper position within the name.

The Cove Inn	Cove Inn (**The**)
Jack the Barber	Jack (**the**) Barber

Coined Words and Trade Names

12.20 A "coined" business name is formed by joining special combinations of phonetic spellings, trade words, prefixes, or suffixes to create a special-sounding, eye-appealing name.

A trade name identifies goods or services as products of a particular company, distinguishing it from comparable items on the market.

Determine if each word in the name can stand by itself. If so, each significant word in the name would be a separate indexing unit.

Stop-and-Go Markets	**Stop** (and) **Go Markets**

If an expression in the name cannot stand alone as a separate word, the name is indexed as one word and one indexing unit to retain the full meaning of the words in the name.

Redi-Maid Cleaners	**Redimaid** Cleaners

Compass Points

12.21 The compass points **north, east, south,** and **west,** when written by themselves, are separate indexing units.

East Sunset Boutique
South Shores Beach Rentals

12.22 When these words are combined, index them as one unit even when separated by hyphens or spaces, for the sake of consistency.

South-Eastern Products	**Southeastern** Products
North West News Service	**Northwest** News Service

Compound Words

12.23 A compound word is a combination of two or more words forming the name of a business, product, or service. These words may be joined by hyphens, spelled as one word, or left as two words (see 12.20–12.22, Coined Words and Trade Names and Compass Points).

Interstate Transportation Lines
Inter-State Packers, Inc.

Interstate	Transportation	Lines
Interstate	Packers	Incorporated

Conjunctions

12.24 The conjunction (**and**) and the ampersand symbol (**&**) are not separate indexing units and are disregarded in filing. However, to retain the complete company name, the word "and" or the ampersand symbol are placed in parentheses.

Benziger Bruce & Glencoe	Benziger Bruce (**&**) Glencoe
Wongworavit and Associates	Wongworavit (**and**) Associates

Compound Geographic Names

12.25 Each English word in a compound geographic name is indexed as a separate unit.

Mt. Ephraim Resorts	**Mount Ephraim** Resorts
Rhode Island Recreation Centers	**Rhode Island** Recreation Centers

A non-English compound geographic name is indexed as one entire indexing unit since the prefix cannot stand alone as a separate unit.

Los Angeles Office Supplies	**Losangeles** Office Supplies
San Simeon Recreation Club	**Sansimeon** Recreation Club

Geographic Names

12.26 Index company names consisting of geographic locations in the order in which the words are written. Geographic names can refer to streets, cities, states, or countries.

Dallas Athletic Club	**Dallas** Athletic Club
Third Avenue Copy Shoppe	**Third** Avenue Copy Shoppe

Hotels and Motels

12.27 If a name begins with the word **Hotel** or **Motel,** transpose the name so that the main, distinctive word appears as the first indexing unit. Then index names of hotels and motels in the order in which the words are written, with such words as **hotel, motel, lodge,** and **inn** indexed as separate units.

Hotel Francisco	**Francisco** Hotel
The Chancellor Hotel	**Chancellor** Hotel (The)
Traveler's Inn	**Traveler**('s) Inn

Hyphenated Compound Company Name

12.28 A hyphenated compound company name consists of the surnames of two individuals joined by a hyphen. Each surname is indexed as a separate unit, followed by the other words in the company name.

Lopez-Tiana Secretarial Services	**Lopez Tiana** Secretarial Services
Luft-Schmidt Appliances	**Luft Schmidt** Appliances

Identifying Elements

12.29 Cities, states, street names, and building numbers are used as identifying elements when all indexing units of two or more companies are identical.

12.30 The **city** is used as the first identifying element when the companies' names are identical.

Broadway Manufacturing Company (**Oshkosh**)
Broadway Manufacturing Company (**Poughkeepsie**)

12.31 The **state** is used as the second identifying element when the companies' names and cities are identical.

Manhattan Sporting Goods (Hollywood, **California**)
Manhattan Sporting Goods (Hollywood, **Florida**)

12.32 The **street name** is used as the third identifying element when the first and second elements are identical.

Jamestown Record Company (Yonkers, New York)
Oscawana Boulevard

Jamestown Record Company (Yonkers, New York)
Richmond Avenue

12.33 The **building number** is used as the last identifying element when all other elements are identical.

Bethlehem Iron Works (Englewood, New Jersey)
Yorkshire Road (**247**)

Bethlehem Iron Works (Englewood, New Jersey)
Yorkshire Road (**401**)

Individual's Complete Name

12.34 When a company's name includes the **full name** (given name, middle name or initial, and surname) of an individual, the individual's name must first be transposed into the proper indexing units: surname, given name, middle name or initial. The other words in the company name are then indexed in the order in which they are written.

Arthur C. Kelley Clothiers
Janice Jackson Fashion Boutique

Jackson	Janice	Fashion	Boutique
Kelley	Arthur	C.	Clothiers

Numbers

12.35 Names containing **numerals** as the first indexing unit are listed, arranged, and filed **before** the alphabetic names. Keeping these names separate from the alphabetic listing enables quicker indexing and filing of information.

The lower numbers would appear before the higher numbers, so that company names containing numerals would be filed numerically in **ascending order.**

4-Hour Cleaners
6th Avenue Reprographics Center
Manhattan Jewelers
Weston's Concrete

When the first indexing unit consists of a number that is **spelled out,** consider the entire number as one indexing unit and index the entire name in the order in which the words are written.

Three-Fifty Data Corp.	**Threefifty**	Data	Corporation
Two-Two-Two Club	**Twotwotwo**	Club	

When a numeral appears **within** the company's name, spell out the number and consider the entire number as one indexing unit. The entire name is then indexed in the order in which the words are written.

Bergie's 200 Diner	Bergie('s)	**Twohundred**	Diner
Bonham 211, Inc.	Bonham	**Twoeleven**	Incorporated

Prepositions

12.36 Prepositions such as **from, for, to, by, on,** and **in** are not separate indexing units and are disregarded. However, the preposition should be placed in parentheses in its proper position within the name.

American Institute of Banking	American Institute (**of**) Banking
Fashions by Renee	Fashions (**by**) Renee

Possessives

12.37 The rule for forming the possessive of a name that does not end in "s" is to add an apostrophe and s ('s) to the name. The rule for forming the possessive of a name that ends in "s" is to add an apostrophe (') to the name. Index the name up to the apostrophe and enclose in parentheses the apostrophe or apostrophe and s.

Behrman's Import-Export Co.
Phillips' Tool & Die Co.

Behrman(**'s**)	Import	Export	Company
Phillips(**'**)	Tool (and)	Die	Company

Single Letters in Names

12.38 Index single letters in a company's name as separate indexing units. In some names, there is a space between the letters; in others, a period is placed between the letters; in still others, the letters are written together. The presence of spacing or periods within the name does not affect the indexing order.

K. P. Restaurants	**K**	**P**	Restaurants		
Triple A Drugs	Triple	**A**	Drugs		
T.T.R. Sportswear	**T**	**T**	**R**	Sportswear	
KWIK Radio	**K**	**W**	**I**	**K**	Radio

Titles

12.39 When a company name includes a title and the complete name of an individual, transpose the parts of the individual's name. The title preceding a complete name is an identifying element, *not* a separate indexing unit. The title is placed in parentheses at the end of the individual's name.

Sir Thomas Drake Caterers
Doctor A. C. Kahoka's Clinic

Drake	Thomas (**Sir**)	Caterers
Kahoka('s)	A	C (**Doctor**) Clinic

When a title precedes only one name as part of a company name, the title becomes a separate indexing unit, and the individual's name (surname or given) is one indexing unit.

Captain Andres' Inn
Doctor Allesio's Foot Clinic

Captain	Andres(')	Inn	
Doctor	Allesio('s)	Foot	Clinic

NAMES OF INSTITUTIONS

12.40 Institutions include **schools, churches, libraries, banks, savings and loan associations, hospitals,** and **sanitariums.** Names of institutions take different forms. Therefore, filing rules should be followed consistently within the office.

Colleges and Universities

12.41 Index colleges and universities by the distinctive words in their names—generally in the order in which the words are written. The words "college," "university," and "school" should be indexed as the *last* unit.

Barber-Scotia College
Texas Christian University
University of Pennsylvania

Barber	Scotia	College
Texas	Christian	University
Pennsylvania	University (of)	

Institution names that include the name of an individual must first be transposed so that the individual's name is in its appropriate indexing order.

George Washington University
Brigham Young University

Washington	George	University
Young	Brigham	University

Elementary and Secondary Schools

12.42 Names of elementary and secondary schools are indexed and filed according to the **cities** in which they are located. Since many schools have identical names of individuals, listing by cities is essential.

The city is the first indexing unit in names of elementary and secondary schools. If the name includes the complete name of an individual, that individual's name must first be transposed.

Brooklyn, Glenn, John, Junior High School
Brooklyn, Lubavitcher High School
Springfield (Illinois), Toland Way Elementary School
Springfield (Ohio), Dearborn Preparatory School

The names of schools can then be indexed and filed in the order in which the words are written.

John Glenn Junior High School, Brooklyn
Lubavitcher High School, Brooklyn
Toland Way Elementary School, Springfield (Illinois)
Dearborn Preparatory School, Springfield (Ohio)

Financial Institutions

12.43 Financial institutions include banks, savings and loan associations, insurance companies, and trust companies. They are indexed according to the **cities** in which they are located; the city name is the first indexing unit, even if it is not part of the institution name.

Any identifying elements such as branch or street names are placed in parentheses after the name.

First National Bank of Athens (Ohio)
First National Bank of Athens (Georgia)
Republic Trust Company, Westville Branch, New Haven
Republic Trust Company, West Haven Branch, New Haven

Athens, First National Bank of (Ohio)
Athens, First National Bank of (Georgia)
New Haven, Republic Trust Company (Westville Branch)
New Haven, Republic Trust Company (West Haven Branch)

Hospitals and Sanitariums

12.44 Hospitals and sanitariums are indexed according to the **significant words** in the name, and the name is generally indexed in the order in which the words are written. When a hospital or sanitarium name includes the complete name of an individual, the individual's name is transposed into its proper indexing units.

Daniel Freeman Hospital	**Freeman**	Daniel	Hospital
Olive View Sanitarium	**Olive**	View	Sanitarium
St. Vincent's Hospital	**Saint**	Vincent('s)	Hospital

Religious Institutions

12.45 Religious institutions include churches, temples, cathedrals, and synagogues. Names of various institutions should be filed according to their **denominations,** if known, with the denomination being the first indexing unit. (If the denomination is not known, use the first significant word other than "Church," "Cathedral," or "Temple" as the first indexing unit.)

Church of the Open Door
St. Alban's Episcopal Church
Jodo Shu Temple
United Presbyterian Church of Hollywood
Sinai Temple

Episcopal	Saint	Alban('s)	Church
Jewish	Sinai	Temple	
Jodoshu	Temple		
Open	Door	Church (of the)	
Presbyterian	United	Church (of)	Hollywood

GOVERNMENT NAMES

12.46 Government bodies or agencies include various departments, commissions, boards, and offices of local, county, state, and federal agencies. At each level of government there may be departments, commissions, boards, and offices that are organized or subdivided into bureaus, divisions, or sections. In a few instances a commission or board is one of the offices of a department. The complexity of these governmental functions and titles creates the need for additional filing rules, although standard alphabetic filing rules generally apply.

Federal Government

12.47 Index and code names of federal government agencies with **United States Government** as the first three indexing units, followed by the name of the department and the name of the bureau, division, commission, or board.

Food and Drug Administration of the Department of Health, Education and Welfare	**United States Government, Public Health Service Food** (and) **Drug Administration**
Internal Revenue Service	**United States Government, Treasury** (Department), **Internal Revenue Service**
Bureau of Indian Affairs Bureau of Land Management	**United States Government, Interior** (Department of), **Indian Affairs** (Bureau of) **Land Management** (Bureau of)

City and Local Government

12.48 Index and code names of city and town governmental agencies under the name of the city or town as the first indexing unit(s), followed by its identification as a city or town and the name of the department, bureau, division, commission, or board.

Long Beach City Board of Education	**Long Beach, City** (of), **Education** (Board of)
Public Utilities and Transportation Department, City of Dallas	**Dallas, City** (of), **Public Utilities** (and) **Transportation** (Department)

County Government

12.49 Index and code names of county governmental agencies under the name of the **county** as the first indexing unit(s), followed by its identification as a county and the name of the department, bureau, division, commission, or board.

Los Angeles County Social Service Bureau	**Los Angeles, County** (of), **Public Social Services** (Department), **Social Service** (Bureau)

State Government

12.50 Index and code names of state governmental agencies under the name of the **state** as the first indexing unit(s), followed by its identification as a state and the name of the department, bureau, division, commission, or board.

Inheritance and Gift Tax Division of the Controller's Office, State of New Jersey	**New Jersey, State** (of), **Controller's** (Office), **Inheritance** (and) **Gift Tax** (Division)

Foreign Agencies

12.51 Index and code names of foreign countries under the name of the country, followed by its designation (republic, union, kingdom, state, etc.,) and the name of the department, bureau, and division.

Department of Transportation Canada	**Canada Transportation** (Department of)
Ministry of Education of China	**China** (**Republic** of), **Education** (Ministry of)

Hints for Filing Government Names

12.52

1. Disregard for indexing purposes such words as *department, commission, bureau,* and *board* that appear within names of government agencies. However, such titles must be coded on all records and typed on file folders for proper identification.

2. Each significant word in the name of a governmental agency is a separate indexing unit. The more words there are in a name, the more indexing units it will have.

3. Disregard for indexing purposes words such as *the, and, for, by,* and *on* appearing within names of government agencies. However, such words must be coded on records and typed on file folders for proper identification. (*The* appearing at the beginning of a name is written in parentheses and placed at the end of the name; *the* appearing in the middle of a name is written in parentheses and placed in its proper sequence within the name. Other words are written in parentheses and placed in their proper sequences within the names.)

4. Index and code names of government agencies by the name of the city, county, state, or nation; then by the major department; then by the name of the bureau, division, commission, or board. (These subdivision names vary from city to city and from state to state. Therefore, it is important to refer to a state government organizational manual or the local telephone directory to determine the major departments and their subdivisions.)

5. Refer to the *United States Government Organizational Manual* published annually by the Government Printing Office, Washington, DC 20402, for organizational charts of all federal government agencies.

6. Refer to local telephone directories and state organizational manuals for guidelines in determining names of major governmental agencies and their various subdivisions.

7. Do not confuse names of government agencies with names of private organizations that may include the name of a city, town, state, or the words "United States."

United States Steel Company or U.S. Steel Company	Pasadena Chamber of Commerce
U.S. Chamber of Commerce	Cincinnati Iron Works
Idaho Manufacturing Co.	Los Angeles Paper Mfg. Co.

8. Establish a separate file for each government agency apart from other correspondence files if an organization does business with one or more government agencies.

9. Establish a separate file for each country apart from other correspondence files if an organization does business with one or more foreign governments.

10. Follow the alphabetic indexing rules for arranging names of government agencies in alphabetic order. Unless there is a large volume of correspondence for government agencies, combine all correspondence within the alphabetic files.

11. Establish files under the name most commonly referred to within the company; cross reference to other possible names.

Example: Internal Revenue Service

File: United States Government, Treasury (Department), Internal Revenue Service

Cross Reference: Internal Revenue Service

See: United States Government, Treasury (Department)

12. Maintain a consistent system of indexing, coding, and filing records for each government agency.

Numeric Filing System

12.53 The numeric filing system involves arranging correspondence, cards, business forms, and documents by the number system, which permits quick and easy identification of records in sequential order and prevents the duplication that often occurs in alphabetic systems.

COMPONENTS

12.54 Numeric filing systems include these elements.

1. Main numeric file, where all records are stored in numeric sequence with numeric guides and folders bearing numeric captions.

2. Miscellaneous alphabetic files, where records are temporarily stored until five or more pieces of correspondence have accumulated for any one correspondent.

3. Alphabetic card index, containing index cards for all customers and correspondents with important information on each company and individual together with the file numbers assigned.

4. Numeric register or log, listing in numeric sequence all numbers assigned to correspondents and the dates files were created.

RULES FOR CONSECUTIVE NUMERIC FILING

12.55 1. Index each digit in a number as a separate unit. The larger the number, the more indexing units a number will have.

142	1	4	2		
1,411	1	4	1	1	
26,401	2	6	4	0	1

2. Compare each number *digit by digit* until a difference is found.

3470	3	4	**7**	0
3465	3	4	**6**	5
3219	3	**2**	1	9

3. Compare the second and subsequent indexing units only when the first units are identical.

4. Disregard for indexing purposes the comma appearing within numbers.

2,546	2	5	4	6
7,002	7	0	0	2

5. Disregard for indexing purposes the hyphens appearing within numbers.

12-45-60	1	2	4	5	6	0
20-95-08	2	0	9	5	0	8
67-33-29	6	7	3	3	2	9

Exception: Some numbers are preceded by a numeric prefix. Such a prefix must be retained as a complete unit during the indexing and coding steps.

12-4560	12	4	5	6	0
20-9508	20	9	5	0	8
67-3329	67	3	3	2	9

6. File records in ascending order; that is, a smaller number is always filed before a larger one.

7. File records in chronological sequence when there are several papers for the same correspondent. The most recent correspondence is placed on top of the file.

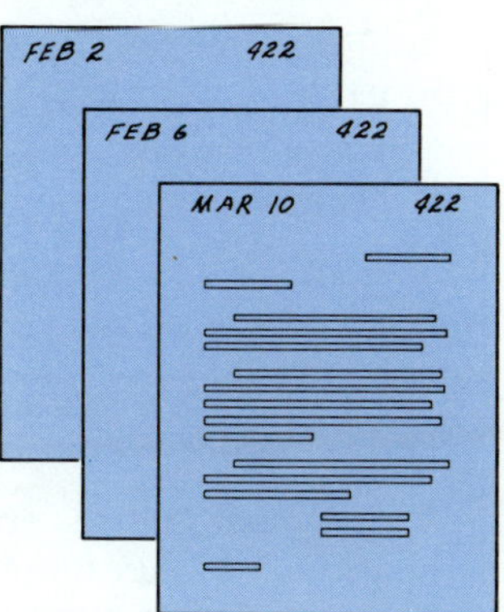

TERMINAL DIGIT FILING

12.56 Terminal digit filing is a numeric filing system in which records are arranged according to the last, or terminal, digits rather than the first units. This system is advantageous for large systems with file numbers of five digits or more.

The advantages of the terminal digit filing system are that files are evenly distributed throughout the system, and file cabinets and drawers can be permanently numbered.

File numbers are assigned in the usual manner—in consecutive sequence as listed in the numeric register—but the numbers are read from right to left. The last two digits—the terminal digits—determine the file drawer number; the middle two digits determine the file folder number in that drawer; and the first digits determine the sequence within the file folder.

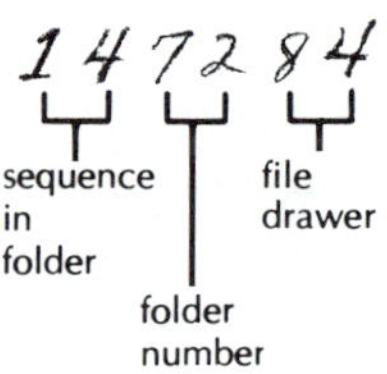

Rules for Terminal-Digit Numeric Filing

12.57 1. Read numbers in groups of two from right to left. (Numbers with more than six digits may be read in groups of three from right to left.)

2. Index each digit in a number as a separate unit, even though the numbers are read in groups from right to left.

497022 becomes	227049			
File drawer number:	22	2	2	
Folder number:	70	7	0	
Sequence in folder:	49	4	9	
6853107 becomes	1075368			
File drawer number:	107	1	0	7
Folder number:	53	5	3	
Sequence in folder:	68	6	8	

3. Index and code records according to the numeric filing rules.

4. File records according to drawer number, folder number, and sequence within the folder.

5. File records in ascending numeric order; that is, a record bearing a smaller number is always filed before a record bearing a larger number—both in terms of folder number and sequence within a folder.

6. File records in chronological order with the most recent item on top, when there is more than one item of correspondence for an individual or company.

HINTS FOR NUMERIC FILING, CONSECUTIVE OR TERMINAL DIGIT

12.58 1. All numbers in a group should have the same number of digits to be compared. Numbers that may appear to be identical should be carefully checked; they could be only similar.

1177110	681144092
117710	6811144092

2. Compare only one indexing unit at a time when arranging papers in numeric sequence. Work with one part of a number at a time to avoid confusing the digits.

3. Sort papers *alphabetically* first so file numbers may be obtained easily and systematically within the alphabetic card index.

4. Sort papers into numeric sequence *before* filing. This saves significant time during the filing process.

5. Begin by sorting papers into small groups by numbers (rough sorting), then sort into numeric sequence by groups. The larger the group of papers or the larger the range of numbers, the more times sorting must be done. Sorting can be accomplished more easily when working with smaller groups of papers.

6. Code each item of correspondence numerically by writing the file number in the upper right corner of each record. This enables a file worker to file and refile records easily.

1 2 3
BR BUILT-RITE CONTAINER CORPORATION 243701

1600 Hyatt Parkway / Atlanta, Georgia 30301 / (912) 337-4500

7. Code each card alphabetically by underlining each indexing unit in the name of the company or individual. This information will stand out so file numbers can be obtained quickly.

Subject Filing System

12.59 The subject filing system is based on the arrangement of records by topic names, or subject classifications, rather than by names of individuals, companies, or geographic locations.

This system works best when records are stored and retrieved according to categories or classifications of information. It follows alphabetic filing rules except that the captions on file folders are names of subjects.

ENCYCLOPEDIC ARRANGEMENT

12.60 A subject file with an encyclopedic arrangement consists of major subject headings with each subject further separated into divisions and subdivisions. Used for larger files, this arrangement is advantageous where small topic divisions are desirable. The components of a subject filing system with an encyclopedia arrangement are:

1. **Main subject files,** containing records on various subjects filed alphabetically by subject captions and divided into divisions and subdivisions.

2. **Relative index** (either an index card file or a typewritten list), showing all the subject headings/captions and the various classifications or sudivisions under each major subject used within the filing system.

DICTIONARY ARRANGEMENT

12.61 A subject file with a dictionary arrangement consists of files set up for the major subjects only, with no breakdown into divisions. This arrangement is advantageous for smaller files, where a person can file or retrieve records without having to check the relative index.

RULES FOR SUBJECT FILING

12.62 1. Follow the indexing and coding rules for the alphabetic filing system, except file by subject names.

2. Each significant word in a subject name is a separate indexing unit.

	First	*Second*
Sales Records	Sales	Records
Production Schedules	Production	Schedules

3. The major subject heading or caption is the first indexing unit(s), followed by the division heading or caption and the subdivision heading, if any.

4. Index and code items of correspondence by writing the subject captions in the upper right corner of the record.

5. File records in chronological order within each subdivision without regard for grouping correspondence from one individual or company. The most recent correspondence is placed on top of the file.

HINTS FOR SUBJECT FILING

12.63 1. Use key words for major subject headings.

Production Schedules instead of Schedules for Production
Expense Reports instead of Reports of Expenses

2. Determine major subject headings and add divisions and subdivisions as the file expands.

Major subject heading:	**Advertising**
Division Headings:	Advertising—**Agencies**
	Advertising—**Newspapers**
	Advertising—**Television**

3. Sort records by major subject headings first, then by divisions within the major subject headings.

4. Code records with their subject headings and divisions; this saves time during filing and refiling of papers.

5. File all related papers under one major subject, cross referencing where necessary under related topics.

Television Ad Agencies **See Advertising—Television**

Geographic Filing System

12.64 The geographic filing system is based on the arrangement of records by names of cities, counties, states, and/or countries, then by the name of the individual or company within each geographic location.

This system is used when information needs to be filed and retrieved by geographic locations—such as district offices, salespersons' territories, and store locations—rather than by names of individuals, companies, or subjects.

RULES FOR GEOGRAPHIC FILING

12.65 1. Index and code with the name of the state as the first indexing unit(s), followed by the name of the city or town, then the name of the individual or company.

Alexandria Pharmacy, Norfolk, Virginia
Lupino Galleries, Lexington, Virginia

Indexing units:	Virginia	Lexington	Lupino	Galleries
	Virginia	Norfolk	Alexandria	Pharmacy

2. Use the street name as an identifying element when the state, city or town, and correspondents' names are identical.

Cheeseboro Electronics, East Armour Boulevard, Kansas City, Missouri

Cheeseboro Electronics, Linwood Boulevard, Kansas City, Missouri

Indexing units:

Missouri	Kansas City	Cheeseboro	Electronics	(Armour)
Missouri	Kansas City	Cheeseboro	Electronics	(Linwood)

3. Code each item of correspondence by circling the names of the state and city or town, then underlining each indexing unit in the name of the correspondent.

<u>*Unique*</u> <u>Office</u> <u>Supplies</u>

909 EMERYVILLE HIGHWAY • OAKLAND, CALIFORNIA 94608

4. Index and code miscellaneous correspondence by the name of the city or town, then alphabetically by the name of the correspondent.

5. Sort records by the state names first, then sort by city or town names.

6. File papers by city or town name, then alphabetically by correspondents' names.

7. File papers within folders in chronological order with the most recent papers on top when there are several items for the same correspondent.

8. File records for an individual correspondent in a separate folder when five or more items have accumulated for that correspondent.

9. Create a separate folder for a city or town when five or more items of correspondence have accumulated for that city or town.

10. File papers in miscellaneous alphabetic folders behind each city or town name until five or more items have been accumulated for the same city or town.

Reading File

12.66 A reading file consists of an extra carbon copy (or photocopy) of each piece of correspondence filed in chronological order with the most recent correspondence on top. The file is kept in a notebook for quick reference.

Correspondence in the reading file is not maintained for more than six months, depending on the volume and the need to refer to previous correspondence. Papers are discarded on a regular basis so the file does not become cumbersome.

Tickler File

12.67 A tickler file or system is a follow-up or reminder file to show what tasks need to be completed, or followed up on, during the month or year.

This file, usually a 5″ × 3″ or 6″ × 4″ card file, is arranged chronologically by months and days. The reminder notices are arranged in order behind guides for the months. All notices for the current month are placed in the front of the file behind guides for the days. As each day arrives, notices for that day are removed and acted upon. The guide for that day is moved to the back of the file, where notices may begin to accumulate for subsequent periods of time.

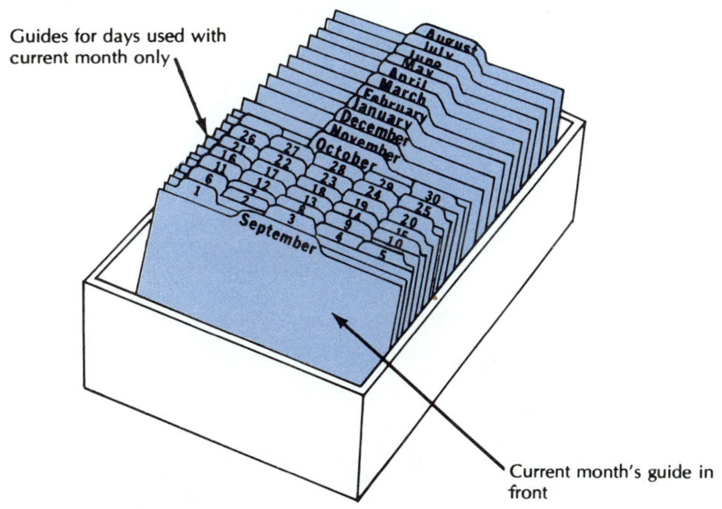

FIGURE 12-2. TICKLER FILE

A tickler file may also be maintained in a notebook where information is written about duties or responsibilities that should be performed on certain dates. This record must be maintained on a daily basis, like the tickler file above, and items should be crossed out or initialed to indicate that action has been taken.

Hints for Finding Misplaced Files

12.68 When a piece of correspondence or a file folder has been misplaced, much time can be spent trying to locate it. Develop a systematic method for locating correspondence or a file:

1. Look in the desk trays on your desk and your employer's desk.

2. Look through the folder to see if the documents are improperly arranged.

3. Look in the folders immediately in front of and behind the proper folder.

4. Look in the *spaces* immediately in front of, behind, and under the proper folder.

5. Look under names that have similar spellings or pronunciations (for alphabetic filing systems).

6. Look under other possible indexing units (for alphabetic filing systems).

7. Look under names or subjects that might be related to the misplaced correspondence, such as possible cross references.

8. In a numeric filing system, look under every possible numeric arrangement.

9. In geographic filing systems, look under similar names in other cities or states.

Thirteen

Office Procedures

Organizing Work

13.1 The systematic organization of work responsibilities places an office employee in command of the job. Good organization is knowing how to make the best use of available time; organizing work on a day-to-day basis helps to maintain a high rate of production. Follow these general suggestions.

1. Set aside a small block of time at the end of each day to **plan** the next day's work. Anticipate important deadlines, prepare for a meeting, plan for additional personnel needs, and be ready for the next day's work.

2. Make a **list** of the specific jobs or tasks that need to be handled. Such a list helps determine the priority of work to be done and serves as a reminder of work to be completed.

3. **Check off** each item as the task is completed. Seeing what is left to be done will help keep the work moving along and keep you organized to complete these jobs.

4. Establish a **routine** for performing routine work to save time, motion, and energy.

5. Prepare a **timetable** and a list of the routine tasks that must be performed on a daily, weekly, or monthly basis.

6. Use a notebook or a 5 × 3 inch card index file to maintain a **record** of those papers or correspondence requiring action that have been routed to others in the office.

7. Use a **notebook** to jot down reminders such as specific tasks to be done; errands to be run; and people to see, call, or write.

8. Place each major job in a separate **file folder** to keep it from prying eyes and to keep related papers together.

Word Processing

13.2 Word processing is a concept involving the processing of an idea. The person who originates an idea to be conveyed is called a **word originator** (or dictator). The idea in its raw form is called **input,** and the end product of processing is called **output.** The output is produced in typewritten, printed, or copied form.

Input is generated through various machine dictation devices and shorthand dictation skills. (See Sections 13.3 to 13.10.)

Hints for producing typewritten work are discussed in Sections 13.26 to 13.42.

Reprographic Processes are discussed in Sections 13.11 to 13.25.

MACHINE DICTATION SKILLS

13.3 Machine dictation involves the word originator (or dictator) initiating and transmitting information into a dictation machine that records the exact message. Machine dictation also involves a secretary or typist transcribing directly from dictation recorded on a tape, belt, card, or disc. A transcription machine is used by the transcriber to transform the spoken message into written form.

13.4 **Routine dictation** responds to requests for information or action, follows up on telephone calls, gives instructions to staff on day-to-day activities. Routine dictation includes short memoranda and letters that need little planning or preparation.

13.5 **Creative (original) dictation** initiates or responds to lengthy or detailed letters, memoranda, and reports that may require several drafts and much editing before the final document is typed.

13.6 **Top-priority dictation** initiates or responds to urgent requests for information or action.

13.7 **Administrative dictation** communicates information or directions of an administrative nature to the staff.

MACHINE DICTATION-TRANSCRIPTION

13.8 1. Follow the operating instructions for using dictation-transcription equipment. Some machines are both dictation and transcription units, while others are separate units.

2. Learn how to handle, process, and store the medium used for dictation—cassette tape, magnetic belt, magnetic card, or magnetic disc.

3. When taking work from a new word originator, determine his or her preferences for a particular format, use of punctuation, etc.

4. Use a folder with a pocket to separate the dictation on each card, belt, disc, or tape. Any notes or related correspondence can be kept in the folder.

5. When transcription work is done for more than one person, keep separate folders for each person and label them clearly.

6. Separate used cards, belts, tapes, and discs from new ones. (If all dictated materials are to be filed rather than reused immediately, file them immediately after transcription. Label each with the date of dictation, the name of the word originator, and your name.)

7. Organize materials efficiently so that stationery and other papers and supplies are accessible. Return the eraser and other correction devices to the same place after each use.

8. Use the eraser and other correction devices so that mistakes cannot be detected.

9. Learn to work with one margin setting for all letters; learn to adjust the lines between letter parts for shorter or longer letters. (Learn to "read" the indicator strip with each dictation to determine the length of material to be transcribed.)

10. Keep a dictionary, word division manual, or reference manual available for reference. Learn to use them properly.

11. During transcription, have all correspondence to which you need to refer assembled in the same order as the dictation.

12. Listen to the dictated material whenever necessary before transcribing. Familiarize yourself with the contents and any changes that may have been made during dictation. Be alert to any special notations or instructions that may have been added, either in the middle or at the end of the dictation.

13. Type a rough draft of lengthy or technical material if necessary, so that the word originator has an opportunity to review the material and make any changes.

14. During transcription, try to keep the typewriter moving —use the controls on the transcription machine to stop, start, or replay the dictated material.

15. Do not hesitate to go to the word originator to clarify spellings of names or addresses or to verify other information.

16. Proofread all work before removing it from the typewriter; corrections are easier to make.

TAKING SHORTHAND DICTATION

13.9 To make the most effective use of the time spent during the dictation session, follow these guidelines:

1. Decide on a regular time of day for the dictation session. Most employers and secretaries prefer the morning hours when they are fresh and alert. Dictation after the morning mail delivery is a convenient time.

2. Have all necessary supplies assembled in one place and ready for dictation—notebooks, two pens, a color pencil, paper clips, and a correspondence folder.

3. Each day, date the notebook at the bottom of the first clean page. This facilitates locating old notes. Marking notes with *a.m.* and *p.m.* is also helpful.

4. Keep a rubber band around the used pages of the notebook so it can be opened to the next clean page.

5. When dictation is taken from more than one person, keep separate notebooks and correspondence folders for each and label them clearly.

6. Use a folder for correspondence to be signed by the dictator. In this way, all correspondence and attachments are kept together for signature.

7. Keep a folder on your desk for all pending work.

8. Keep an extra notebook on your desk to jot down messages or instructions or to take dictation on the spot.

9. Use a pen. It increases dictation speed and ease, and transcription speed is increased because notes are more easily read.

10. During the dictation session, number each letter in your notebook and code it with its related correspondence. Place the correspondence face down in the folder so everything will be in sequence for transcription.

11. Skip two or three lines between each dictated letter for those special notations and instructions that the dictator may mention after the dictation.

12. If the dictator is one to change his or her mind frequently, use only one column of each notebook page. Any changes can be made in the other column without disturbing other notes.

13. Number each insertion made in your notes, and indicate its place in your notes by a caret (^). A blue pencil notation can be spotted readily.

14. Do not hesitate to ask the dictator about the spelling of a name or address that may not be in the files.

15. Use a color pencil (preferably red) to flag important correspondence to be transcribed first or to call attention to special notations. Fold the relevant notebook page so the edge sticks out; then you can find this urgent letter more quickly.

16. If interrupted by telephone or by a visitor during dictation, review your notes—especially the last few sentences. After the interruption, you may need to review the last few sentences before receiving additional dictation.

17. Write down changes, special notations, and instructions. Don't trust your memory.

18. When the dictation session is over, make an effort to transcribe notes immediately. If this cannot be done, review your notes and remind yourself to raise any questions that might require clarification.

SHORTHAND TRANSCRIPTION

13.10

1. As soon after the dictation session as possible, review your notes and locate any priority correspondence that should be transcribed first.

2. Always read through your notes before attempting to transcribe. Insert any necessary punctuation marks and paragraphs if they were not dictated. Obtain correct spelling(s) of proper names, cities, and states; obtain correct addresses and ZIP code numbers; verify days, dates, and amounts of money.

3. Keep your eyes on the shorthand notes while transcribing. This increases transcription speed.

4. Organize your materials efficiently. Keep stationery and other papers and supplies accessible. Return your eraser and correction materials to the same place after each use.

5. Use the eraser and other correction devices so mistakes cannot be detected.

6. Learn to work with one margin setting for all correspondence; learn to adjust the lines between letter parts for shorter or longer letters.

7. Draw a diagonal line through the shorthand notes after the letter is transcribed, so you won't have to read them again.

8. Keep a dictionary, word division manual, or reference manual available.

9. When transcribing, have all correspondence to which you need to refer assembled in the same order as the dictation. (The correspondence should already have been placed face down in the folder used during dictation.)

10. Proofread all work before removing it from the typewriter; corrections are easier to make.

REPROGRAPHIC PROCESSES

13.11

Reproducing information for distribution—by using carbon paper, photocopiers, mimeograph or liquid duplicating machines, or offset printing—is an important aspect of the output phase in the word processing cycle.

Each office has its own reprographic processing needs. The following questions should be asked in determining the most appropriate method of reproducing information.

1. What quality of copy is desired?

2. How many copies are required?

3. How much can be spent on materials and labor?

4. How soon must copies by ready?

Carbon Paper

13.12 Up to ten legible copies of a document can be made using carbon paper. At least one carbon copy of correspondence for the files is required in most offices, and several carbon copies of documents are often required for distribution to all persons concerned.

It is important that carbon copies be legible and neat, with no wrinkles or creases. Since photocopies may be made from carbon copies later, it is essential that any mistakes be corrected at the time the original is corrected.

Carbon copies are usually prepared on onionskin paper, manifold paper, or colored paper of a lighter weight than company letterhead stationery.

The grade of carbon paper used depends on the number of copies made at one typing and the number of times carbon is used. Typewriter carbon paper is different from carbon paper used with pen or pencil.

13.13 **Carbon packs.** A carbon pack consists of alternating layers of stationery, carbon paper, and carbon copy paper (called second sheets). A carbon pack is assembled and inserted into the typewriter as follows:

1. Place the second sheet on the desk or on top of the typewriter. Place a sheet of carbon paper, carbon side down, on top of the second sheet. Place the letterhead or other stationery on top.

2. Lift the entire pack up so that the back of the second sheet is facing you. Tap the pack to straighten the sheets.

3. Hold the pack with the back of the second sheet facing you and drop it into the typewriter, using the paper release lever to insert the pack into position.

4. Adjust the carbon copy indicator on the typewriter to loosen the pressure against the cylinder if several carbon copies are made.

5. To remove the carbons from the pack, hold the upper left edge of the entire pack and shake the carbons from the pack. (Most carbon papers are notched in the upper left and lower right corners for ease in removing from packs.)

Hints on Using Carbon Paper

13.14 1. Do not handle carbon paper more than is necessary.

2. When carbon paper is not in use, place it flat in its box in a cool, dry place.

3. Keep carbon paper carbon-side down on a protective sheet on the desk between uses to prevent carbon from smudging the desk, other papers, or clothing.

4. When inserting and removing a carbon pack from the typewriter, use the paper release lever to prevent typewriter roller marks on the copies and wrinkles or creases on the carbon paper.

5. Keep hands clean—use a non-greasy lotion or cream to prevent carbon from accumulating on the fingers.

6. Throw away carbons as soon as copies begin to be illegible. (Faded copies are difficult to read and to photocopy.)

7. Use carbon paper that is one-half to one inch longer than the paper. It is easier to handle than carbon that is the same size as the stationery.

8. Always use an eraser shield (a plastic or metal guard that fits over the cylinder between the paper and the carbon paper) to prevent wearing out the carbon by rubbing against it during erasing.

9. Extend the life of carbon papers by alternating them from top to bottom to distribute their use more evenly.

10. Use the correct weight of carbon paper for the number of copies being made. Use lightweight carbon paper for several carbon copies; use medium-weight carbon paper for normal typing.

Photocopy Process

13.15 Photocopiers make it possible to reproduce copies of an existing record without preparing a master. They are widely used, both for their convenience and the high quality of copies produced.

The two most popular photocopying processes are the thermal and electrostatic.

13.16 **Thermal process.** The thermal process is a dry copying process that works on a heat and light principle. Heat-sensitive paper is inserted with the master into a thermofax (heat transfer) machine to produce the copy. The thermal copy is useful only for temporary copies because the paper is thin and sensitive to light and heat, and becomes brittle with age.

Advantages	Disadvantages
• Machine is easy to operate. • Copies are quickly made. • No special training is needed to operate the machine.	• Copies are not as clear as other methods. • Materials containing pen inks, rubber stamp marks, colors, and dittoed copies do not reproduce.

13.17 **Electrostatic process.** The electrostatic process includes the xerographic or transfer method and the direct method.

13.18 The **xerographic method** uses a light-reflection process where an original is "photographed" and the image is transferred from a drum to the copy paper. The image is then fused to the paper by heat.

Advantages	Disadvantages
• Copies are easy and fast to make. • Machine uses regular bond or duplicator paper.	• Equipment is expensive to operate. • Photographs, colors, and solid areas cannot always be reproduced.

13.19 **Direct method** photocopies are made by forming the image directly on the copy paper itself and then fusing the impression by heat.

Advantages	Disadvantages
• Machine is fast to operate. • Most colors can be copied. • Photographs, halftones, and solid areas can be reproduced.	• Specially coated paper must be used. • Copies are easily scratched.

Fluid (Liquid) Process

13.20 The fluid or liquid process is also referred to as the ditto or spirit duplicating process.

13.21 A **masterset** is used to prepare the copies. It consists of a sheet of special carbon-coated paper attached to a sheet of white paper. A thin protective sheet separates the two sheets until the master is to be used. The carbon substance is transferred to the back of the paper by writing, typing, or drawing on the front of the masterset.

When the masterset is separated and the prepared master is placed on the drum of the duplicating machine, the liquid takes some of the carbon off the master, thus producing the copies. Up to 300 clean, clear copies can be made with this process with proper machine adjustments.

Advantages	Disadvantages
• Copies can be made in quantity inexpensively. • Copies are legible and easy to read. • Masters can be stored and reused if few copies are run at a time. • Several colors are available. • The machine is easy to operate.	• A master must be prepared for each set of copies desired. • The number of copies obtained is limited. • Correcting errors on the master is time-consuming and messy. • Copies are not professional in appearance. • Copies cannot be photographed on many machines.

Stencil (Mimeograph) Process

13.22 The stencil or mimeograph process produces more professional-looking copies than the fluid process, and most kinds of material can be produced. Electronic stencil-cutting machines cut and transfer typewritten, handwritten, or drawn work onto a stencil master.

13.23 The **stencil master** consists of a waxy sheet of paper that does not absorb ink. When information is typed, drawn, or written on the master, it is actually cut onto the stencil. Electronic stencil-cutting machines transfer and cut information from a typewritten, handwritten, or drawn work, thus eliminating the need to prepare a stencil master.

The mimeograph machine allows the ink to go through the cuttings on the stencil master, and the impression is transferred to the paper copies. Up to 1,000 copies can be made from an average stencil; other qualities of stencils provide more copies.

Advantages

- Copies are inexpensive to make in quantities.
- Copies are professional looking and easy to read.
- Corrections are easy to make on the stencil.
- Copies can be reproduced on photocopying machines.
- Stencils can be stored for future use.

Offset Printing Process

13.24 The offset printing process is more time-consuming than the other processes, but it produces professional-looking copies.

Material is typed, drawn, or written on a paper master, which is then transferred to the plate by a photochemical process. Between 50 and 100 copies can be made with paper plates; up to 10,000 copies can be made with long-run metal plates.

Advantages

- High-quality, professional copies are obtained.
- All copies are of the same quality.
- Printing can be done in various colors.
- The master is filed for future use.

Disadvantages

- Cost of equipment is higher than other processes.
- Special training is needed to operate the machine.
- Cost of supplies and maintenance is higher than other machines.

Hints for Using Reprographic Processes

13.25 1. Do not make more copies than are needed.

2. Use a routing slip with one set of materials rather than preparing copies for everyone.

3. Do not use the photocopying machine indiscriminately.

   a. Use only when a single high-quality copy is required.

   b. Do not photocopy the same item more than once. Unless a perfect copy is required (which is seldom), a copy that is clear and legible will serve its purpose.

c. Make carbon copies of correspondence rather than photocopies unless a photocopier is easily accessible.

4. Use an appropriate reprographic process for the job, based on the quality of copies needed, quantity needed, cost factor, and time element (see Table 13-1).

5. Keep a log sheet of everyone using the photocopier—make everyone accountable for its use.

6. Determine the "needs" versus the "wants" of copying. Unless copies are necessary, they only clutter files and take up valuable office space.

Process	*Number of Copies*	*Supplies Cost Per Copy*
Carbon paper	1–10	Much less than 1 cent
Photocopy	1–10	1 cent to 10 cents
Fluid	10–300	Less than 1 cent, within suggested quantity range
Stencil	50–1,000	Less than ½ cent, within suggested quantity range
Printing (offset)	50–several thousand	Less than ½ cent, within suggested quantity range

TABLE 13-1. REPROGRAPHIC PROCESSES: COST COMPARISON

Joyce Kupsh, *Duplicating: Machine Operation and Decision Making* (Beverly Hills, Calif.: Glencoe Press, 1972).

Typing Hints

ASSEMBLING PRINTED LETTERS OR FORMS

13.26 If printed letters or forms must be assembled into sets for typing with carbon paper, collate forms into sets. Staple each set on the top of the page parallel to the top edge so the pack can be inserted easily into the typewriter.

Interleave carbon paper into the pack before typing.

Use spare minutes to assemble small supplies of these sets of letters or forms so they will be available when needed.

BLIND CARBON COPY

13.27 A blind carbon copy of a letter or memorandum is prepared when the writer does not want the addressee to know another person is receiving a copy of the communication (see also 7.60).

1. Type the entire letter or memorandum to the point on the page where the blind carbon copy (*bcc* or *bc*) notation is to be typed.

2. Disengage the paper release lever.

3. Pull the original letter and the first carbon paper out of the typewriter with one hand while the other hand holds the remaining pages and carbons in position.

4. Straighten the remaining pack of papers and carbons.

5. Type the blind carbon copy notation in its appropriate place on the page.

or

1. Type the entire letter or memorandum to the point on the page where the blind carbon copy notation is to be typed.

2. Insert a small piece of paper between the original and the type guide of the typewriter.

3. Move the carbon copy indicator back two or three notches to release the tension on the cylinder.

4. Type the blind carbon copy notation in its appropriate place.

CARBON COPIES

13.28 1. Make carbon copies of correspondence rather than photocopies; they are less expensive and less time consuming.

2. Use the back of incoming letters and memoranda for the carbon copy of a reply to the writer. This results in less paperwork.

CHAIN FEEDING ENVELOPES

13.29 Use this method when many envelopes are to be addressed; chain feeding allows a continuous supply of envelopes to be fed into the typewriter.

1. Place a stack of envelopes on the desk, address side down, with the flap end pointing away from you.

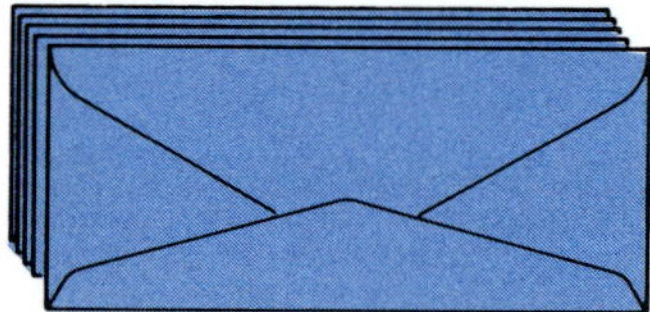

2. Pick up each envelope and drop it into the typewriter.

3. Type the first envelope address.

4. Insert a second envelope in the back of the typewriter immediately behind the first envelope.

5. Remove the first envelope using the cylinder knob and/or carriage return (carrier return) to bring the second envelope into typing position.

6. As each envelope is addressed, insert the next one to form a "chain."

COMPOSING AT THE TYPEWRITER

13.30 Save time by learning to compose short messages, letters, and memoranda as you type. This involves thinking and organizing thoughts at the typewriter.

1. Decide what needs to be written, jotting down notes as necessary.

2. Organize the ideas in your mind: important points, details, overall form, and the appropriate words.

3. Think and type simultaneously. Try to type the final communication the first time through. If changes are necessary, type them on the page; then use this page as a rough draft as you retype the communication in final form.

FOLDERS

13.31 Use various folders with pockets to keep work together and away from prying eyes.

1. Keep a folder for **WORK TO BE DONE.**

2. Keep a folder for your employer of things **TO BE SIGNED.**

FOLLOW-UP CORRESPONDENCE

13.32 When it is necessary to send a follow-up letter or memorandum, send a photocopy of the original correspondence with a handwritten note mentioning the follow-up. A standard form letter or printed reminder notice may also be used to save typewritten work.

GUIDE PAGE

13.33 A guide page is a specially ruled and/or numbered page containing guide lines or numbers to indicate the various margin settings for letters and reports. The guide page is placed behind the original page so lines and numbers are visible; the typist can see how much space is left on the page for side and bottom margins. (See Figure 13-1, p. 294.)

HANDLING SIMPLE INQUIRIES

13.34 Use incoming letters and memoranda to write responses or make simple inquiries. This eliminates dictation and transcription time and the need to create additional papers for the files.

INDEX CARDS AND LABELS

13.35 Fold a quarter-inch pleat in the center of a sheet of paper.

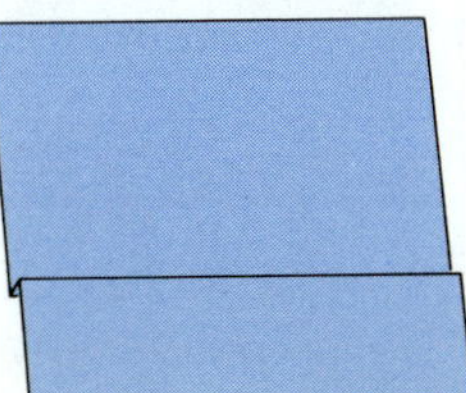

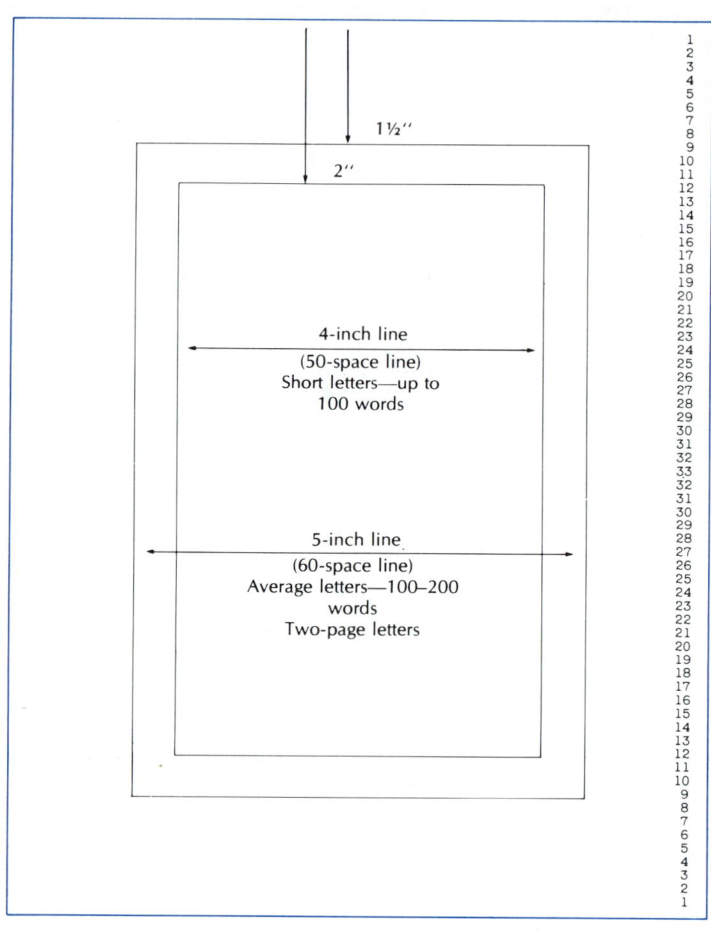

FIGURE 13-1. GUIDE PAGE

Insert the paper into the typewriter so the pleat is visible. Insert the index card or label inside the pleat. Roll the paper backward to type the desired information.

MARGIN SETTINGS

13.36 Use a standard margin setting for all letters. Adapt the margins for shorter letters by allowing more space between the letterhead and date, and date and inside address. Adapt for longer letters by leaving less space between these parts.

13.37 Use Table 13-2 to calculate margins for different paper and type sizes.

NAMES AND NUMBERS

13.38 Verify names, addresses, dates, and amounts *before* beginning to type the letter or memorandum in which they appear. It takes less time to verify this information beforehand than it does to retype a page of information.

	PICA (Pie-ka)	*ELITE (ay-leet)*
Determine your type size:		
It will look like this	Pica Type	Elite Type
There will be	10 spaces to an inch	12 spaces to an inch
On a sheet of paper 8½ inches long, your carriage position scale should read from	0–85	0–102
On a sheet of paper that is		
5½ inches (half sheet), there are	55 spaces	66 spaces
8½ inches (standard), there are	85 spaces	102 spaces
11 inches (standard lengthwise), there are	110 spaces	132 spaces
8 inches (official), there are	80 spaces	96 spaces
7¼ inches (executive), there are	72 spaces	87 spaces
6¾ inches (No. 6 envelope), there are	68 spaces	81 spaces
9½ inches (No. 10 envelope), there are	95 spaces	114 spaces
5½ inches (postal card), there are	55 spaces	66 spaces
When planning margins for a manuscript or report, it sometimes is necessary to convert inches to spaces.		
if there are		
4 inches in a line, there are	40 spaces	48 spaces
5 inches in a line, there are	50 spaces	60 spaces
6 inches in a line, there are	60 spaces	72 spaces
7 inches in a line, there are	70 spaces	84 spaces
Set the margins for a	Left – Right*	Left – Right*
40 space line at	22 – 62	30 – 70
50 space line at	17 – 67	25 – 75
60 space line at	12 – 72	20 – 80
70 space line at	7 – 77	15 – 85

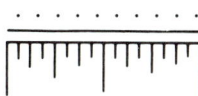

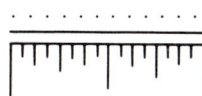

*You may wish to add 5 spaces to each right margin, allowing you to type 5 additional spaces after the bell rings.

TABLE 13-2. PLANNING MARGIN SETTINGS

Kenneth Zimmer and Vauncille Jones, *Basic Typewriting for the College Student* (Beverly Hills, Calif.: Benziger Bruce & Glencoe, 1972). Reprinted by permission.

OFFICE SUPPLIES

13.39 Keep office supplies such as stationery, carbon paper, second sheets, and envelopes within easy reach and organized in the desk drawer. Place them in the order in which they are to be assembled for typing. Use spare time to replenish supplies, sharpen pencils, fill stapler, etc.

ROUGH DRAFTS

13.40 1. Type correspondence and business reports in final form at the first typing unless a rough draft is requested or necessary.

2. When material is to be typed from rough drafts that include special headings, indentions, or special features, refer to the files to locate similar projects to obtain the appropriate form and style.

3. If columns of information or figures are to be typed, insert a page from a previously typed table into the typewriter to determine the margin settings and tabulator stops. This eliminates the need to calculate the spacing.

TYPING TABLES

13.41 When high-priority work is to be typed and you are in the middle of typing statistical data in columnar form, jot down the numbers of margin settings, tabulator stops, and other spacing on the page so that you may return to the table quickly.

USING THE TELEPHONE

13.42 Use the telephone to obtain or to verify information urgently needed or when communication of technical or detailed information can more effectively be conveyed and discussed by telephone. (Be sure to take notes of the conversation and date and initial the notes for future reference.)

Proofreading

13.43 Proofreading is an essential skill that everyone should develop to ensure that correspondence, reports, and business forms sent within and outside the company will be error free. Proofreading involves four steps.

1. **Look at the overall document.** Is it attractively placed on the page? Is the general format correct? (If the answers are "No," it is not necessary to proofread further.)

2. **Scan the document for obvious mistakes.** Are there any typographical errors, errors in spacing, or incorrectly divided words at ends of lines? (If the answer is "Yes," can these errors be easily corrected?)

3. **Read the entire document for meaning.** Does the information make sense? Is it grammatically correct? (If the answer is "No," how can the information be rewritten?)

4. **Verify names, addresses, numbers,** and **amounts.** Are words and names spelled correctly? Are the numbers and amounts correct?

Proofreading Techniques

13.44 1. Concentrate on the material being proofread. If necessary, proofread a second time.

2. Proofread with another person on tables, charts, graphs, legal descriptions, measurements, and other technical information. (The person who typed the material should read from the *original* material while the second person proofreads the typewritten copy.)

3. Place the original and copy side by side and proofread using two fingers—one on the original and the other following the typewritten copy. (As the bottom portion of a page is proofread, one page may be overlapped to make the distance between the original and the copy easier for the eye to read.)

4. Place a light check mark with a pencil in the right margin next to the line where an error exists. (For a lengthy document, it may be more desirable to place a paper clip at the right edge to spot errors on each page.)

5. Try to correct a mistake if it can be corrected in an acceptable manner. Determine how much needs to be corrected and retype the page if necessary.

6. Whenever a page needs to be retyped, do not type by reading from the incorrect sheet. Instead, read from the original. (This prevents compounding errors or making the same mistake again.)

7. When extensive corrections need to be made, use standard proofreading symbols (see section 6.47).

Making Corrections

13.45 There are five ways to correct errors on typewritten work; eraser, correction fluid, correction paper, correction tape, and self-correcting typewriter. Each method has its advantages and disadvantages (see Table 13-3).

ERASER

13.46 The eraser requires the most time and skill. Erasing is a permanent method that involves the use of several "tools"—an eraser suitable for the type and color of paper used, an erasing guide, and a plastic or metal eraser shield.

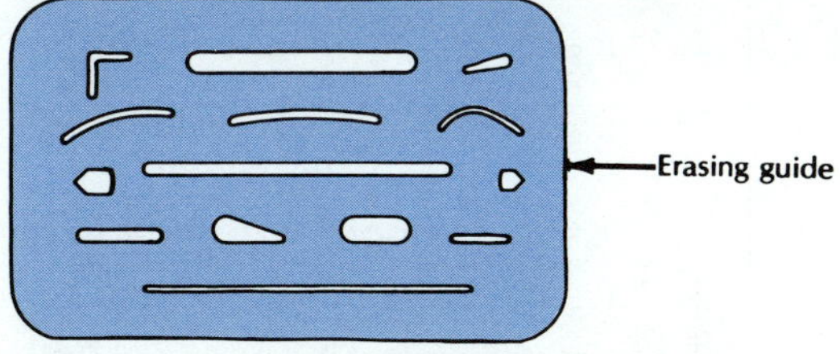

Erasing Techniques

13.47 Before beginning to erase an error, study it carefully to determine whether it can be corrected easily or whether the page should be retyped. It is more efficient to retype the entire page than to spend several minutes, for example, erasing several words or a line.

1. Move the carriage (or carrier) to the extreme left or right side. Use the margin release key.

2. Raise the paper bail or pull it forward.

3. Advance the paper several lines to allow space to make the correction. (If the error appears on the top part of the page, advance the paper forward; if the error appears on the bottom part of the page, roll the paper backward.)

4. Place an eraser shield over the letter or word to be erased so that only the letter or word is visible. (See 13.46.)

5. Hold the paper firmly in place with clean fingers so the paper does not slip.

6. Use a typewriter eraser (abrasive) for originals and a pencil eraser (nonabrasive) for carbon copies.

7. Sharpen the eraser to a blunt end, not to a point.

8. Use short, up-and-down strokes while erasing. Brush or blow away eraser crumbs.

9. Roll the paper to its original position, check the alignment of the line of typing, and type the correct letter or word. Strike the correct letter or word again if necessary to obtain an even stroke on the page.

10. Keep erasers clean by rubbing them on a sheet of paper or emery board after each use.

11. Return the eraser and correction materials to the same place after each use.

Erasing Original and Carbon Copies

13.48

1. Erase last carbon copy first, using techniques listed in 13.47.

2. Place an eraser shield behind the next-to-last copy.

3. Erase the next-to-last carbon copy; then remove the eraser shield and place it behind the next carbon copy.

4. Proceed in the same manner to erase all carbon copies.

5. Place the eraser shield behind the original and correct the original.

CORRECTION FLUID

13.49 Correction fluid is perhaps the easiest way to correct typing errors. However, this method also takes skill to use, and its uses are limited.

The main advantage of correction fluids is that they can be used to block out a letter, a word, or a line from typewritten, handwritten, or printed material and then be photocopied with no trace of the error on the copies. The original is used as the master and kept in the files until additional photocopies are desired.

Correction fluids are available in many colors to match the various colors of paper and card stock in use.

Correction fluids should not be used on original correspondence or reports unless the material is to be photocopied. The fluid does cover up the error, but it can be detected on the page.

Using Correction Fluids

13.50 1. Roll the cylinder forward or backward several lines so the error is visible.

2. Shake the correction fluid well.

3. Remove excess fluid from the brush.

4. Apply sparingly by dotting the fluid over the error.

5. Replace the cap on the bottle to prevent drying up.

6. Allow the fluid to dry thoroughly. (A water-base fluid takes longer to dry than an oil base.)

7. Return paper to the line of typing and correct the mistake.

CORRECTION PAPER

13.51 Correction paper is used for making corrections on originals and carbon copies. This chalk-coated paper is available in all colors but is not a permanent correction device.

Correction paper must be used in conjunction with an eraser. A correction made with this chalk-coated paper is detectable on the original as well as any photocopies.

Use correction paper only when the correction involves letters of the same size and shape (e.g., to correct an "e" to an "a").

Do not use correction paper when the correction involves letters that are different sizes or shapes. Use an eraser to erase all or part of the letter and type the correct letter.

Do not use correction paper when the correction involves a mistyped letter between two words. Use an eraser, as the letter with the chalk coating is quite detectable.

	Eraser	CORRECTION FLUIDS Chemical	CORRECTION FLUIDS Water-base	Correction Paper	Correction Ribbon	Correcting Typewriter
Time Required	Done correctly, the most time consuming method.	Fast-dry formula dries in 10–12 secs.	Takes about 45 secs. to dry.	Extra backspace time is needed.	Extra backspace time is needed.	Fast.
Permanency	Permanent.	Permanent.	Permanent.	Temporary; chalky substance may flake off in mail or file.	Temporary; chalky substance may flake off in mail or file.	Permanent.
Effect on Paper	Makes indention on paper surface; can make paper fuzzy.	Bonds itself to paper making like-new surface for typing.	Bonds itself to paper making like-new surface for typing.	Chalk-like substance adheres to paper.	Chalk-like substance adheres to paper.	Lifts carbon ink off paper, or covers carbon ink with chalk-like substance.
Technique Involved	Practice needed to acquire technique.	Practice needed to acquire technique.	Practice needed to acquire technique.	Little technique needed.	No technique needed.	Knowledge of correcting typewriter required.
Materials Required	Eraser, index cards, type cleaner, metal letter protector.	Bottle of correction fluid, thinner.	Bottle of correction fluid.	Appropriate type of correction paper for paper being corrected.	Correction ribbon.	Self-correcting typewriter, special ribbons.
Corrections on Colored Paper	Many times erases pigment; spots.	Comes in white and colors.	Comes in white and colors.	Comes in white and limited colors.	Comes in white only.	Corrects on all colors.
Other Possible Corrections	Corrects typewritten or pen errors; corrects before or after removed from typewriter.	Corrects typewritten or pen errors; corrects before or after removed from typewriter.	Corrects typewritten or pen errors; corrects before or after removed from typewriter.	Corrects only typewritten errors; once removed from typewriter, very difficult to reinsert.	Corrects only typewritten errors; once removed from typewriter, very difficult to reinsert.	Corrects only typewritten errors; once removed from typewriter, very difficult to reinsert.
Carbon Copies/ Photocopies	Corrects carbon copies; smears chemical surface on some photocopies.	Corrects carbon copies; can smear some photocopies.	Corrects carbon copies; will not smear photocopies.	Corrects carbon copies; will not correct photocopies.	Will not correct carbon copies or photocopies.	Will not correct carbon copies or photocopies.

TABLE 13-3. CORRECTION METHODS: ADVANTAGES AND DISADVANTAGES

Using Correction Paper

13.52 1. Backspace to the error.

2. Insert the correction paper over the error between the paper and the card holders.

3. Retype the incorrect letter to coat it with the chalk covering.

4. Remove the correction paper and check to see if the incorrect letter has been completely covered with chalk.

5. Backspace to the error and type the correct letter. Strike it again if necessary to obtain an even type.

CORRECTION TAPE

13.53 Correction tape is a thin strip of self-adhesive tape that comes in varied widths used to cover a letter, word, line, or paragraph. This device is used for making corrections on original work that will be photocopied and work on liquid duplicating masters.

Do not use correction tape on originals unless they are to be photocopied.

Using Correction Tape

13.54 1. Roll the cylinder forward or backward several lines so the error is visible and so the area of the error rests on the cylinder or against the top of the typewriter. (It may be desirable to remove the paper from the typewriter to make the correction.)

2. Tear off the appropriate length needed to cover the error.

3. Apply the tape over the error. To cover up an entire line, hold both ends of the tape to be sure the line is completely covered.

4. Return the paper to the line of typing and type the correct letter, word, or line.

SELF-CORRECTING TYPEWRITER

13.55 A self-correcting typewriter contains a special backspace-correction key that backspaces once to the error while changing the typing mode to "correction." The special cartridge contains the adhesive correcting ribbon that literally lifts the error off the page.

The correction made with this special typewriter is permanent.

Using a Self-Correcting Typewriter

13.56 1. Depress the backspace-correction key on the typewriter.

2. Retype the mistyped letter.

3. Type the correct letter.

Maintaining Office Calendars

13.57 Office calendars should be kept on a regular basis—daily, weekly, and/or monthly. They are essential in planning future events and in reviewing events of the past.

1. Maintain a monthly calendar to show at a glance the month's activities. Being able to look ahead to projects, important meetings, and deadlines increases office efficiency.

2. The secretary should maintain a weekly calendar in some detail to plan for the week's activities. In scheduling appointments and meetings, the secretary can work around other activities of the week.

3. A daily calendar or appointment book is a must for employer and secretary alike. Draw a line through the hours for each activity so you and the employer can anticipate the length of each meeting, schedule other appointments around those meetings, and arrange for work within the office.

4. Use the daily calendar for a tickler file also to remind you or your employer to follow up on a previous matter on a particular day.

5. Go through the calendars at the beginning of each month, or sooner if necessary, and write in standing appointments and meetings.

SCHEDULING APPOINTMENTS

13.58 Schedule appointments for the executive so they do not conflict with other activities. Some executives prefer to meet with clients at certain specified times, thus freeing other times for conferences and other office tasks.

Keep these guidelines in mind when appointments are being made.

1. Determine which people the executive wishes to see whenever they call for an appointment.

2. Determine which callers may see the executive without an appointment.

3. Determine an appropriate procedure for scheduling appointments and dealing with salesmen.

4. Determine which individuals the executive prefers not to see.

5. Determine whether the executive will accept telephone calls or other interruptions during meetings.

When a caller requests an appointment, these steps should be followed.

1. Determine the purpose of the proposed appointment. Is the matter something that the executive must handle or could someone else—perhaps the secretary—take care of the caller?

2. Determine the approximate length of the proposed visit. Is it something that can be handled in a few minutes, or is a longer conference necessary?

3. Determine whether others will be meeting with the executive and the caller so schedules can be coordinated if necessary.

4. Check to see whether the executive wants to make the appointment if he or she is available. In some instances, the matter may be handled over the telephone. If the executive is not available to confirm the appointment, make a tentative appointment with the caller and confirm it later.

5. Check the executive's calendar to determine the best time and date for such a meeting. Try not to schedule too many meetings in succession if possible.

6. Verify the time, date, and place with the caller. If the meeting is to take place somewhere other than the executive's office, verify this information too.

7. Immediately after the appointment has been verified, write it on the executive's calendar as well as on yours.

PREPARING FOR APPOINTMENTS

13.59 To help the executive prepare for the appointment, certain tasks should be performed before the caller arrives.

1. Remind the executive of the day's scheduled appointments.

2. Determine beforehand whether your presence will be needed either at the meeting or at your desk to handle work that may need to be processed.

3. Gather any necessary correspondence, files, or notes that may be needed by the executive during the meeting before each caller arrives.

CONFIRMING APPOINTMENTS

13.60 It is sometimes necessary to change the time and/or date of meetings previously arranged. Ideally, an appointment should be changed or canceled well in advance.

1. All appointments made can be considered confirmed at the time they are made unless the conversation indicates otherwise.

2. Confirm appointments when they involve luncheon dates, meetings out of the city or state, and meetings arranged several weeks or months ago.

3. When an appointment has to be changed, notify the other persons as soon as possible so other plans can be made and another time or date can be arranged.

4. When a meeting involves several individuals, be sure to notify everyone and verify the new time and date.

5. When in doubt about an appointment, always call the other person(s) to verify the appointment time and date. It is better to be safe than to have the employer miss the meeting.

Planning Meetings

13.61 Meetings—regular activities for most executives—enable participants to exchange ideas and establish a common basis for business operations.

Documents prepared for meetings and during meetings include the agenda, the minutes of the meeting, and the resolution.

AGENDA

13.62 An **agenda** is a list of the order of business for a meeting. The person calling the meeting prepares the tentative agenda based on the items to be discussed. An agenda should be distributed to the participants before the meeting begins—or mailed out well in advance if detailed or technical matters are involved.

Preparing an Agenda

13.63 An agenda usually includes the following:

- Call to order by presiding officer
- Roll call
- Reading of previous minutes
- Approval of minutes
- Reports of officers
- Reports of standing committees
- Reports of special committees
- Discussion of old business
- Discussion of new business
- Date, time, and place of next meeting
- Adjournment

MINUTES

13.64 The record of topics discussed at a meeting, decisions voted upon, and other actions is called the **minutes.** Taking minutes is more than a skill; it involves careful detail work and an ability to stay alert. The secretary is often called upon to take the minutes.

Taking Minutes

13.65 Here are some guidelines to follow in taking minutes effectively and accurately.

1. Before the meeting, review the agenda and other materials that will be covered to gain an understanding of what will be discussed (note that the agenda serves as an outline for taking the minutes).

2. Before the meeting begins, jot down participants' names and seating positions. It may be helpful to devise a coding system for each person, to facilitate identification of each speaker.

3. During the meeting, take notes on the important information discussed. Record all motions made and any accompanying discussion. Include the names of individuals who make and second motions. Record motions as they are made. Other points may be summarized.

4. Organize notes, keeping all discussion on any one subject together to simplify transcription of notes.

5. Do not hesitate to interrupt politely to ask for a restatement of the motion or to determine names needed for the minutes.

RESOLUTIONS

13.66 A **resolution** is a statement made by those at the meeting to express a group opinion. Resolutions are often formulated to express sympathy for the loss of a member or colleague, to show appreciation to an individual for the work contributed to the organization, and to recognize an outstanding person in the group.

Processing Mail

13.67 With the exception of correspondence marked *Personal* or *Confidential,* incoming mail should be opened, dated, and read as quickly as possible. Correspondence should be answered within **48 to 72 hours** of receipt. If an answer cannot be given immediately or if information must be obtained, notify the correspondent by telephone or letter so he or she knows the request is being processed.

OPENING MAIL

13.68 Use a letter opener. If mail often includes checks, money orders, or other valuable papers, open three sides of the envelopes to be sure everything has been removed.

13.69 Check to see if the writer's return address is included within the letter. If not, copy the address from the envelope onto the letter. Unless the postmark on the envelope is needed for legal purposes, the envelope should be discarded.

13.70 Verify any enclosures that should have been included with the letter. Notify the correspondent if the enclosure is missing.

SORTING MAIL

13.71 Sort mail into the following categories.

1. Urgent or special mail (registered, airmail, and special delivery)

2. Regular mail (first class mail, interoffice correspondence to be answered)

3. Routine mail (to be routed to others or answered by the secretary)

4. Bulletins, magazines, advertising circulars, etc.

DISTRIBUTING MAIL

13.72 Before placing correspondence or other information on the employer's desk, attach any previous correspondence or files that might be needed in processing the correspondence.

13.73 When mail is to be routed to another office or department for processing, the person who originally receives the mail should be responsible for it. Record in a notebook or 5″ × 3″ card file, the following information for all such correspondence.

name of correspondent
date of letter
subject matter
person or office where routed
date routed

ROUTING SLIPS

13.74 When bulletins, circulars, magazines, or supplements to books are routed on a regular basis to office personnel, use a printed routing slip to expedite the material from person to person.

13.75 The routing slips should list the name of everyone in the office who reads the information distributed. One form should be used to route items for everyone to see (containing everyone's name). Another form should be used to route items for a few to see (containing selected names).

Routing slips save time because lists do not have to be handwritten each time and each person sends the material directly to the next person.

Fourteen

Telephone, Telegraph & Postal Services

Telephone Services

14.1 The telephone is the most commonly used communication device in modern business. It is considered a necessity; the farthest sections of the country and the world are accessible by telephone. Correct use of the telephone saves time and reduces correspondence and travel costs.

USING THE TELEPHONE EFFECTIVELY

14.2 Follow the suggestions below to make your business calls as efficient, productive, and gracious as possible.

1. Speak distinctly to be understood. Pronounce your words carefully.

2. Take your time and speak slowly. Telephone speech should be neither too fast nor too slow.

3. Speak directly into the mouthpiece. Your voice is carried most clearly when you hold the transmitter directly in front of your mouth without touching the mouthpiece.

4. Use your normal tone of voice. A loud voice may irritate the person on the telephone and disturb those nearby. A weak voice can be equally annoying because the listener must strain to hear what is being said and may ask for frequent repetition.

5. Make your voice interesting, pleasant, and helpful.

6. Plan your conversation. Jot down notes on the topics to be discussed. This saves time for both the caller and the person called and creates a better impression of the caller.

7. Be sure you have the correct number. Keep an up-to-date list of frequently called numbers and use the telephone directory to locate others (call directory assistance—information—only if a number is not listed in the directory).

8. Place your own calls whenever possible instead of having another person call for you.

9. Let the telephone ring for about a minute to give the person called sufficient time to get to the telephone and answer.

10. Identify yourself and the name of the person or department to whom you wish to speak.

11. If the person called is not available, leave your name and telephone number, the time you can be reached, and a message or request to expedite the return of the call.

12. Always keep a note pad handy for messages. Indicate the name and number of the caller and the message. Obtaining the nature of the call helps the caller gather necessary information when the call is returned.

13. Always verify dates, numbers, amounts, and addresses over the telephone. Never hesitate to ask someone to repeat information.

14. Spell out any names that may be difficult to understand or to spell. Clarify each letter by giving a well-known word that begins with the same letter.

15. Pronounce numbers carefully.

16. Apologize for errors or delays but be sincere and natural.

17. Use the hold button when you must leave the line for even a few minutes. The telephone is very sensitive and can transmit extraneous office noises and conversations.

18. Suggest a time when the caller may call you again if you will be out of the office part of the day.

19. Do not argue with a caller, especially one who is upset or disturbed. Allow the caller to "let off steam" before asking questions or trying to solve the problem.

20. Check the time difference before calling across the nation. A three o'clock call from the west coast would be received at six o'clock on the east coast.

21. Let the caller hang up the receiver before you do. If *you* are the caller, put the receiver down gently.

OUTGOING CALLS

14.3 Outgoing calls include local and long-distance calls.

Local Calls

14.4 Local calls are those made between persons within the same city, community, or telephone service area without any additional cost to the caller. Local calls are placed by dialing the seven-digit number.

Long-Distance Calls

14.5 Long-distance calls are those made to any telephone outside the local service area. Charges are based on the distance of the call, the length of time the line is used, the type of call made, and the time of day the call is placed. Long-distance calls include toll calls, station-to-station calls, person-to-person calls, collect calls, and conference calls.

Consult the front pages of local telephone directories for information about each type of long-distance telephone service.

INCOMING CALLS

14.6 Follow these guidelines for handling incoming calls.

Receiving Calls

14.7 1. Answer the telephone promptly—by the end of the first or second ring if possible.

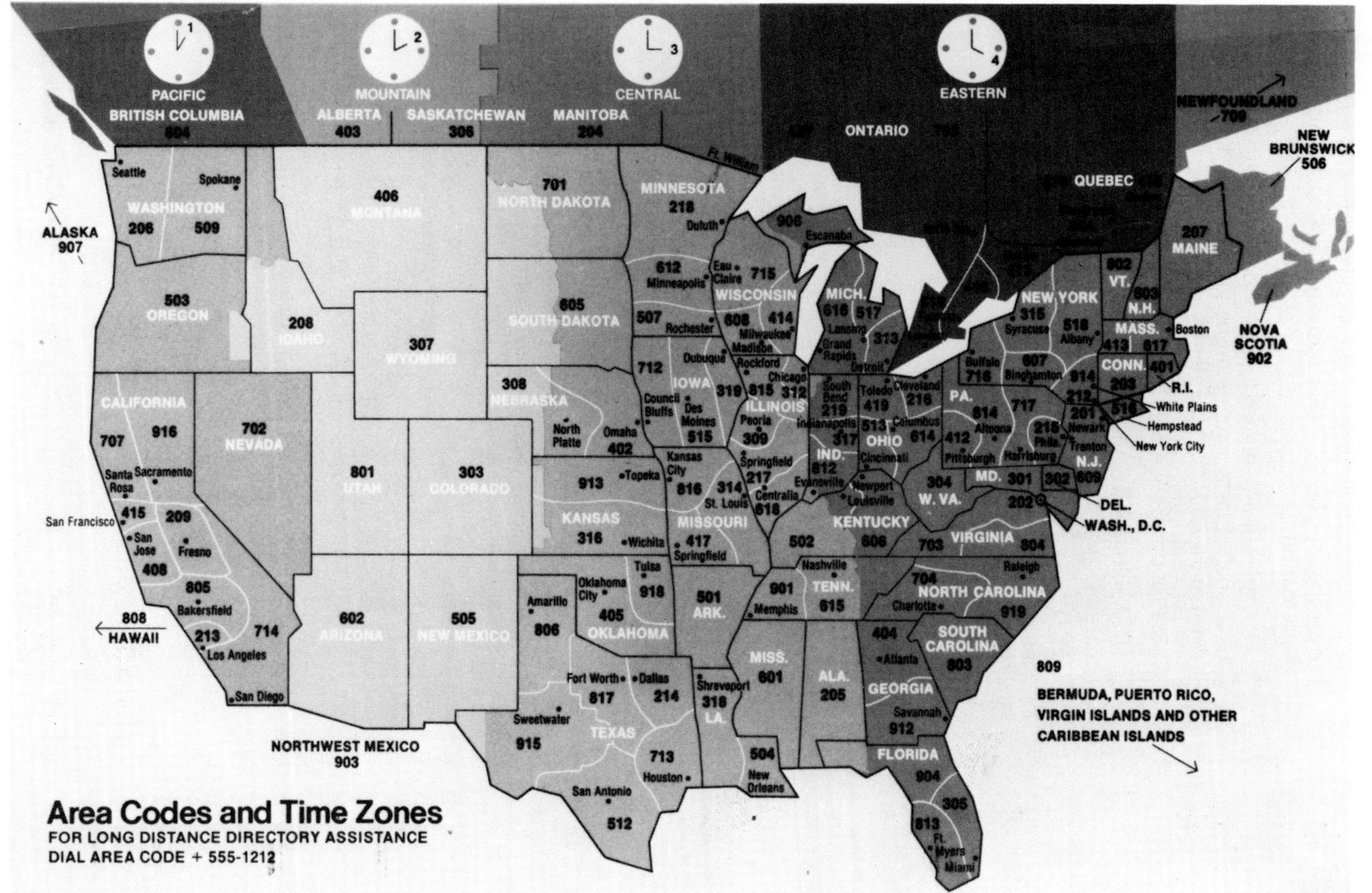

Photo courtesy of American Telephone & Telegraph Company.

2. Be ready to talk as soon as you pick up the receiver.

3. Greet the caller pleasantly and identify the office and yourself.

4. Jot down the appropriate information. Do not trust telephone information to memory.

5. Let the caller conclude the conversation.

Transferring Calls

14.8 1. Transfer a call only when it is necessary.

2. Be tactful with the individual, especially when he or she might have reached the incorrect number.

3. Explain why the transfer of the call is necessary; then indicate what you are going to do: "I will transfer you to our Sales Department. One moment, please."

4. Be sure the caller is willing to be transferred. It may be advisable for the caller to note the complete telephone number so he or she can place the call directly at a later time.

5. Transfer the call correctly.

Placing Calls on Hold

14.9 1. Explain why you would like the caller to hold and determine if the caller would care to wait.

2. Depress the hold button.

3. Check back on the caller periodically so the caller knows he or she has not been forgotten and that you are aware the person is still waiting on the line.

4. If the caller has waited more than a reasonable length of time, obtain his or her name and telephone number.

Answering Calls for Others

14.10 If the employees in the office are responsible for answering calls in each other's absence, be sure to tell the person in charge of the telephones when you will return to the office.

1. Take calls for others as efficiently and as courteously as you would expect them to take your calls.

2. Identify the office and yourself.

3. Inform the caller that the person called is not available. Offer to help the caller.

4. Note the caller's name and number.

5. Give the message to the person called promptly.

Telegraph Services

14.11 Telegrams are advantageous when speed and a printed record of transmitted message are essential. When a conversation between persons or companies is not necessary, telegrams may be the best choice for urgent messages.

Telegraph service is generally less expensive than the telephone when the message must travel a great distance. As a means of calling attention to the message, a telegram is superior to a written letter because people associate telegrams with important and urgent messages. And, unlike letters, telegrams can be sent to travelers on buses, trains, ships, and airplanes.

DOMESTIC MESSAGES

14.12 Domestic telegraph messages include the full-rate telegram, overnight telegram, and mailgram. Relative advantages, limitations, and costs are explained below.

Full-Rate Telegrams

14.13 The full-rate telegram, also called the fast-service telegram, is sent at any time of the day or night when received by Western Union. The minimum charge is based on fifteen words, with an extra charge for each additional word. Messages may be in code or a foreign language.

Full-rate telegram messages are accepted for immediate delivery, which is usually made within a few hours. It is the fastest and most expensive kind of domestic telegraph service. The urgency and importance of the message determines whether this type of service is used.

Overnight Telegrams

14.14 Overnight telegrams (or night letters) are accepted up to midnight for delivery the next morning. This class of telegraph service is especially useful when a lengthy message is sent and immediate delivery is not essential.

The minimum charge for overnight telegrams is based on 100 words, with an additional charge made for each additional group of five words. Messages may be in code or a foreign language. This is the least expensive kind of domestic letter service.

Mailgrams

14.15 A mailgram is a combination letter and telegram that provides overnight service to addresses in the continental United States. Mailgrams may be sent via a **TELEX, TWX, Info-Com,** or **computer terminal,** or through a **voice-originated telephone system** to an operator.

A message of up to 100 words is presented to a Western Union telephone operator. The message is sent by electronic devices to a teleprinter at a post office near the destination, where it is teleprinted, placed in a special envelope, and delivered to the addressee by a U.S. Postal Service letter carrier. Most mailgrams are delivered the next day.

INTERNATIONAL MESSAGES

14.16 The two kinds of international messages—**full-rate telegram** and **international letter**—may be sent as either cablegrams or radiograms. The *cablegram,* used for intercontinental messages, is transmitted by means of a cable laid across the ocean floor. The *radiogram,* used to communicate with aircraft and ships, is a message sent by wireless systems.

When messages are to be transmitted by radiogram or cablegram, contact the telegraph office about the classes of service, the charges, and the features of each type of service. In sending international telegrams, the time differences around the world should be considered.

Full-Rate Telegrams

14.17 The full-rate telegram (FR) is the fastest service for international messages. It may be written in any foreign language that can be expressed in the roman alphabet and type or code numbers.

The minimum charge is based on seven words including the address and signature, and the rates depend on the distance the message is to be relayed.

International Letters

14.18 The international letter telegram (LT) is a less expensive service for longer, overnight, plain-language (without numbers) messages. A minimum is charged for 22 words, with an extra charge made for each additional word.

TYPING TELEGRAMS

14.19 Telegram forms, available in Western Union offices, should be used to expedite messages. Type the forms as follows:

1. Determine the number of copies (usually four) to be made of all telegrams.

   a. original for Western Union

   b. confirmation copy to be mailed to addressee

   c. file copy

   d. Accounting Department copy

2. Set the left margin at a point where all information can be typed beginning at the same point. This eliminates the time-consuming process of setting various tabulator stops across the page.

3. Type the body of the message in double spacing with triple spacing between paragraphs. Paragraphs may either be indented or blocked.

4. Complete the entire telegram form so the message can be transmitted without delay.

   a. kind of service desired

   b. account to be charged, if any

   c. date message filed

   d. complete name and address of addressee

   e. message (see 14.20)

   f. name, address, and telephone number of sender

5. To send a telegram to a person arriving on a train or bus, the address should include:

name of passenger	station
destination	arrival time
name and number of bus or train	city and state
car/berth number on train	

6. To send a telegram to a person arriving on an airplane, the address should include:

name of passenger	airport
name of airline	arrival time
flight number and destination	city and state

7. To send a telegram to a person sailing or arriving on a ship, the address should include:

name of passenger	pier
name of steamship line	sailing time
name of ship	port of departure
stateroom number	

COUNTING WORDS

14.20 The charges made for sending domestic telegrams and international messages are based on the length of the message, measured by number of words. Because charges for domestic and international services vary, consult your local telegraph office for specific rates. Some of the major differences between the rates charged for domestic telegrams and international messages are listed below:

Domestic	*International*
1. The address and one signature are free.	1. Each word in the address and the signature is counted and charged as one word.
2. Common punctuation marks such as the hyphen and apostrophe are free.	2. Each mark of punctuation is counted as one word.
3. Each dictionary word counts as one word regardless of its length.	3. Each dictionary word is counted as 15 letters to the word or a fraction thereof.

SENDING TELEGRAPHIC MESSAGES

14.21 Telegraph messages may be filed in person at any Western Union branch office or (as in most businesses) telephoned to a nearby branch office. Businesses that handle large volumes of telegraph messages may install special equipment, such as the TELEX teleprinter and the Desk-Fax, to handle telegraphic messages within the company.

TELEX Teleprinter

14.22 TELEX service is a worldwide direct-dial system linking one company's teleprinter with others around the world to enable instantaneous written communication at the rate of 66 words per minute. Five characters and one space are counted as one word.

The advantages of TELEX service are that messages are transmitted as fast as they are typed and a two-way "conversation" can take place easily and inexpensively with someone across the continent.

Desk-Fax

14.23 The Desk-Fax or Telefax is a compact unit that facilitates the sending and receiving of telegrams within a business office rather than through Western Union. Companies using this equipment are assigned certain call letters by which to identify themselves.

SPECIAL TELEGRAPHIC SERVICES

14.24 In addition to transmitting messages across the country or around the world, Western Union offers the following services.

Telegraphic Money Order

14.25 Telegraphic money orders are used to transmit money (via cable) to almost any point in the world. A request is filed at any Western Union office, and money is paid to the addressee-payee at the destination, usually within a few hours.

Telegraphic money orders are fast and safe. The sender pays the telegraph company the amount to be sent by money order plus the fee and a charge for any message sent with the money order. The payee of the money order is notified by the receiving telegraph office and is paid the amount of the money order upon showing proper identification.

Messenger Service

14.26 Messengers may be hired from Western Union for such personal and business errands as delivering documents, packages, advertising material, and gifts. Messenger service also may be used to fill pharmacy prescriptions, carry baggage, and deliver rush materials.

Gift Services and Greetings

14.27 Western Union can deliver gifts, flowers, candy, dolls, and similar gifts for birthdays, holidays, and other special occasions. They can also provide special anniversary and holiday greetings.

Hotel and Travel Reservations

14.28 Hotel and motel reservations can be made through the Western Union Hotel Reservations Desk. Rail, water, and air transportation tickets also may be reserved by telegraph.

Postal Services

14.29 The U.S. Postal Service is responsible for mail service within the United States. Postal rates and regulations change occasionally, so the Postal Service should be consulted regularly for current information.

Using the proper postal services not only expedites mail to correspondents and customers but also saves on postage costs.

ADDRESSING HINTS

14.30 Follow these guidelines to ensure that you get the most efficient mail service.

1. Type all envelope addresses—including the return address—in single spacing.

2. Include a complete return address on all mail, including postal cards.

3. Include the personal titles *Dr., Miss, Mr., Mrs.,* and *Ms.* on all envelopes addressed to individuals.

4. Include the personal titles *Dr., Mrs.,* and *Ms.* in the return address of correspondence.

5. Include the five-digit ZIP code on all mail, in the return address as well as in the addressee's address.

6. Type the ZIP code one space after the two-letter state abbreviation, on the same line.

7. Use the two-letter state abbreviations adopted by the U.S. Postal Service. Refer to the National ZIP Code Directory, which lists codes for every postal delivery zone in the United States.

8. Type postal notations (such as AIRMAIL, REGISTERED MAIL, SPECIAL DELIVERY, and CERTIFIED MAIL) in the upper right corner of the envelope below the postage stamp.

9. Type addressee notations (such as PERSONAL, CONFIDENTIAL, PLEASE FORWARD, and ATTENTION) in the upper left corner of the envelope below the return address.

10. Mark the class of mail on the front when oversize manila envelopes or jiffy bags are used; otherwise, they are processed as fourth class.

ADDRESS PROCEDURES

14.31 The use of automated equipment for processing mail has helped to expedite the handling and delivery of mail, but addresses must be accurate, complete, and legible to avoid delays in mail processing and delivery and higher costs. See 7.18–7.24 and 7.71–7.79 for correct address procedures.

DOMESTIC MAIL CLASSES

14.32 Domestic mail may travel first class, second class, third class, fourth class, special fourth class, airmail, or air parcel post.

First Class

14.33 First-class mail service and rates are based on overnight delivery within the local area, if deposited in a collection box by 5 P.M. or at a post office by 6 P.M. Mail that can be sent first class includes letters, postcards, postal cards, bills and statements, cancelled and uncancelled checks, business reply letters and cards, and sealed greeting cards.

Regulations are as follows:

1. Rates are based on each ounce or fraction of an ounce (up to twelve ounces), to (a) any place in the United States, (b) United States territories and possessions, (c) armed forces outside the United States, addressed to APO (Army Post Office) or FPO (Fleet Post Office), and (d) Mexico and Canada.

2. The minimum size for mailable envelopes and cards is 3 inches by 4¼ inches.

3. Mail is returned to sender if undeliverable.

Second Class

14.34 Second-class mail consists of newspapers and magazines issued four or more times a year. Postal rates vary according to the weight and type of publication and the distance to destination.

Third Class

14.35 Third-class mail consists of all other mailable matter within the weight limitation (less than sixteen ounces) not included as first- or second-class mail—circulars, books, catalogs, and other printed matter; proof sheets and corrected proofs with related manuscript copy; keys (hotel, motel, and steamship); merchandise; farm and factory products; seeds, cuttings, bulbs, roots, scions, and plants; and photographs and printed drawings.

The rate is determined by weight and distance, on either a single-piece or bulk basis (over 200 pieces of the same size and weight, or with a total weight of fifty pounds addressed to different persons).

Fourth Class

14.36 Most fourth-class mail is domestic parcel post and includes special catalog mailing rates, special fourth-class rate, and a library rate for material weighing one pound or more. It includes merchandise, printed matter, farm products, catalogs, and printed advertising material.

Weight limitations are one to seventy pounds; size restriction is 100 inches (in combined length and girth). Rates are determined by weight and mailing distance.

Special Fourth Class

14.37 This service excludes books that contain advertising for other merchandise, telephone directories, corporation reports, house organs, and periodicals. It includes books of 24 pages or more, 16mm films or narrower, printed music in bound or sheet form, printed test materials, sound recordings, playscripts and manuscripts for books, and loose pages and binders containing medical information.

Airmail

14.38 Airmail service should be reserved for high-priority and international mail since most first-class mail is designated for next-day or second-day delivery. Airmail rates are based on each ounce or fraction of an ounce. Any mail that can be sent on a first-class basis may be sent airmail.

Air Parcel Post (Priority Mail)

14.39 Use priority mail to send heavier pieces over long distances, where speed of delivery is important. Priority mail is given full airmail handling, and includes all first-class mail over twelve ounces and all airmail over nine ounces. Maximum weight is seventy pounds, and maximum size is 100 inches (in combined length and girth). Rates are determined by weight and mailing distance.

INTERNATIONAL MAIL

14.40 International mail does not include APO (Army Post Office) or FPO (Fleet Post Office) addresses. Mail sent overseas may be letters, letter packages, printed matter, small packages of merchandise or samples, or parcel post. Classes of international mail are described as follows.

Surface

14.41 Mail rates for letters are based on each ounce up to twelve ounces, with higher rates based on total weight.

Air Rates

14.42 Air rates to Canada and Mexico are based on each ounce; rates to other international points are based on the half ounce.

Aerogrammes

14.43 Aerogrammes are printed on special lightweight stationery that folds into a self-envelope. They provide an economical means of overseas communication. No enclosures are allowed.

Air Parcel Post

14.44 Air rates vary from country to country. There are specific weight and dimension limitations as well as ways of packing goods for shipment. Goods sent abroad must meet customs regulations for both the United States and the destination country.

MAILING HINTS

14.45 Follow these suggestions to ensure the quickest arrival of mail.

1. Mail early in the day for the most efficient handling.

2. Write or print legibly all envelope addresses.

3. Mark any postal notation clearly, in the appropriate place on the envelope.

4. Use the correct amount of postage. When in doubt about the weight of a letter or package, have it weighed at the post office.

5. Use postal cards for short messages. Postal cards are handled as first-class mail, but the rate is lower, and the cost of stationery and envelope is also saved.

6. Do not use airmail within the United States since most first-class mail is sent by air anyway.

7. Use airmail only for high-priority and international mail.

8. Use airmail envelopes to expedite handling of mail by the office staff and the post office staff.

9. Use special delivery service only when the extra speed is crucial.

10. Do not send mail by special delivery to a post office box.

11. Use preprinted mailing labels (or other addressing devices) for regular correspondents or customers.

12. Request an original certificate of mailing when a return receipt is essential.

NON-MAIL POSTAL SERVICES

14.46 The U.S. Postal Service provides a number of services not connected with mail delivery.

Documentary Internal Revenue Stamps

14.47 These stamps are used to pay taxes on documents such as stock certificates, transfer of capital stock of corporations, and real estate deeds. They are sold at most post offices.

Post Office Box Rentals

14.48 Boxes and drawers may be rented at most post offices for the convenience of individuals and businesses. These boxes provide privacy for the renter and are a convenience when it may not be desirable to have mail delivered to a home or business address. Mail is delivered to the post office box number where it may be picked up by the renter, even when the post office is closed. Box rentals vary according to the classification of the post office and the size of the box.

Postal Money Orders

14.49 Postal money orders provide a means of sending money through the mail safely. They may be purchased and redeemed at any post office. Fees vary according to the amount of the money order.

United States Savings Bonds and Stamps

14.50 The U.S. Postal Service acts as the agent of the Treasury Department for the sale of Series E Savings Bonds and Stamps in communities where banks do not have this service or where there are no other issuing agents.

PREMIUM SERVICES

14.51 Premium mail services were developed for large-volume mail users and businesses.

Express Mail

14.52 Express mail service provides businesses with high-speed intercity delivery of important papers and products where time is crucial. Consult the customer service representative of the U.S. Postal Service for information on the different options that involve postal employees picking up shipments, taking them to the airport, and delivering them to the addressee.

Business Reply Mail

14.53 Business reply mail simplifies the addressee's task when the sender needs a response. The sender obtains a special permit from the Postal Service and guarantees the postage on all replies returned, based on first-class mail rates plus an additional fee for the service (there is no charge for the permit itself).

Preprinted envelopes designating business reply mail must state *No postage stamp necessary if mailed in the United States* and *Postage will be paid by addressee.*

Cash on Delivery

14.54 First-, third-, and fourth-class material may be sent on a cash-on-delivery (COD) basis where the addressee pays for the postage plus the value of the goods contained in the letter or parcel. The amount collected by the mail carrier is sent to the sender by a postal money order.

The COD fee, paid by the sender, includes insurance against loss, damage, and failure to collect payment from the addressee.

Certificate of Mailing

14.55 A certificate of mailing is a post office receipt furnishing evidence of mailing only. It may be used for all classes of mail except second class. This certificate does not provide protection against loss or damage but is available at a nominal fee (less than that charged for return receipt).

Certified Mail

14.56 This service, available for first-class mail and airmail, certifies proof of delivery to the addressee of valuable documents or other items for which a record of delivery and receipt are needed. There is no insurance value, as certified mail carries no liability for lost mail.

Return receipt is available at a nominal fee to indicate the type of delivery requested: to addressee only or to any one at the address.

Insured Mail

14.57 Third- and fourth-class mail can be insured against loss or damage to content. Maximum liability is $200, with fees based on the value of the contents.

Return receipt and restricted-delivery services are available at nominal fees.

Registered Mail

14.58 Registered mail offers protection for valuable papers, stocks, bonds, jewelry, money, etc., up to $10,000, with liability limited to the value declared by the sender. This is available for domestic first-class, air, and priority mail.

The customer is provided with a receipt at the time of mailing and the Postal Service keeps a record of mailing. Return receipt and restricted-delivery services are available at nominal fees.

Special Delivery

14.59 All classes of mail may be sent special delivery, which means mail is delivered to the addressee as soon as possible upon arrival at the local post office, with limitations in distance and time. See 14.45, Mailing Hints, for information on when it is appropriate to use special delivery.

A special delivery service fee is charged in addition to the regular postage for the letter or parcel.

Special Handling

14.60 Special handling provides expeditious service for third- and fourth-class mail, but does not include special delivery service.

The special-handling fee, charged in addition to the regular parcel-post postage, assures that packages will be handled almost as efficiently as first-class mail.

Fifteen

Annotated References

Introduction

15.1 References and source materials with which office managers, secretaries, and other office workers should be familiar are almanacs, biographical books, dictionaries and word books, directories, encyclopedias, indexes, secretarial handbooks and textbooks, and such general references as atlases and the ZIP code directory. Each category of reference book is defined and discussed below, followed by an annotated bibliography of key titles.

Almanacs

15.2 An almanac is a collection of historical, social, economic, and political facts published on an annual basis. It contains information about important events of the past year, including such items as names of government officials by names and departments; election statistics; athletic events and sporting records; data about each state, the United States, and foreign nations; the calendar, the weather, and astronomical facts; memorable dates and holidays; and facts of interest about many other subjects.

Information Please Almanac, Atlas, and Yearbook. New York: Simon & Schuster, Inc. Annually.

Contains information on such diversified topics as geography, politics, sports, taxes, vital statistics, and social and political conditions.

New York Times Encyclopedic Almanac. New York: New York Times Co. Book and Educational Division. Annually.

Reader's Digest Almanac and Yearbook. Pleasantville, N.Y.: The Reader's Digest Association, Inc. Annually.

World Almanac and Book of Facts. Garden City, N.Y.: Doubleday & Co., Inc. Annually.

Contains information on economic, social, educational, and political events.

Biographical Books

15.3 Biographical books supply factual data about prominent men and women, noting such information as their background, age, parentage, schools attended, occupation or profession, marital status, affiliations, achievements, and honors.

Various professional associations and national and regional organizations also publish biographical books.

Current Biography. New York: The H. W. Wilson Co. Monthly and cumulated year.

Covers such celebrities as kings, prime ministers, presidents, senators, cabinet members, Supreme Court justices, and radio, television, film, stage, and sports personalities. The yearly cumulation is entitled *Current Biography Yearbook.*

Dictionary of American Biography. New York: Charles Scribner's Sons.

Contains information on American men and women no longer living.

Webster's Biographical Dictionary. Springfield, Mass.: G. & C. Merriam Co.

Contains biographical sketches from a few lines to more than a page in length. Useful for identifying persons of any nationality from any period of history.

Who's Who. New York: St. Martin's Press, Inc. Annually.

Listing of internationally famous men and women, primarily British.

Who's Who in America. Chicago: Marquis-Who's Who, Inc. Biennially.

Biographies of best-known living men and women in all lines of useful and reputable achievement.

Who's Who in Commerce and Industry. Chicago: Marquis-Who's Who, Inc. Biennially.

Biographical data of outstanding business professionals throughout the world.

Who's Who of American Women. Chicago: Marquis-Who's Who, Inc. Biennially.

Biographical data on notable living American women.

Other biographical reference books published by Marquis-Who's Who Inc., include:

Who's Who in the East

Who's Who in the Midwest

Who's Who in the South and Southwest

Who's Who in the West

Dictionaries

15.4 The dictionary is perhaps the most important general reference book for office workers. Dictionaries are published in various sizes, from the abridged small pocket editions to the large unabridged volumes. Abridged dictionaries contain information about the more common words, while unabridged dictionaries give authoritative information about virtually every word in the English language. Both volumes are indispensable tools for written and oral communication.

Office workers need to know how and when to use the dictionary properly—to know the contents and organization of the dictionaries found in their offices. The main entry for each word provides information on spelling, syllabication, pronunciation, part of speech, etymology (origin of the word), meanings, usage, capitalization, synonyms, and certain irregular forms.

Most dictionaries also provide interesting and useful supplementary information in the appendixes.

The American College Dictionary. New York: Random House, Inc.

The American Heritage Dictionary of the English Language. Boston: American Heritage and Houghton Mifflin Co.

Anderson, Ruth I., Lura Lynn Straub, and E. Dana Gibson. ***Word Finder.*** Englewood Cliffs, N.J.: Prentice-Hall, Inc.

Bartlett, John. ***Familiar Quotations.*** Boston: Little, Brown and Co.

Funk & Wagnall's Standard College Dictionary. New York: Harcourt Brace Jovanovich, Inc.

Kahn, Gilbert, and Donald J. D. Mulkerne. ***The Word Book.*** Beverly Hills, Calif.: Glencoe Press.

Leslie, Louis A. ***20,000 Words.*** New York: Gregg Division, McGraw-Hill Book Co.

The Original Roget's Thesaurus of English Words and Phrases. New York: St. Martin's Press, Inc.

The Random House Dictionary of the English Language. New York: Random House, Inc.

Roget's International Thesaurus of Words and Phrases. New York: Crowell Collier and Macmillan, Inc.

Webster's Eighth New Collegiate Dictionary. Springfield, Mass.: G. & C. Merriam Co.

Webster's New Dictionary of Synonyms. Springfield, Mass.: G. & C. Merriam Co.

Webster's New International Dictionary of the English Language. Springfield, Mass.: G. & C. Merriam Co.

Webster's New World Dictionary of the American Language. New York: World Publishing Co.

Hints on Using the Dictionary

15.5 1. Know what material is contained in the dictionary, to save time in looking for information.

2. Read the explanatory notes in the front of the dictionary concerning the main entries and the pronunciation guides so that you will know how to read and use the symbols.

3. Use the alphabetic guide words found at the top of each page to help locate a particular word on the page.

4. Study the spelling, pronunciation, and definitions of a word when you look it up in the dictionary. If two or more spellings are shown for the word, the first one is the preferred spelling.

5. Note the various definitions and uses of each word. Because words assume different meanings in different contexts, it is important that the correct word be used to convey the precise thought desired.

6. Note the synonyms for a given word. This helps to increase your vocabulary and adds variety to your writing.

Directories

15.6 A directory is an alphabetical listing (in booklet or book form) of names and addresses of people within a particular community or a given business, industry, or profession. Directories are helpful in verifying the spelling of an individual's name, finding an address or a telephone number of a person or company, and identifying a company's officers, products, and/or services.

Directories are available for many specialized areas such as manufacturing, shipping, hotels and motels, newspapers, attorneys, educational institutions, insurance firms, and sales executives.

City directories. Compiled, published, and sold commercially for most of the cities of the United States and Canada.

Each directory lists names, addresses, and businesses of all residents of the city.

Congressional Directory. Washington, D.C.: Superintendent of Documents, U.S. Government Printing Office.

Lists the names and addresses of members of Congress and executive personnel.

Dun & Bradstreet Ratings and Reports. New York: Dun & Bradstreet, Inc.

Gives credit and capital ratings of firms, addresses; type of business.

Fortune Directory. Published by *Fortune* Magazine, New York.

Contains listing of major industrial firms in the United States, with their sales and assets.

Moody's Investors' Service. Weekly and semiweekly.

Provides detailed financial data on various companies that offer investment opportunities.

Poor's Register of Directors and Executives.

Contains information on executives and directors in the United States and Canada, in various industrial classifications.

Rand McNally Bankers Directory. Chicago: Rand McNally & Co. Semiannually.

Contains names of the officers and directors of all banks in the world. Also includes information on domestic and foreign banks, statements, U.S. banking and commercial laws.

Telephone directories. Compiled and published by telephone companies and distributed to telephone subscribers annually.

List subscribers, their telephone numbers and addresses. Also include information on types of telephone services, long-distance rates, etc. *The yellow pages* list subscribers by particular product or service.

Encyclopedias

15.7 After the dictionary, the encyclopedia is perhaps the most frequently used reference book. It provides authoritative information on a great number of subjects and topics arranged in alphabetic order and discussed briefly in articles written by specialists in the various fields. Many encyclopedias are illustrated with pictures, graphs, maps, and charts that help the reader understand the written material.

Specialized encyclopedias that relate to a particular field or subject are found in school and public libraries, and in the libraries of professional and technological societies or organizations.

Columbia Encyclopedia. New York: Columbia University Press.

A general encyclopedia, written in nontechnical language.

Columbia Viking Desk Encyclopedia. New York: The Viking Press, Inc.

Encyclopaedia Britannica (30 volumes). Chicago: Encyclopaedia Britannica, Inc.

The oldest encyclopedia, with contributions from top authorities in every field.

Encyclopedia Americana (30 volumes). New York: Grolier Incorporated.

Emphasizes American topics in condensed fashion. Specializes in biographies and the sciences.

Lincoln Library of Essential Information. Buffalo: Frontier Press Company.

Indexes

15.8

Indexes to the contents of books and periodicals are helpful when information on a particular subject must be located. These indexes list book and article titles, often grouped by subject, and identify the sources (name of publisher for books, name and date of periodical or newspaper for articles).

Books in Print, U.S.A.: An Index to the Publishers Trade List Annual. New York: R. W. Bowker Co.

Gives author, title, price, publisher, and year of publication of all books included in publisher's trade list annual.

Business Education Index. New York: Delta Pi Epsilon Fraternity and Gregg Division, McGraw-Hill Book Co. Annually.

Author and subject index of business education articles, yearbooks, textbooks, and research studies.

Business Periodicals Index. New York: The H. W. Wilson Co. Monthly except July.

Subject index to periodicals selected by subscribers to the Index in accounting, advertising, banking, general business, and other fields.

Cumulative Book Index. New York: The H. W. Wilson Co. Monthly, and cumulated twice a year.

Indexes all books published in the English language by author, title, and subject.

Education Index. New York: The H. W. Wilson Co. Monthly, cumulated annually.

Comprehensive index of periodicals, yearbooks, bulletins, and monographs in the area of education.

The New York Times Index. New York: The New York Times Co. Biweekly, with annual cumulation.

Classifies material in the *New York Times* alphabetically and chronologically under subject, title, person, and organization names.

Reader's Guide to Periodical Literature. New York: The H. W. Wilson Co. Semimonthly.

Indexes by subject and author articles of a popular and general nature.

Secretarial Handbooks and Textbooks

15.9 For the secretarial or clerical worker who must be familiar with a wide range of information and skills, the following selected list of reference sources should be consulted. Such handbooks and textbooks provide the latest office procedures and techniques.

Anderson, Ruth I., Dorothy E. Lee, Allien A. Russon, Jacquelyn A. Wentzell, and Helen M. S. Horack. ***The Administrative Secretary: Resource.*** New York: Gregg Division, McGraw-Hill Book Co.

Clark, James L., Jr., and Lyn R. Clark. ***HOW: Handbook for Office Workers.*** Belmont, Calif.: Wadsworth Publishing Co.

Doris, Lillian, and Bessie May Miller. ***Complete Secretary's Handbook.*** Englewood Cliffs, N.J.: Prentice-Hall, Inc.

Flynn, Patricia. ***The Complete Secretary.*** New York: Pitman Publishing Corp.

Gavin, Ruth E., and William A. Sabin. ***Reference Manual for Stenographers and Typists.*** New York: Gregg Division, McGraw-Hill Book Co.

Hanna, J Marshall, Estelle L. Popham, and Rita Sloan Tilton. ***Secretarial Procedures and Administration.*** Cincinnati: South-Western Publishing Co.

House, Clifford R., and Apollonia M. Koebele. ***Reference Manual for Office Personnel.*** Cincinnati: South-Western Publishing Co.

Hutchinson, Lois Irene. ***Standard Handbook for Secretaries.*** New York: Gregg Division, McGraw-Hill Book Co.

Janis, J. Harold, and Margaret H. Thompson. ***New Standard Reference for Secretaries and Administrative Assistants.*** New York: Macmillan Co.

Taintor, Sarah, and Kate M. Monroe. ***Secretary's Handbook.*** New York: Macmillan Co.

Whalen, Doris H. ***The Secretary's Handbook.*** New York: Harcourt Brace Jovanovich, Inc.

General References

15.10 Important additional reference sources include books that give shipping rates or hotel information and atlases.

Bullinger's Postal Shipper's Guide for the United States, Canada, and Newfoundland. Westwood, N.J.: Bullinger's Guides, Inc.

Contains post office and railroad stations with the railroad or steamer line on which every town, or the nearest communicating point, is located, and the delivering express for every town. Also lists railroads and water lines with their terminal points.

Hotel and Motel Red Book. New York: American Hotel Association Directory Corp. Annually.

Lists hotels and motels alphabetically by city and state, gives information about number of rooms, services, location, telephone numbers, and rates.

Johnson, H. Webster. ***How to Use the Business Library.*** Cincinnati: South-Western Publishing Co.

Guide for training in the use of the business library. Includes comprehensive list of sources and description of methods used to secure exact information needed in business.

Leonard's Guide. New York: G. R. Leonard & Co., Inc.

Contains a complete shipper's guide with rates and routings for freight shipments, express, and parcel post. Guide also includes information concerning Canadian and foreign parcel post.

National ZIP Code Directory. Washington, D.C.: Superintendent of Documents, U.S. Government Printing Office. Revised periodically.

Gives information on how to use ZIP code in addresses, how it works, address abbreviations, ZIP code prefixes, state list of post offices, and numerical list of ZIP codes.

Postal Manual. Washington, D.C.: Superintendent of Documents, U.S. Government Printing Office.

Provides information about regulation, rates, and postal service.

Rand McNally Commercial Atlas and Marketing Guide. Chicago: Rand McNally & Co. Annually.

Gives general information for the United States, population and reference maps for Canada, and reference maps and general information for the world.

Rand McNally New Cosmopolitan World Atlas. Chicago: Rand McNally & Co.

Book of maps with geographical statistics and population figures for each area.

Index

G

H

Q

R

S

T

U

V

W

X

Y

Z